After the Breakup of a Multi-Ethnic Empire

After the Breakup of a Multi-Ethnic Empire

Russia, Successor States, and Eurasian Security

SUSANNE MICHELE BIRGERSON

Westport, Connecticut
London

#46884235

Library of Congress Cataloging-in-Publication Data

Birgerson, Susanne Michele, 1968–
    After the breakup of a multi-ethnic empire : Russia, successor states, and Eurasian
security / Susanne Michele Birgerson.
        p.   cm.
    Includes bibliographical references and index.
    ISBN 0–275–96950–9 (alk. paper)—ISBN 0–275–96965–7 (pbk. : alk. paper)
    1. National security—Former Soviet republics.   2. Former Soviet republics—Foreign
relations.   3. Former Soviet republics—Politics and government.   4.
Post-communism—Former Soviet republics.   5. World politics—1989–   I. Title.
DK293.B57   2002
    947.086—dc21   2001032903

British Library Cataloguing in Publication Data is available.

Library of Congress Catalog Card Number: 2001032903
ISBN: 0–275–96950–9
        0–275–96965–7 (pbk.)

First published in 2002

Praeger Publishers, 88 Post Road West, Westport, CT 06881
An imprint of Greenwood Publishing Group, Inc.
www.praeger.com

Printed in the United States of America

The paper used in this book complies with the
Permanent Paper Standard issued by the National
Information Standards Organization (Z39.48–1984).

10 9 8 7 6 5 4 3 2 1

To my parents
Sandra and Donald Birgerson

Contents

Introduction

The dissolution of the Soviet Union in 1991 was one of the most momentous and unexpected political events of a century chockfull of extraordinary political events. The breakup of the largest political entity in the world has security implications spanning Asia and Europe. Though commentators and leaders in the Western world at first rejoiced at the collapse of communism, it soon became clear that the power vacuum left by the dissolution of the Soviet Union would be filled either by the newly formed Russian Federation or by regional powers in Europe, the Middle East, South Asia, and East Asia. Western powers now had to take into account the potential for adventurism by countries such as China, Iran, Pakistan, and Afghanistan. Porous borders, communal violence and civil war, and the general breakdown of law and order in the post-Soviet territories contribute to a climate of opportunism. Chaotic conditions along the frontiers of the Russian Federation also provide opportunities for the rise of extremist groups and the spread of terrorism.

The breakup of the Soviet Union represented the fall of the last empire of the twentieth century. When empires dissolve, chaos and disorder are the result. This simple truth is evident by even the most cursory examination of history: the fall of the Roman Empire, the Imperial dynasties that arose in China, the Austro-Hungarian Empire, the Ottoman Empire, and countless others. Even the breakup of the colonial empires of European powers wreaked havoc and devastation as seen in the Belgian Congo, Angola, Mozambique, Indochina, and so on. In the turmoil following the breakup of the Soviet Union we see nothing new.

What is new is the political aftermath; that is, the virtually automatic formation of new political entities from what was the periphery of the Soviet Empire. These entities are the legal result of an internationally sanctioned System of

States as exemplified by the United Nations that serves as its forum. Historically, the fall of an empire resulted either in anarchy, where order was established on a local basis by small political groupings such as tribes or city-states, or in the territorial conquest by a neighboring empire. Now we have a situation where even regional rivals recognize the "sovereignty" of these new states, at least formally, where as in earlier centuries they would have most certainly taken advantage of the weakness of their rival by conquering or raiding its territory. Would the Germans, Han Chinese, Persians, or Turks have hesitated in conquering the territories of the Baltic Littoral, Middle Asia, Central Asia, or the Caucasus in earlier centuries?

But how enduring are these newly independent states? In their present geographical forms, they have no historical precedent. This begs the question of their viability. How well can they defend their territory, control the traffic of people and goods, and provide for the needs of their citizens? These questions generate others: How far did the former center of the empire, Russia, actually fall? The center of the former Soviet Empire also automatically became a state. How weak is the center vis-à-vis its former periphery? How much has really changed since the breakup?

The relationship between the Russian Federation and the 14 non-Russian Successor States is unequal, with the Russian Federation as the dominant power. This power imbalance is a holdover from the Soviet system that was dominated by the RSFSR (the Russian Republic). In the course of this argument, I resurrect the old-time construct of the empire as a specific type of political system fundamentally different from that of the modern state. This difference explains the asymmetrical pattern of power that emerged between the Russian Federation and the non-Russian Successor States. In seeking systemic (internal) causes for the breakup, causes peculiar to empires, I hope to avoid the reductionist reasoning that typically accompanies economic explanations for the dissolution.

In looking at the distinctive features of empires, it becomes clear that a contracting economy was only the catalyst in sparking the Gorbachev reforms which had the unintended consequence of undermining the very foundation that held the Soviet empire together; that is, the political and social relations between the leaders in Moscow and their counterparts in the Republics. Economic problems inspired the Gorbachev reforms, especially the anti-corruption campaign that targeted the republics. However it is also the case that economic difficulties were exacerbated by the breakup for all parties including Russia.

Gorbachev surely did not intend to disrupt relations between central and Republican Party cadres. It is easy to see in retrospect that he badly miscalculated when he thought he could use the authority of the central government to purge corrupt elements in the republics without causing a rift between All-Union and Republican elites. Since Republican elites were given carte blanche by no less a personage than Leonid Brezhnev, whose ties to elites in the Caucasus and Central Asia were notorious, dislodging ensconced interests in the Republics was bound to be unpleasant and difficult. But who could have foreseen the chain reaction Gorbachev's anti-corruption campaign triggered? In this milieu, independence from the center became a desirable option for Republican leaders who formerly had a vested interest in preserving the status quo. In many cases independence was more than a desirable political option; it was a form of self-preservation.

A clear parallel exists between the dominance of the Russian Republic in the Soviet System and the dominance of the Russian Federation over the non-Russian Successor States. Given the superiority of the Russian Federation, this book focuses on the endurance of power structures, both economic and political, that were established during the Soviet era and how their endurance has compromised the independence of the non-Russian Successor States.

Chapter 1

The Dissolution of Empires

What are the effects of the Soviet political structure on the sovereignty of the non-Russian Successor States? How well has the former center, Russia, adjusted to the loss of its periphery? What might be the lingering effects of the Soviet administrative apparatus in the Successor States, particularly in regards to the Russian minority living there? Legacies of Soviet rule complicate post-Soviet inter-ethnic relations between Russia, the former imperial "center," and the Successor States, the former "periphery." This problem is not easily resolved by the governments of the Successor States, given their continued dependence on Russia and the fact that Russia remains their biggest security concern. The continued dominance of Russia and the centrality of Russia in policy considerations constitute the principle similarity among the otherwise very different Successor States. Given their weakened position vis-a-vis Russia, none of these governments can afford to dismiss Russia in their state-building endeavors.

Lasting consequences of the empire include the following. First, the Soviet Union was an empire based on relations between an imperial center as represented by Russia, and a periphery, as represented by the titular nationalities of the former Republics. Because the center was Russia, the Russian nationality was the one which was equated with the Soviet state. This fact was reflected, not by any measure of economic or even political well-being vis-à-vis the titular minorities (indeed it has often been noted that the Russians did not enjoy a higher standard of living and in fact had significantly lower standards of living than many national minorities including the Estonians, Latvians, Lithuanians, Georgians, and Jews), but by the dominance of Russian culture, especially the Russian language, which was the language of higher culture, science, and government. Learning Russian was necessary for social and economic advancement. Russian effectively became the *lingua franca* of the Soviet Union. This bias served to raise the number of bilingual non-Russians whose first language is the language of their nationality, while their second language is Russian. This process is generally what is referred to as "russification."

Second, the indigenous populations regarded the Russians residing in "their Republic" as foreign, despite the fact that most Russians living in the non-Russian Republics had been born there. Among central and Republican authorities there was an unspoken agreement that the Republics were the domain of the titular nationalities where native customs rightly took precedence over others including those that were Russian. In contrast the Russians largely viewed the Republics as an extension of their own homeland.[1] The perception of the Russians as foreign was undoubtedly heightened by the fact that the Russian minorities by and large did not assimilate, as there had been no compelling need for them to learn local languages and adopt local customs. Non-indigenous, non-Russian minorities who lived in the periphery—Ukrainians, Germans, Belarusians, the Baltic nationalities—were generally Russophones and were grouped together with Russians by the indigenous people.

Third, given the abruptness of the breakup, the Russian minorities identify the country of their citizenship as the Soviet Union to a greater extent than do the Russians living in Russia, a fact which alienates them even more from the emerging, nationalist governments in the former Republics. The introduction of stringent language and citizenship laws and the day-to-day pressures of living are forcing them to choose between assimilation or repatriation to Russia, a choice most are reluctant to make. The result has been a readjustment on the part of the Russians to a minority mentality as seen in the establishment of cultural and political institutions based on ethnicity. These endeavors are the result of the perceived need on the part of nationalities to preserve their ethnic heritage and are generally associated with minority status.[2] The demise of the Soviet empire and the unwillingness on the part of most Russian minorities to return to Russia, some out-migration not withstanding, raises the question of minority rights in the Successor States.

Last, despite Russia's weakened position in the international arena, it still possesses considerable capabilities vis-à-vis its neighbors in the "near abroad."[3] First, the countries of these regions are still heavily dependent on Russian credits for their economic survival, especially in the areas of energy and raw materials. In addition, Russia remains the primary trading partner of the Successor States, even the Baltic States. The largest percentage of Lithuanian and Latvian exports went to Russia; 23.8 percent (1996) and 22.8 percent (1996) of Lithuanian and Latvian exports went to Russia respectively while by 1996 Russia ranked second to Finland in Estonian exports.[4] Second, Russia's military strength dwarfs that of its neighbors, despite difficulties. Third, the existence of ethnic conflicts, both manifest and latent, in the near abroad serve to weaken the Successor States internally and provide potential opportunities for interference by Russia. Furthermore, the international climate is hardly favorable for the future of the Successor States. Outside powers are unable, or unwilling, to provide aid in the massive amounts needed for the Successor States to rid themselves of their dependence on Russia. And with the exception of the Baltic states, countries have been reluctant to invest in, and slow to expand bilateral trade with, the Successor States.

The breakup of the Soviet Union, unlike the dissolution of smaller states, has potential security implications for an area spanning two continents including several regions: South Asia, the Middle East, and East Asia and the Pacific rim, and all of Europe. In the Baltic States, there are several outstanding issues: the dispute over the Russian military presence in Kaliningrad and the Baltic Sea; the treatment of the Russian minorities living in the Baltic States; trade arrangements, especially the supply of energy resources; and border disputes. For Tallinn, Vilnius, and Riga, the successful resolution of these disagreements will be crucial for successful entry into European economic and security regimes, that is, the European Union (EU) and the North Atlantic Treaty Organization (NATO).

In South Asia instability is evident in skirmishes along the Tajik-Afghan border involving Russian and Uzbek military troops and by sporadic communal unrest in Uzbekistan, Tajikistan, and Kazakhstan. The fighting in Transcaucasia, territorial disputes over the Caspian Sea and the division of its petroleum reserves, and the resulting polemics over the placement of pipelines promise to complicate the political situation in the Middle East and South Asia. Now that the Central Asian Republics are independent, the number of political actors with varying interests in the region—for example, Turkey, Iran, Pakistan, China, and various multinational corporations—has increased, while the political rules of engagement are unclear due to the power vacuum left in the wake of the dissolution.

In the Far East, the Sino-Russo border as well as the unregulated character of cross-border trade have become areas of contention between Beijing and Moscow. Unregulated border trade with China is also prevalent in Kyrgyzstan. The Japanese have raised the issue of dominion over the Kuril Islands with Russia. Russia promises to play an active role in any security arrangements of the Pacific rim; whether the role will be that of an active participant or the disruptive force of an excluded outside power remains to be seen. Last, given the superpower status of the Soviet Union and the alliance structures established during the Cold War, the dissolution of the Soviet Union affects all of Europe and the countries of NATO.

THE BREAKUP OF MULTI-ETHNIC POLITICAL SYSTEMS

There is a need to analyze the causes and circumstances surrounding the dissolution of multi-ethnic political systems in order to effectively assess various outcomes. In order to posit a strategy for reconciliation among ethnic groups and the successful establishment of independent states, the dynamics of the dissolution of multi-ethnic political systems need to be understood.

The point of departure for this study is that political systems break up largely as the result of demands for sovereignty from minorities. The creation of smaller states that have as their basis a nationalist ideology is a familiar, typical outcome. Furthermore, these smaller states themselves are rarely homogeneous; they are beset with the problems and dilemmas that plagued the former political system.

In fact, they may have *greater* difficulties in dealing with minority pressures for several reasons. First, the very newness of the state and the inexperience of the new government in general, and their inexperience in minority matters in particular, complicates the adoption of effective minority policies. Second, the nationalism movement that brought about independence in the first place also brought with it a nationalist ideology which may make the new government unable or unwilling to take a conciliatory approach towards its own minorities. Third, the success of nationalist movements in gaining independence sets a precedent which may make minorities in Successor States unwilling to accept any limitations or encroachments on *their* cultural integrity.

Last, if the minorities in question have outside benefactors such as a foreign government or diaspora group to which they can appeal, then the benefactors may be able to pressure the government on behalf of their countrymen. And depending on the relationship between the successor state and the state dominated by the nationality of the minority group, the effects of such pressure can range from mild irritation to blatant intimidation which, given a continuing dependency on the latter, would be impossible to disregard.

The fact remains, the breakup of large multi-ethnic political systems typically produces smaller multi-ethnic states. That the Soviet Union was an empire further complicates the process of dissolution, with the former imperial center willing and able to disrupt the political processes of the newly formed states. The nationalist component therefore, becomes central in understanding the political dynamics within multi-ethnic political systems, and why some dissolve along ethnic lines. The nationalist component becomes a bone of contention in the post-breakup period between opposing groups which previously had managed ethnic disagreement within the framework of a single, shared government. After the breakup, the management of ethnic disagreements becomes the province of foreign policy between independent states.

In the eighteenth, nineteenth, and twentieth centuries, empires broke up into smaller political entities called states. The value in considering the Soviet case includes analyzing the potentially destabilizing effects of a breakup of multi-ethnic political systems and to address ways in which negative consequences might be mitigated or even avoided altogether. The inability of national actors to come to terms with the dissolution of the former political system and the failure to establish normal interstate relations perpetuate instability.

What are the applications of such a study to the understanding of international relations?

For one thing, the breakup of multi-ethnic empires has a direct and immediate impact on inter-ethnic relations among rivaling nationalities formerly belonging to one political system which brings with it the potential for future conflict. In the post-Cold War international political system, there has been a trend towards the breakup of large political systems and the establishment of smaller political units. Germany, Vietnam, and Yemen are exceptions. In most, if not all, of these cases, the political systems were multi-ethnic, with one national group over-represented in the government apparatus, and nationalist separatist movements and subsequent fighting were the result of minority demands for greater autonomy and/or independence.

The breakup of empires increases the potential for general political instability. In the case of empires that have dissolved during the twentieth century such as the Austro-Hungarian and Ottoman empires, the instability and upheavals that followed overlapped the general chaos of WWI. Intrastate and/or interstate conflict, the displacement of populations, the problem of resettling refugees, and general political violence weaken chances for democracy and peace in the international system. Continuing conflict could entangle other actors (be they states, national and transnational organizations, diaspora groups, or individuals), particularly if there was protracted fighting and bitterness between those who wanted to preserve unity and those who opted for succession. As a matter of fact, there is typically some degree of disagreement over such issues as the appropriate division of foreign debt, management of trade agreements, and the demarcation of international borders. In effect, the breakup of states can be destabilizing in its impact on the system of states if there is no reassessment of relations between opposing factions, and no attempt at reconciliation with current realities.

Ideally, opposing factions should come to terms with the change in political order: The core of the former state should recognize the independence and integrity of the new states while the new states should recognize the responsibilities that come with independence. Responsibilities include the willingness and ability to take control of tasks previously managed by the former government, for example, managing minority issues, establishing armed forces, and taking over the costs associated with the implementation of government programs and economic restructuring. Newly formed governments need to recognize and deal with the difficulties involved in conducting foreign relations in an international system often insensitive to small states, and especially with conducting bilateral relations with the Successor States of the former union.

CHARACTERISTICS OF TWENTIETH-CENTURY EMPIRES

Eisenstadt distinguishes among various types of empires. Essentially though an empire is an old, historic form of political organization that predates the rise of the modern state, and that must possess certain characteristics in order to be successfully transformed into a modern state. Among these traits are the institutionalization of the orderly transfer of power and an efficient administrative apparatus capable of functioning regardless of who is in power. Eisenstadt termed this type of empire as "historic bureaucratic empires."[5] Of interest to this study are those historic bureaucratic empires that survived into the twentieth century.

In order to understand the effects of an imperial political structure on the readjustment of inter-ethnic relations and their impact on the establishment of sovereign nation-states, it is necessary to consider cases that might be pertinent to the Soviet Union. The most significant factor to consider is the historical epoch in which empires existed. The only cases comparable to the Soviet Union are those empires that lasted until, and eventually broke down during, the twentieth century.

Empires that survived into the twentieth century differ from ancient empires in two important ways that are crucial to understanding of imperial collapse in contemporary times. First, nationalism as an ideology and political movement emerged in the nineteenth century and plagued the Austro-Hungarian Empire. The notion of nationalism transformed and gave voice to agitators and anti-imperial movements that proved critical in furthering imperial decline. In the decline of colonial empires, this voice became the national independence movements in the overseas colonies.

Second the nineteenth and twentieth centuries mark a major transition of the international state system from a system based primarily in Europe to one that embraced the former colonies of European powers after they achieved independent statehood. With the addition of so many more states, the state system became truly international in scope. Before the twentieth century, when empires collapsed, their peripheral territories descended into chaos where they were either left to the mercy of warring clans or were eventually swallowed up by another empire. With the advent of the state system, the collapse of empires has resulted in the formation of states. When Austria-Hungary dissolved as a result of WWI, several states were created. In effect, empires that collapsed after the establishment of the system of states resulted in the formation of states, all of which are theoretically equal in status. In the case of the Soviet Union, the maintenance of an old empire (i.e., Russian empire) was incompatible with modern ideas of nationalism. Nationalist movements were organized in the Republics and found their ultimate expression in the creation of states from the territories of the Republics.

There are two main types of empires which survived into the twentieth century, both of which are based on territorial configuration, that is, the territorial structure of the empire: those that were territorially contiguous, and those that were not. Only two empires, the Austro-Hungarian and Ottoman empires, were territorially contiguous *and* survived into the twentieth century. The colonial empires of the European powers typify the latter imperial territorial structure, their centers being the mother country in Europe and their peripheries consisting of overseas colonies. Certain European countries seized and held overseas colonies that were utilized primarily as sources of raw materials and later as markets. Colonial empires include the British, French, Belgium, and Portuguese empires that dissolved in the mid-twentieth century due to independence movements of colonial peoples. Decolonization of what was generally referred to as the Third World resulted in the formation of dozens of new states and the expansion of the state system.

The Soviet Empire differs significantly from the other two types of empires. First, the causes for the collapse were internal rather than external. Typically specialists have emphasized poor economic performance and growing political dissent as factors which served to bring about the downfall of the Soviet system. In fact, the policies of Gorbachev were largely credited for its ultimate collapse. One could focus on the policies of Glasnost and Perestroika and the effects they had in the creation of a nascent civil society which was to act as a democratic alternative to state institutions. But in reality, these measures would only have served to place new limits on the power of the Communist party; they would not have dismantled the entire state apparatus.

In point of fact, the dissolution of the Soviet Union was the result of a permanent rupture between central and peripheral elites. This amounted to the dismantling of the cadre system that developed in conjunction with the policy of *korenizatsiia* or indigenization that was adopted by the party in 1923, weakened under Stalin, and bolstered under Brezhnev. This policy essentially ensured that national cadres in the union Republics dominated the Republican party apparatus. The leadership position, that is, the position of First Secretary, was customarily reserved for a non-Russian Republican national (a Kazakh in Kazakhstan, a Georgian in Georgia, etc.) who worked closely with Moscow and who had a seat in the Central Committee and sometimes the Politburo. The cadre system refers to the practice of placing trusted party cadres in authority positions and, in return for their loyalty, ensuring them almost unlimited perks and privileges, particularly job security. Cadres were guaranteed their status and were not subject to any limits on their tenure in their positions. This policy was in direct contrast to, and indeed was a reaction against, Khrushchev's policy of rotating cadres among different posts within the party apparatus. The Brezhnev system of "trust among cadres" created a system which fostered the development of Republican enclaves where local leaders were given a carte blanche in the administration of their Republics.

This system tied local elites to the Soviet system, and it was this same system which Gorbachev attacked in his program to purge corruption in the party. His anti-corruption campaign was directed primarily against Republican elites and it resulted in the purge of local officials from party and state posts. Despite the anti-Russian backlash that followed many of these purges—as in Uzbekistan, Kazakhstan, and Georgia—the backlash became open rebellion only after Gorbachev began to replace local cadres with Slavic ones.[6]

The federal structure of the Soviet Union created the vehicle for local elites to rebel against the center, and after the cavalcade of sovereignty proclamations, and later, independence declarations, the Soviet Union dissolved along Republican borders established by the Soviet leadership. The besieged Republican elites, no longer bound to the center (especially since the center was determined to purge local cadres and replace them with Slavs), used nationalist strategies to rally the populations of the Republics.[7]

Although on the surface it could be argued that the rebellion of the Republics is similar to what occurred in the overseas territories of the colonial empires, the effects of secessionist movements had very different implications for the Soviet Union than they did for the colonial powers of Europe. The comparison is a fallacious one; the relationship between center and periphery in each case differed drastically. And it is the *quality* of this relationship that shaped the post-imperial environment. Unlike the European colonial powers, Russia has enduring historical, economic, political, and cultural links with the former Soviet Republics. These links directly impacted inter-ethnic relations.

In the Soviet case, the degree of imperial incursion into the periphery is very high. Historically, Russia has occupied and administered these territories for centuries and had regarded them as integral to the empire. The establishment of the Soviet Union furthered center/peripheral integration in its efforts to instill loyalty to the Soviet regime. The Soviet Union took an active role in integrating these regions into the Soviet Union. It did this in several ways.

First, the introduction of mass education served to socialize the population not just of the Republics, but of Russia as well, into the duties and responsibilities as Soviet citizens. Mass education was not the province of Tsarist Russia but was introduced only with the advent of the Soviets and for the first time provided a common denominator among all citizens.

Second, the policy of *korenizatsiia*, as mentioned earlier, gave local elites a stake in the Soviet system.[8] The Soviet Union extended the administrative, legal, and political apparatus of the state to the Union Republics. To this end, the policy of *korenizatsiia* also encompassed the establishment of a wide range of political and social institutions for the titular nationalities including their own universities, academies of sciences, and so forth. In fact most of the all-Union political and social institutions have their counterparts in the Union Republics. In this way, the Soviet system facilitated the integration of the Republics into the Soviet system.[9]

Third, mass migrations of peoples occurred under Soviet rule. Some of these population movements were forced, such as the expulsion of the Tartars from the Crimea, the evacuation of the Chechens from Chechnya, and the condemnation of millions of Russians and non-Russians to forced labor camps across Russia and Siberia. Other migrations were more or less voluntary, for example, the movement east of Slavic peoples in search of work and career opportunities. Most significant is the migration of large numbers of Russians to the Union Republics. Russians moved to the Republics in large numbers, drastically altering the demographic balance in the Republics. Since most were employed in the industrial or military sectors of the economy, they represented an important link between the center and periphery.

The level of post-breakup relations remains high because of the continued Republic's dependence on Russia. Russia provides credits to countries of the near abroad for the purchase of energy and raw materials. In addition, Russia is by far the largest export market for the Successor States, accounting for over fifty percent of all trade. This is true even for the Baltic States.

The issue of minorities complicates the situation further. Although there are many minority groups, the Russian minority is the most politically sensitive. First, fully twenty-five million Russians live in the near abroad according to the 1989 census. The Russian minority comprises seventeen percent of the entire Russian population and eighteen percent overall of the population of the former Republics.[10]

Second, the Russians in the near abroad represent the imperial minority to a greater extent than do the Russians in Russia. Although there is significant variance among Russian minority populations living in the former Republics, overall their status has been appreciably lowered vis-à-vis the indigenous nationals.

Third, the abrupt change in status made the Russian minority a volatile issue both for Russia and the Successor States. The very newness of minority status has created anxiety among the Russian minorities to the point where they are forced to make concrete decisions about their political loyalties. The process is by no means complete nor is it clear what role they will play in the Successor States. The issue continues to color Russia's relationships with its former Republics.

THE SOVIET UNION AS AN EMPIRE

The Soviet Union differs from other twentieth-century, multi-ethnic political systems in that it was an *empire*, a fact that serves to complicate the establishment of states in the post-Soviet environment. Empires consist of a center and periphery: Both terms have overlapping territorial, political, and national components to them. Territorially, the center represents the geographic heart of the empire, while the periphery refers to the outlying areas that border other foreign political entities.[11] Politically, the center dominates the periphery and in fact organized the polity in such a way as to facilitate the maintenance of its power. Nationally, the center represents the homeland[12] of a nation that is distinct from the nations of the periphery. Empires are political systems based on a power relationship between the center and the periphery and involves the political control of the center *over* the periphery. Logically then Imperialism is simply " the process of establishing and maintaining an empire."[13] Hence the distribution of power overlaps with the issue of nationalism.

The former relationship between Russia and the nations of the former Republics led directly to the following outcomes, both of which complicate political relations. Russia finds it particularly difficult to reconcile itself to the loss of superpower status and to the loss of territories that had long been considered an integral part of its national/political identity. The former Republics, most having no history of independence, must grapple with the twin burdens of governance and nationalism. In addition to the daily burdens of administering a country, they are also responsible for inter-ethnic relations within their borders, a responsibility which is complicated by the fact that the most significant minority group both in numbers and influence, the Russians, represent the nationality of the former imperial center. This last responsibility may be made difficult due to persistent feelings of injustice among indigenous ethnic groups who may be tempted to take out their frustrations on the Russian minorities. But Russia continues to exercise economic, political, and military influence over the territories of the former empire, and it has the tacit support from the West that views the near abroad as part of Russia's sphere of influence.

THE POLITICAL SIGNIFICANCE OF THE RUSSIAN MINORITY

The breakup of the Union has initiated processes of state building, both in Russia and the former Republics, which have been accompanied by attempts to define or redefine the nation. The Russian minorities in the near abroad are reminders of the Soviet Union and the former imperial position of Russia. For Russia, the issue brings into question the political versus national boundaries of the Russian Federation. For the former Republics, the issue is potentially explosive on two fronts: rising nationalism on the domestic scene, and potential interference by their formidable neighbor. The Russian minorities pose a challenge to the development of a Russian state and the maintenance of independence of the former Republics.

The significance of the issue within the Russian Federation reflects the abruptness of the breakup and the attempt by the political elite to construct a new state with the Russian nation as its basis. The political rhetoric in the Russian Federation supports the position that Russia somehow has an obligation to protect their ethnic brethren in the near abroad. The real debate concerns just *how* the Russian Federation should go about this. Proposals range from economic and diplomatic pressure to direct military intervention. Regardless of which strategies Russia may employ in the future, it is clear that this matter continues to provide Moscow a platform for interfering in the near abroad.

The Russian minorities are a pressing problem for the non-Russian Successor States. First, they pose a political problem regarding statehood and national identity. The Successor States are in the process of defining national identities that are to be embodied in the state. To this end, the Successor States seek to increase their independence vis-à-vis Russia. The Russian minorities pose obstacles to these endeavors. They are perceived as outsiders, foreigners, or even colonizers. Knowledge of the official local language became mandatory for citizenship in several instances. Citizenship became mandatory for housing, jobs, education, and health care. There are domestic political pressures in several Successor States to exclude Russians from the political system due to the perception that any laxity in the area of language somehow compromises national integrity. This effort has typically taken the form of establishing laws of citizenship, gaining control over borders, especially the movement of people and goods, and the creation of armed forces. All of this is occurring against a backdrop of heightened national awareness among the indigenous populations with varying degrees of intensity. The wave of nationalist sentiment has in many cases manifested itself in a resentment of the Russian population as witnessed by exclusionary policies such as strict language laws that restrict the number of Russians eligible for citizenship.

Second, the Russian minorities are a potential threat to continued independence. Essentially, their treatment is the most significant issue between Russia and the Successor States. The Russian government has suggested that the former Republics allow dual citizenship whereby the Russians themselves can decide where they want to reside. The Republican governments oppose it on the grounds that it would compromise their sovereignty by transforming the Russian population into a fifth column. On the other hand the consequences for not making concessions to Russian minorities may potentially lead to other difficulties including deteriorating relations with Russia and the disapproval of international bodies such as the Organization for Security and Cooperation in Europe (OSCE) which in the past has criticized the Baltic States for their restrictive citizenship laws.

The issue of the Russian minorities holds somewhat different implications for the Russian Federation. The issue is a contentious one in Russian politics. Political leaders, especially leaders of nationalist parties, have incorporated this issue into their political platforms. The ultra-nationalists proclaim that Russia has a responsibility to the Russians living outside its borders. The nationalist revivals in the former Republics have provoked a Russian nationalist backlash along with fears that the Russian minorities will be targeted for discrimination.

Along with the effects on the rivalry between political parties, the issue is of critical concern to the government for other reasons. It is widely perceived that should the situation grow intolerable in the former Republics, there will be a large influx of Russians from these areas. Hence the legal status and treatment of the Russian minorities is of great concern because repatriating Russian nationals on a large scale would create many problems, and Russia lacks the administrative facilities and financial resources needed to deal with large scale immigration.

GENERAL OUTLINE

This study examines the effects of Russia's continued dominance of the former Republics in a post-Soviet environment by comparing and evaluating the state-building processes in the Successor States of three broad regions: the Slavic, Central Asian, and Baltic states.

The grounds for looking at regions rather than individual states stem from analytical and organizational concerns. The Slavic, Central Asian, and Baltic regions differ from each other, and any focus on individual countries would obscure the similarities among countries of a region and the differences between regions. First, the similarities among countries of a region are more significant than their differences, particularly in the context of relations with Russia. To cover each successor state separately would quickly result in redundancies. For example, separate descriptions of strict citizenship laws adopted by Estonia, Latvia, and Lithuania would quickly become repetitive. What are important are the similarities in the content of citizenship laws in the Baltic States. Second, differences between regions are significant, yet a country by country case study would obscure this fact by providing too much detail on the individual traits of each country rather than what some have in common with others and how some differ from others. The regions are regarded as different in several key areas: geography, political culture, and history. The emphasis on the latter consists of the length and circumstances of their tenure under Russian, and later Soviet, rule; their experience, or lack thereof, with independence; and the existence, or relative absence, of political divisiveness within the Successor States themselves.

The similarity they all share however is the centrality of Russia in their respective domestic and foreign policy considerations. Russia is still the principal trading partner of all of the Successor States including the Baltic States. All of the states in the three regions have a significant number of Russians living within their borders. Relations with Russia are a priority because Russia continues to be the dominant concern in foreign policy decisions, whether because Russia is regarded as the principal security threat or because of a continued military dependence on Russia.

Chapter 2 will examine the value of empire and imperialism as theoretical constructs. How is the classification of the Soviet Union as an empire useful? There is a significant difference between a modern state and an empire. The ideological and normative connotations of the terms "empire" and "imperialism" will be addressed with regards to the Soviet Union.

Chapter 3 will examine the historic origins of the Russian State in the context of Russian nationalism and empire building. The contention that the Soviet Union was an empire, as was the pre-revolutionary Russian state before it, assumes the development of a nationalism that linked state-building with the territorial conquest of non-Russian peoples. Because the building of the Russian state predated modernization, the industrial age, ideas of democracy, and mass participation in politics, it is necessary to demarcate where the national borders of Russia end and conquered foreign lands begin. National boundaries have, in the course of history, shifted with changes in the national makeup of inhabitants resulting from population movements. It is also important to gain some insight as to the development of imperial ideas and how those ideas were transmitted from the Russian bureaucratic elite to the general population, and from Tsarist Russia to Soviet Russia. By the time of the Russian revolution and the establishment of the Soviet Union, the idea of the imperial periphery as the proper domain of Russia took hold.

Chapter 4 examines the issue of the Russian minority living in the near abroad through the prism of Russian nationalism and the Russian political debate over Russia's proper role vis-à-vis the Slavic, Central Asian, and Baltic Successor States.[14] As suggested previously, the Russian minority would not be a volatile issue were it not for Russia's firm stance on this problem. Remnants of the former imperial structure are most clearly visible in the ongoing political debate over the future of the Russian nation. What is needed here is the illumination of the correlation between Russian nationalism and the Russian minority issue; a correlation that is directly related to the broader issue of redefining the Russian nation in the post-Soviet environment. Redefining the Russian nation entails many things, most notably the reconfiguration of relations between Russia and the former periphery of the Soviet empire. Hence the link between this process and Russian nationalism is by no means clear, especially given the huge number of competing conceptions of Russian nationalism.

Chapters 5 through 7 cover the three regions of the study, the Slavic, Central Asian, and Baltic regions respectively. These chapters will focus on the following: (1) the historical background of these regions regarding their contacts with Russia; (2) the relationship between the Soviet central government and the respective regions, with an emphasis on their national and economic development and their respective roles within the Soviet Union; (3) the relationship between the Russian and the national governments of the Successor States of each region following the breakup; and (4) the prospects for the eventual establishment of viable independent states in the areas of the former Soviet Republics.

Chapter 8 pulls together the conclusions drawn from the study. Against the backdrop of their former diminutive status in the Soviet Union, the Successor States can expect to confront serious obstacles in their attempts to strengthen their independence from Moscow. It reaffirms the common difficulties of these very different regions with regards to enduring imperial ties to Russia and Russia's aggressive attitude toward them in turn. The course of state-building in the former Republics will be determined by Russia's eventual reconciliation to the loss of its empire and the ability of the Successor States to overcome the conditions within their own territories that make them vulnerable to Russian pressure and intervention.

NOTES

1. Rasma Karklins, *Ethnic Relations in the USSR* (Boston: Allen & Unwin, 1986) p. 53.

2. See Emil Payin, "The Disintegration of an Empire and the Fate of an 'Imperial Minority,'" in *The New Russian Diaspora* (ed.) Vladimir Shlapentokh, Munir Sendich, and Emil Payin (Armonk: M.E. Sharpe, 1994).

3. A term used by Russian political analysts and politicians to designate the territories of the former Republics. The term reflects the ambiguous status of the Successor States in the eyes of Russians. The "near abroad" is used correspondingly with the term "far abroad" which is used to refer to foreign countries outside the territory of the former Soviet Union.

4. *The Economist Intelligence Unit Country Report: Estonia, Latvia Lithuania, 1st quarter* (London: The Economist Intelligence Unit, 1998), pp. 6, 21, 34.

5. S. N. Eisenstadt, *The Political Systems of Empires* (New York: Free Press of Glencoe, 1963) pp. 10–12.

6. Helene Carrere d'Encausse, *The End of the Soviet Empire* (New York: BasicBooks, 1993) pp. 24–26.

7. Philip Roeder, "Soviet Federalism and Ethnic Mobilization," *World Politics*, vol. 43, January (1991) pp. 199, 212–213.

8. Georgiy I. Mirsky, *On the Ruins of Empire: Ethnicity and Nationalism in the Former Soviet Union* (Westport: Greenwood Press, 1997) pp. 1–3.

9. See Alexander Motyl, *Will the Non-Russians Rebel?* (Ithaca: Cornell University Press, 1987).

10. Ramazan Abdulatipov, "Russian Minorities: The Political Dimension," in *The New Russian Diaspora*, p. 37.

11. Michael W. Doyle, *Empires* (Ithaca: Cornell University Press, 1986) pp. 22–26.

12. The term "homeland" is used to refer to the geographical territory from which members of a nationality originally came. The homeland becomes associated with a given nationality and forms an integral part of national consciousness.

13. Doyle, *Empires*, p. 19.

14. The term "near abroad" is used by Russian government officials and politicians in referring to the territories of the former Soviet Republics. The usage of this phrase carries with it the implication that the Successor States fall within Russia's sphere of influence and therefore remain a legitimate area in which to project Russian power.

Empires and the Case
of the Soviet Union

EMPIRES AND STATES

As previously noted, an empire is understood as a unit of analysis that differs fundamentally from the state. States are understood to be modern, small (relative to empires), and administered in ways that are substantially different from those of empires.

First, there is no center or periphery in a state; the actions of the center as well as the response from the periphery (to the center) serve to keep empires functioning. In a state, there is no dominant nation; that is, that nation does not dominate minority groups in the way in which dominant nations in empires would. Though a state may contain minorities and a nation that is in a numeric superiority, that nation can not be said to have conquered its minorities or their "homeland," though they might, using their larger numbers, be guilty of discrimination. This does not preclude inter-ethnic strife or even violence. But the dominant nation of an empire is sufficiently strong enough to "keep the peace" in their territory. A state differs from an empire in this respect in that serious ethnic unrest leads to a general breakdown in order and an inability of the government to restore order; or the conflict seriously disrupts the day-to-day workings of the government.

Second, the origins of states and empires are different. Hobson suggests that imperialism and empire-building occurs when a nation conquers territory and exceeds its "natural boundaries." States by contrast have not been formed in this way. States formed in three rough periods. The first states emerged in Europe and their borders roughly corresponded to the natural borders of nations. Many minorities of Europe did not achieve their own states either because they were too small and weak, or because their numbers were not sufficiently concentrated in any given territory. The second stage of state formation occurred with the breakup of empires such as the Ottoman and Austria-Hungarian empires. The third stage of state formation occurred with the dissolution of overseas, colonial empires. Most of the states of the developing world had their origins in this stage. As a result, the character of inter-ethnic relations (whether harmonious or discriminatory) emerged *after* the state's formation. An imperial political system by contrast *begins* with the expansion of one nation into territories of others.

Third, the term "empire" does not include states that have one nation that oppresses and/or persecutes another. Empires are more than the elimination of one nation (i.e., its customs, language, and people) by another. Empires involve a complex administrative structure that, though dominated by one nationality, governs impartially; that is the dominant nationality in an empire is not interested in destroying a minority group(s) as such. Priority is in maintaining control, and an all-out ethnic war does not accomplish this purpose.

There is a need to define empires, to explain how they function, and to pinpoint the reasons for their decline. Although the Soviet Union was frequently referred to as an empire, this label is generally applied without systematic explanation or elaboration. Also its usage typically carries with it pejorative connotations, biases, and value judgments.[1] Its application to the Soviet Union and later the Russian Federation was typical in the literature on Soviet nationalities and nationalism. This usage usually evokes the image of a dominant nation, generally understood to be the Russians, restricting the sovereignty of the weaker, smaller nations as represented by the non-Russian Republics.[2] However it was never the aim of such works to elaborate on what constitutes an empire, nor was it their aim to focus on the mechanics of the Soviet political system in a developed theoretical context. Rather the use of the term "empire" was largely descriptive. While this term most often alluded to the multi-ethnic nature of the Soviet Union, the presence of different nations within the same political borders—while certainly a necessary ingredient of empires—is not in and of itself sufficient for the designation of empire.

The remainder of the chapter is divided into three parts. The first explains the characteristics of empires. The second describes the Soviet Union as an empire. The third compares the three regions in their attempts at building state institutions in the post-Soviet period.

In the first part divergent conceptions of empires and imperialism will be examined. The use of the term "empire" implies that there are characteristics peculiar to empires that distinguish them from other political orders. Existing literature falls into two broad categories: narrow, historical definitions of empires (Eisenstadt, Hobson, and Doyle), and the broad, systemic notions of imperialism which focus on the world system (Lenin, Galtung, and Wallerstein). Next I will outline the functional definition of empires used in this study. This section examines the interworkings and administration of empires, how empires function, and the reasons for their decline.

In the second part, this definition is applied to the Soviet Union. Relations between Russia and the Successor States as they have evolved in the last decade are examined. The imperial aspects of the political and economic structure and the Soviet administrative apparatus are considered. The center, as defined by Russia and the Russian nation, is analyzed with an emphasis on its dominant role in the political and economic structures of the Soviet Union as well as its power vis-à-vis the non-Russian union Republics. Finally, relations during the Soviet and post-Soviet periods between the periphery (as defined by the fourteen non-Russian Republics) and the center (understood here to be Russia) are clarified.

The third and final part of the chapter outlines the study and details the basis for comparing different regions of the periphery: the Slavic states, Central Asia, and the Baltic States. Though the former imperial center, Russia, is likely to exercise continued dominance over the former Republics, there has been considerable variance among them in how they have pursued independence. The most important component of constructing a viable and independent state has been, and will continue to be, the tenor of the relationship between these new governments and Moscow, which will in turn impact the state-building processes in these states.

CHARACTERISTICS OF EMPIRES

Some Conceptions of Empires

In using the term "empire," authors, analysts, and social scientists implicitly formulate or have in mind certain characteristics associated with empires. These characteristics are at times quite vague and usually involve some notion of "dominance" or "absolutism." Not uncommonly, theories contradicted one another. For instance, both Lenin and the later dependency and neo-Marxist theorists postulated that imperialism is the spread of capitalism by a small group of "capitalist" or "imperialist" states that deliberately manipulate patterns of international trade to their advantage, thus retarding economic development in non-imperialist countries and perpetuating global inequalities. Joseph Schumpeter on the other hand regarded imperialism and capitalism as diametrically opposing processes and posited that, as capitalism spreads, it will eventually invalidate imperialism.[3]

This study draws on the existing literature on empires and imperialism to define core characteristics of empires. This literature can be divided into two broad categories: empires as political systems and systemic theories of imperialism. Some of the former includes the works of S.N. Eisenstadt, J.A. Hobson, and Michael Doyle; the latter consist, among others, of V.I. Lenin, Immanuel Wallerstein, and Johan Galtung.

Eisenstadt regarded empires as political systems distinct from feudalism and the modern state system. He argues that a specific type of empire, historic bureaucratic empires, can, under certain circumstances, develop from feudalism and further evolve into modern states. Thus the argument goes that historic bureaucratic empires are "more advanced" than feudal systems and "less advanced" than the modern state as a form of political organization. Among the different types of historic bureaucratic empires identified by Eisenstadt are "the West, Central, and East European states, from the fall of feudal systems through the Age of Absolutism."[4] This includes Tsarist Russia and later, the Soviet Union, because he argues the "Age of Absolutism" never really ended but in a sense was actually restored following the Russian Revolution and Communism.

Two definitive characteristics of historic bureaucratic empires distinguish them from feudalism. In historic bureaucratic empires political power is highly centralized, and bureaucratic and administrative functions are independent from social status. Feudalism differs from empires in both of these features. First, feudal systems are decentralized, in that loyalties are given to local lords or local nobility but not a distant ruler. No outside authority controls the social structure or the economy of feudal estates. The very *idea* of feudalism was local self-sufficiency; estates produced what they needed and provided their own military security.

Second, feudal bureaucratic and administrative functions are not autonomous from social position and corresponding societal obligations. A medieval English Knight's military duties were tied to his title. After the decline of feudalism and the rise of empires, a man who could preface his name with a "Sir" did not wear armor and fight with a lance on horseback. Aristocratic titles were divorced from the responsibilities that accompanied them in medieval times; they became inherited indicators of a life of privilege. But in medieval times, administrators had inherited titles. Feudal systems are ascriptive and traditional; administrative positions are not assigned via merit but by one's inherited social status. Social hierarchy is determined not by achievement, but by ascriptive means, such as heredity or personal ties to those with high-ranking status.[5]

The transformation from a feudal system involves centralization and the creation of an autonomous bureaucracy and administrative apparatus. These are the distinguishing characteristics of historic bureaucratic empires. The impetus for these changes originates from a ruler who wants to enlarge his domain either through conquest, expansion, or economic development. Whatever the means, the core desire is the desire to *expand*.[6] To do so requires two things from the onset: maintaining power and mobilizing resources.

To maintain a position of power, a ruler strove not to be merely "first among equals," but to concentrate as much power in his own hands as possible.[7] This meant being released from the obligations and restrictions of the traditional social hierarchy that might impede him from attaining his goals. It also meant creating another social class independent from the traditional social hierarchy (though members may be recruited from its ranks) as a basis for support; this class forms the bureaucracy and administration of the empire.

Through this stratum the ruler is able to mobilize resources and implement policies largely at his own discretion.[8] Centralized power and the existence of a non-traditionally based bureaucratic and administrative caste give rulers broad latitude in pursuing goals because they provide the ruler with an independent and continual supply of resources. The lord of a feudal system depends on his vassals to provide him with equipment and muscle for military endeavors; the vassals comply or abstain according to their personal interests. In an empire, the ruler does not rely on the upper classes from whence he came originally for material support because he has an alternate and more dependable supply of resources. This is the key to the ruler's success. The ruler of a centralized bureaucratic empire "could realize his political objectives only in so far as there existed . . . power and resources that were neither entirely dependent on other groups, nor committed to their use, nor obtainable only through their good will."[9] The regime does not become dependent on the bureaucracy because the traditional upper social ranks retain their societal power and status, a fact that counterbalances the influence of the bureaucratic classes.

In fact, it is in the ruler's best interests that neither these nor any other groups within society have exclusive access to any necessary resource, lest they use this power against the ruler. In spite of the creation of new social strata, the social structure of historic bureaucratic empires is still based mostly on ascriptive, or subjective, criteria. Rulers have an interest in preserving traditional values and orientations because they come from this stratum and hence their legitimacy is grounded in its continued existence.[10] And while the procurement and accumulation of resources is more fluid, this fluidity has its limits and does not resemble any sort of market exchange of the type characteristic of modern societies.[11]

This is the point of departure for most systemic theories of imperialism including those of Lenin, Wallerstein, and Galtung. Hobson's seminal work, *Imperialism*, was the first to pursue the notion that capitalism and imperialism were linked. The state as the tool of big business uses its military, financial resources from its collection of taxes, and the ability to mobilize its population in the pursuit of overseas colonies as new sources of raw materials as well as captive markets for finished goods.[12] The principal preoccupation of Hobson was the spread of capitalism that he equated with imperialism. It was his seminal work on imperialism that influenced thinkers such as V.I. Lenin, Karl Kautsky, Nikolai Bakunin, and Rosa Luxemburg.[13] Lenin's *Imperialism: The Highest Stage of Capitalism* owes a considerable debt to Hobson; it was Hobson who first explored the effects of the spread of capitalism and the impetus behind its expansion, that is, the manipulation of the state apparatus by capitalists in their overseas business ventures.

Nevertheless, Hobson's definition of imperialism, unlike Lenin's, Wallerstein's, and Galtung's, assumed the independent existence of the polity that gave rise to imperialism, that is, empires. In this way Hobson's work acts as a bridge between traditional conceptions of empires, such as that offered by

Eisenstadt, and systemic notions of imperialism. While detailing the accumulation of capital and the acquisition of overseas markets through colonial expansion, Hobson ultimately measured imperialism by the expansion of the colonial powers of Europe, in particular Great Britain, and by the formal annexation of non-native territories.[14]

Hobson emphasizes the significance of nationality in imperial conquest and in the subsequent makeup of empires, noting that annexed territories are inhabited by nations different from that of the colonial power and who are regarded as inferior by the colonial nation, in this case Britain. In fact, for Hobson, imperialism begins when a state expands past the "natural" boundaries of its nation, or nationality, and attempts to absorb territories inhabited by other nations for whom assimilation is impossible.[15]

Hobson also speaks of an attitude of superiority and moral righteousness on the part of the imperial nationality toward the subjugated nations, which serves as the justification for colonialism.[16] This attitude is one that emphasizes the generosity of the imperial power, Britain, in taking on the burden of "civilizing" inferior nations by providing them with Western political, economic, and social know-how. At the very least the imperial mentality incorporates the position that indigenous cultures are far better off being colonized by Britain, as opposed to other, less progressive European powers; if Britain does not fulfill that role, then some other European power will, to the detriment of the non-European natives. The tragic consequences of colonial policies are consistently downplayed or misrepresented.[17] Yet Hobson insists that imperialism is not hypocrisy; rather that it is an elaborate exercise in self-delusion whereby politicians, colonial administrators, and other proponents of imperialism are largely unconscious of the deleterious effects of their actions and attitudes. Hobson maintains that "much of the brutality and injustice involved in imperialism would be impossible without this [unconscious] capacity."[18] Thus the imperial nation perpetuates imperialism through self-delusion, a sense of superiority, and self-righteousness. Those in government service, the educated classes as well as the broader public, are either deluded or kept ignorant of two sets of facts: that injustice accompanies imperialism, and that imperial policies are expensive and come at the cost of the taxpayer for the benefit of financial and business interests.[19]

From systemic theories of imperialism come the concepts of center and periphery. This territorial and national differentiation is what ultimately distinguishes empires from other political orders, though systemic theorists do not subscribe to the existence of more than one empire or even more than one type of political system since all political entities are subordinate to (or part of) one world system. As mentioned previously, systemic theories of imperialism focus on the spread of capitalism to the developing world and attempt to explain the dynamics of this process. In Lenin's *Imperialism: The Highest Stage of Capitalism*, this process is an extension of that which Marx predicted in *Das Kapital*, the evolution of capitalism to the point where it can no longer expand and therefore must give way to another, more progressive force. The mode of transformation as envisioned by Marx and Lenin was of course revolution. But Lenin's work is an attempt to explain why capitalism has endured. His conclusion: the delay in the crisis of capitalism is the result of the internationalization of capital, the exporting of capital (as opposed to goods) for profitable investment (no longer possible in the mother country) to the colonies by colonial powers. He defines this process as imperialism.[20]

Dependency and neo-Marxist theories about the international political economy ultimately owe a debt to Lenin and to Hobson before him. However from the neo-Marxist school come the concepts of center/periphery so useful to the notion of empires.

Immanuel Wallerstein divided the world into three groups of states: core, semi-periphery, and periphery states. This division was a reflection of an international division of labor whereby core states produced and exported manufactured goods utilizing a highly skilled workforce; periphery states were consigned to exporting raw materials and agricultural goods. Because of the value added to manufactured goods, core states could demand comparatively higher prices for them; likewise the highly skilled workforce of the core could demand higher wages.[21] The periphery was left undeveloped and impoverished. Roughly speaking the classical class structure of Marx could be said to apply to the world system of states whereby the capitalist/imperialist states comprise the core while the proletariat states form the periphery.[22] In contrast to modernization theory which stipulates uneven though inexorable world development, dependency and neo-Marxist theorists claim that the development of the core takes place *only at the expense of the periphery*.

Wallerstein's contribution comes not from his analysis of capitalism but his notion of the role states play in shaping the world economy. By designating states as either core or periphery, he was emphasizing the *political* control that core states exert over the world economy at the expense of periphery states. In fact he takes this a step further by recognizing the strength of the state mechanism in the core states and the weakness of the state mechanism in peripheral states as the principal cause for the international division of labor. Hence the *political* leverage of core states consistently exceeds that of peripheral states. The core dominates the world economy because it uses *political* means—military intervention, subversion, and diplomacy—to ensure that the world market operates in its favor.[23]

Johan Galtung further refines the concepts of core/periphery by identifying sub-units within both the center (he uses the term "center" instead of "core") and periphery, sub-units that highlight the imperial relationship between center and periphery. The key to the success of imperialism lies in the alliance between rulers in the core and administrators in the periphery. Accordingly, he identifies a separate "center" in the periphery, a "center" that acts as an outpost for the original imperial center.[24] Galtung, like Wallerstein, views political power as ultimately determining economic relations.

Michael Doyle's work, *Empires*, is an attempt to firmly nail down the concept of empires and imperialism. He draws from earlier works, including those of Eisenstadt and Hobson, and attempts to fuse together characteristics of empires into a comprehensive whole that includes both ancient and contemporary political orders (e.g., colonial empires). He rejects out of hand definitions of imperialism that "do not test whether imperialism actually led to the postulated outcome, empires . . ."[25] and precisely defines concepts such as formal and informal control.

A Functional Definition

Michael Doyle presents the following definition: "Empire: A system of interaction between two political entities, one of which, the dominant metropole, exerts political control over the internal and external policy—the effective sovereignty—of the other subordinate periphery."[26] Imperialism then " . . . is simply the process or policy of establishing or maintaining an empire."[27] Thus the defining features of empires are as follows. An empire is a tangible political unit with finite borders that allow for measurement and analysis. There exists a distinct center (metropole) and a distinct periphery. And the power relationship between the two is an asymmetrical one that favors the center.

Three things need to be explained regarding the political order of empires. First, it is necessary to define and distinguish between "center" and "periphery." Second, the asymmetrical relationship between the center and periphery in empires needs to be elucidated. Third, what do "political control" and "effective sovereignty" mean in this context?

First, the notion of empires assumes an imperial relationship between a center and a periphery that in turn assumes a sharp division between the center and periphery. By "imperial" I mean an unequal relationship based on the preponderance of power in the center, and the ability and willingness on the part of the center to wield its power over the periphery in pursuit of certain goals such as resource extraction, the maintenance of law and order, or the repression of seditious elements. In order to make this distinction meaningful, two conditions must be met. The center and periphery must occupy separate distinct territories; and the periphery must be inhabited by nations different than those of the center.[28]

The second task is to account for the power of the center. In the first place, the central ruling class must have a monopoly of power in the political system; the type of political system is necessarily some variant of an authoritative government. Two, power is concentrated in the center; the latter governs through "agents" whose duty is to collect information and extract resources—two functions essential for the center's continued hold on power.[29] These "agents" or the administrative apparatus that carries out these tasks are usually located in the central part in each national region in the periphery, or what is termed the *center in the periphery*.

To clarify the relationship among the various populations—the regime, the "agents," the population of the center, and the population of the periphery—Galtung subdivides the territory of the center and periphery.[30] The center as a territory has its center (CC) and its own periphery (CP); likewise the periphery of an empire has its own center (PC) and periphery (PP).[31] The urban/rural divide is one example of what Galtung illustrated with this subdivision of the center and periphery. For example, the capital city (that which is usually the largest and contains the bulk of economic and political activity) in the periphery is culturally, socially, and economically very different from the rural areas. The capital links the entire periphery to the center. These cities, when located in the periphery of an *empire*, become the administrative centers of the periphery through which the principal imperial tasks, the collection of information, and the extraction of resources are carried out.

An empire is thus held together by a strategic relationship between the rulers in the center and the imperial administrators in the periphery.[32] Galtung thus summarizes the relationship of the central and peripheral ruling elite. The *center* nation and the *center in the periphery* have common interests. There is a higher level of discord in the periphery than in the center nation. And the interests of the *periphery of the center nation* and the *periphery in the periphery* are dissimilar.[33] The imperial relationship is characterized by the dependency of the periphery nations upon the center. The political arrangement reinforces the unequal relationship between the center and periphery. The relationship is an enduring one because the center maintains close relations with the periphery via its agents in the periphery.

The imbalance of political and economic power is the defining factor of the relationship. Several things account for the weakness of the periphery vis-à-vis the center. First, the periphery is more unstable than the center, partially as a result of the tension between peripheral administrators (who are in alliance with the center) and their constituent populations. This configuration of power typically increases the inequality between the PC and the PP, more so than might be true within the center. The insecurity of the periphery makes it reliant on the center for the maintenance of order necessary for the normal functioning of an integrated economy, which in turn increases the power of the center over the periphery. If the power of the center wanes, creating a power vacuum, peripheral administrators would become exposed and vulnerable to their own constituent populations. According to Doyle, the imperial center, what he terms the "metropole," differs from subordinated peripheries precisely by its political unity. Disunity is what makes peripheral territories vulnerable to imperialism in the first place.

Second, the PC is aligned with the CC, not with its own periphery. Galtung suggests that economic and political interaction is vertical; patterns of interaction stress each of the individual PC's link with the center, resembling the spoke of a wheel. This pattern of interaction likewise illustrates the *lack* of multilateral contacts among the administrative capitals of peripheral territories;

horizontal linkages are missing. The peripheral territories do not face the center united; each deals with the center on its own.

Third, what do "political control" and "effective sovereignty" mean? Political control in empires is both formal and informal in nature.[34] Formal political control involves the official annexation of territories that assumes the center's control over the annexed territories. The distinction is a fine one designed to exclude polities that are unable or unwilling to exercise anything but nominal control over their territories.[35] Examples of regimes not having total, effective control over their territories include empires in decline as well as those polities which never had effective control over territories claimed. Empires can acquire territories through conquest, treaties, and/or dynastic ties, but their ability to administer territories tends to decline over time. It is not uncommon for imperial maps to show dominion over territories that is at variance with reality. An empire in decline and unable to defend its borderlands, such as Rome, remains an empire in that it retains control over many of its peripheral territories. However in areas detached from central control, there can be no imperial relationship between that particular peripheral territory and the center. Herbert Kaufman suggests that since an empire, or any large polity, must ultimately rely on bureaucracy and an administrative apparatus to carry out the mandates of its rulers, an empire's "real" borders are determined by the effective *reach* of its bureaucracy.[36]

Effective political control can also be exercised informally. Domination of one power over another need not be through formal channels, such as annexation. Informal domination exits when(1) the relationship between the dominant and subordinate is "close," with high levels of continued interaction, and (2) the power ratio is highly uneven—enough of a ratio so that the "effective sovereignty" of a territory is eliminated altogether.[37]

Formal control and informal control are both necessary components of imperial rule. One existing without the other is inadequate. Formal control (that is annexation) in the absence informal control would make any discussion of imperial dominance of one nation over others meaningless. It would indicate that the administrative apparatus of the center is either absent or ineffectual; in either event, dictates of the center cannot be implemented.[38] Similarly, informal control in the absence of formal control presents certain conceptual problems. Measurement is problematic because the domination of strong states by weak states in the international arena would be indistinguishable from imperialism and the political systems of empires. Also, in the absence of a formal, homogenous political system, establishing who has control over whom and to what degree is also problematic. Such a conception of empires and imperialism crosses over into the sphere of systemic theories of imperialism.

Here the problem lies with theory testing. If the world is one big imperial system, to what other parallel systems can it be compared? Also, imperialism is the world system yet the nature of the world system is ostensibly the cause of imperialism; imperialism then becomes both the cause and the effect. And, as is the problem with any all-encompassing grand theory, it tends to dismiss or ignore processes that contradict or are not easily reconciled within the framework of the theory. For example, with the emphasis on economic exploitation as the basis of imperialism, the autonomous behavior of disadvantaged states and the economic and social disparities within the "imperialist" states become problematic for systemic theories of imperialism. However, it should be stressed that systemic theories of imperialism and the more classic conceptions of empires address different phenomena; the confusion lies in the use of the term "imperialism," derived from "empire," in the works of Hobson, Lenin, Schumpeter, Wallerstein, and others.

The phrase "effective sovereignty" encompasses control over the internal political system of a country and its external policies such as its relations with other states, that is, foreign policy. In empires eliminating the effective sovereignty of peripheral territories means the center controls both the internal and external policies of the periphery; the political system is imposed on the periphery by the center and foreign policy is handled directly by the center. For instance, in international relations there are numerous examples of strong states effectively dictating the external, or foreign, policies of weak states without taking control over the domestic political regimes of these states. For example, the United States informally influences the foreign policies of the Central American countries. Yet the United States plus Central America does not constitute an empire (although many characterize the relationship as "imperial," the term is used in a broader context than the one in this study). Control is not absolute, because it does not include control over internal policies; nor is the United States always able to influence the foreign policies of these states, for example, Nicaragua and Cuba. Despite the unequal relationship between strong and weak states, the latter remain sovereign. Doyle would characterize this type of relationship as dependency; dependence being understood as "unequal influence" which constrains the actions of weaker states but which falls short of formal and informal control.[39] Hence empires control both the internal political apparatus and the foreign policies of peripheral territories.

An empire then has the following characteristics: (1) it is a political unit with finite and measurable boundaries, (2) it is controlled by a center, and (3) the center exerts both formal and informal control over some number of conquered and/or annexed territories. The administrative center of an empire as well as the surrounding territory primarily inhabited by peoples of the same nationality is referred to as the center, while the annexed territories are termed collectively as the periphery or individually (when distinguishing among nations of the periphery) as peripheral territories.

The Empire and the Modern State

In conceptualizing the differences between empires and modern states, it is useful to do it on two levels: historical and national. Historically, empires predate states. Empires are older forms of political organization. The origins of those empires that have survived into the twentieth century lie in an earlier period. The following is indicative: Austria-Hungary in the seventeenth century when the Hapsburgs came to power; the Ottoman empire, heir to an imperial tradition stretching back to the Byzantine and Roman empires; and the colonial empires of Britain and France which began their quest for overseas colonies in the seventeenth century. States by contrast are modern creations based on clear territorial boundaries and some type of ideology that serves to legitimize their existence, such as nationalism.

One historical trend relevant to any discussion of empires and states has been the increasing acceptance of "democracy" as a political system. Empires are by definition both centralized and non-democratic, and while states can also exhibit these characteristics, most have at least pretensions of being responsive to the popular will and generally observe the outer trappings of democracy such as legislative structures and elections. Those states that are based on a specific nation claim to rule on its behalf and frequently employ chauvinistic rhetoric to mobilize popular support. Empires that survived into the twentieth century were something of an anachronism. Certain conditions were necessary for them to become states. They include economic development (rural and urban) independent of the state; the emergence of autonomous centers of political power; political organization among government and non-government groups who draw their membership from the general population (rather than from already connected groups); clear links between government bureaucracies and popular cultural and political activities; and "strong universalistic elements in the . . . goals, and policies of the rules . . ."[40]

Both empires and states can have more than one nation within their borders. The principal differences between the two types of political systems have to do with whether a single ethnic group controls the political structure, and whether there are distinct *ethnic* territorial boundaries. In empires, one nationality tends to dominate the political machinery, giving that nation inordinate power vis-à-vis others. The dominant and subordinate nations occupy distinct territories in an empire. Hence the relationship between the dominant and subordinate nations tends to be one of conquest as a result of one nation expanding to swallow other.[41] In states, different ethnic groups are not generally confined to a distinct territory far from the political center nor are entire groups necessarily excluded from political power purely on the basis of ethnicity.

Empires: How They Function and Why They Collapse

In outlining how empires function, it is useful to work backwards and first explain what is meant by collapse. In analyzing the collapse of empires, it is logical to assume that when the conditions for their maintenance are not met, they cease to function, and decline can be assumed to follow. In describing their collapse we are describing how they are *not* being maintained.

Norman Yoffee defines collapse as the "drastic restructuring of social institutions," from which political institutions are ultimately derived.[42] Similarly Kaufman argues that despite the differences among empires across time and space, the conditions of their collapse have in common the "dissolution of large-scale political systems encompassing many local groupings of people and institutions."[43] More concretely, the perpetuation of an empire requires that the center be able to extract and procure resources from its territories. When the center can no longer do so, then collapse can be said to have occurred; the loss of extractive capabilities signals the impotence of the political and economic institutions responsible for administering the periphery on behalf of the center. "Economic disaster, political overthrow, and social disintegration . . . " are not the causes but are the consequences of collapse.[44] It must be noted that collapse does *not* mean the termination of a civilization or a people and their culture or traditions. In fact with few exceptions such as that of ancient Mesopotamia, the collapse of empires has not coincided with the end of civilizations.[45]

How and why does collapse occur? Scholars have suggested many factors instrumental in the fall of empires: bad leadership, natural disasters, defeat in war, steady economic decline as the result of changing international trade patterns, and so on. In the latter case, markets for a key revenue-generating export disappear or perhaps the price of key goods imported from abroad becomes prohibitive. Another factor in the decline of government revenues that affects the standard of living of the general population might be environmental degradation.[46] In any event, a precipitous decline in government revenues has dire consequences for imperial administration. Defense of borders becomes more expensive and internal unrest may result from decreased social spending at home on infrastructure, hidden subsidies, and other government services which inhabitants had previously taken for granted. In addition, to raise revenues the center may raise taxes. Either way the standard of living is likely to fall. The negative consequences of this include decreased production and perhaps civil unrest further reducing the capacity of the center to govern.[47]

Rather than produce a general list of the many possible reasons for the fall of disparate empires throughout history, it might be more useful to look to the center and periphery for clues. What conditions are necessary for the creation and maintenance of an empire, and why and how might those conditions change over time? The strength of this sort of approach is that it avoids the pitfalls of reductionist reasoning. The explanations for imperial collapse offered above do offer insight, yet there are too many counter cases where empires appear on the decline but are able to overcome obstacles and avoid collapse. Ancient China is a classic example. The imperial order remained intact for over a millennium. China was first unified under the Chin dynasty which lasted from 221–206 BC, and was ruled by a succession of dynasties almost uninterrupted until this century.[48] So despite certain crisis periods, some empires wax and wane without completely collapsing.

In addition, the provision of a lengthy list of causal factors begs the issue of sufficiency. Would any of the above causes, in and of themselves, be sufficient for the downfall of an empire or must certain combinations of these factors be present before collapse can occur? And at what point do political, economic, and/or ecological tragedies become fatal to the survival of an empire? It is preferable to focus less on these causes than their effects on the functioning of the center and the response of the periphery.

An empire cannot be maintained unless the center wants to rule and conditions in the periphery make central rule possible. In looking at the origins of empires, Doyle hits upon a method that not only serves to account for the origins of empires, but also serves to explain how they are able to function and why they collapse. Doyle has examined theories of empires that consider the origins of imperialism. Some emphasize political dynamics of the center while others focus on the periphery. He suggests that both approaches are valid and should be combined. If the center is prepared to carry out imperialist policies and the periphery is resistant, then creating and maintaining imperial rule over peripheral territories becomes expensive and ultimately futile (unless conditions change in the periphery to favor the acceptance of imperial rule). Likewise, it is impossible to conceive of empires in the absence of an imperial mind-set on the part of would-be emperors. If the Caesars of Rome did not believe in the superiority of Roman civilization that included a mission of conquest as well as a practical and utilitarian method of administration, there would have been no conquest and hence no Roman empire.

Basic conditions in the center are necessary for the creation and maintenance of empires. They include the following: a nation united by a common purpose and organized and mobilized by a leadership with an interest in imperial expansion and a belief in the superiority of the nation. The leaders must be able, at least in the formative phase of an empire, to imbue their subjects with a sense of purpose and the notion that imperialist expansion is of benefit to both themselves and the peoples of the conquered territories.

Nationalism however is an emotive issue and does not hold up to hard logic. One cannot argue that imperial expansion is a decision reached by a rational consideration of potential strategies; that is, the impetus for empire-building cannot be accounted for using a "rational choice" model of decision making. A classic example of a state pursuing imperialist policies to its own detriment would be interwar Germany that pursued aggressive, nationalistic and expansionist policies after 1932.[49] Rather, imperial expansion is based on a belief system of national superiority or belief in some sort of manifest destiny. Imperial expansion becomes synonymous with national will; expansion is justified for any number of reasons. Belief is the key.

In the periphery, the following conditions facilitate imperial conquest: a politically divided population, a lack of popular national mobilization, and general instability. Eisenstadt has suggested that the maintenance of empires depends on the political involvement of a minority of the population and the political noninvolvement or apathy of the majority.[50] This would seem to be true of both the center and periphery: the majority of the former are most likely unaware of the cost it bears for imperial expansion and maintenance, while the latter are unaware of, or indifferent to, the lack of national sovereignty. Elite/mass divisions in both center and periphery vindicate Galtung's division of the center and periphery into the CC/CP and PC/PP sub-units outlined previously.

The Behavior of the Center Following the Dissolution of the Empire

Once empires crumble, what characterizes the behavior of the former imperial center? What can be expected from the center once its formal power has waned? Plainly, the behavior of the center will be heavily influenced by its past imperial position. The relationship between the center and periphery would not therefore be expected to change drastically after the formal dissolution of the former empire. Though the specifics of the center's behavior and the duration of the adjustment period will differ from case to case, the general patterns of behavior will be similar for all empires.

First, a lingering imperial attitude on the part of the former center can be expected. Accustomed to being in a position of power and of dominating the territories of the periphery, the center continues its superior attitude in its relations with the former periphery. It follows that the center will continue to interfere in the internal politics of the former periphery, with the former center using various means to influence political outcomes favorable to its interests.

Second, this lingering attitude is the result of the center's initial inability (which may or may not be long-term) to reconcile and adjust itself to the decline of its power. The breakup of an empire can be expected to produce heightened feelings of insecurity and inadequacy on the part of the center. This can make relations with the periphery uncomfortable, for the behavior of an insecure center that was accustomed to being in a position of power will be unpredictable and occasionally belligerent. And should foreign powers attempt to take advantage of the weakened position of the center by establishing a presence in the former periphery, the center can be expected to react negatively.

In short the center of any empire will take its dissolution badly, with a heightened sense of insecurity; the former periphery will suffer the consequences for the insecurity of the former center because it will bear the brunt of the former center's unpredictable, aggressive behavior. Such is certainly the case of Russia, the former center of the Soviet Union.

THE CASE OF THE SOVIET UNION

What is necessary then for collapse to become irreversible is a change in the circumstances in the center and periphery. This is well illustrated in the Soviet case. In essence the center was demoralized by infighting among the ruling elite. The Gorbachev reforms led to the destruction of the cadre system, that is the patron-client relationship between the central and peripheral leadership that effectively negated the center's power to mobilize resources. The economic reforms and conflicting policies led to confusion and in some instances insubordination among bureaucrats resulting in the immobilization of the government's administrative apparatus. This demoralization permeated the general population resulting in public apathy.

The center was no longer "unified" by a common goal or even a common sense of national identity. There has emerged a strain of Russian nationalism that is decidedly anti-Soviet; that is, completely alienated from the very wellsprings of Russian imperial expansion in the twentieth century.[51] This brand of Russian of nationalism rejects the Soviet heritage and asserts that the Russians as a nation suffered as much if not more than the non-Russian nations. This is because Soviet ideology attempted to destroy Russian national identity while actively preserving the ethnic identities of Republican nationalities though the policy of *korenizatsiia* (see chapter 3). It is Russia that was used as the model for a new Soviet national identity that was based on an abstract ideology derived from a foreign philosophy.

In the periphery, or non-Russian Republics, there has been a mixed reaction to the collapse of the center. In the Baltic States, Moldova, and the Caucasus, national mobilization during the Gorbachev years created resistance to continued Soviet rule. In contrast, the working relationship between the Moscow leadership and Republican Party cadres in Central Asia survived the collapse of Soviet authority. In the former Slavic Republics of Ukraine and Belarus, the reaction to the dissolution was more complex. In Ukraine a certain segment of Ukrainians concentrated in Galicia and far-western portions of Ukraine supported separation from Russia and view Ukraine as a part of Central Europe. But Russians living in Ukraine and russified Ukrainians see a close relationship, if not reunification, with Russia as pragmatic and even essential. Belarus sees its future even more closely bound to Russia.

However it is conditions in the former center which prevent the recreation of the Union. Because the Russia under the leadership of Yeltsin lacked the will and resources to reconstruct the old empire, the Republics have no recourse to anything except independent statehood. Even if the center did not lack the will, conditions of heightened national awareness in the former Republics would make attempts at reannexation extremely costly.[52] Nevertheless, Russia does remain a formidable regional power whose political players agree on one point: that informal, if not formal, control over the territories of the former Republics is essential for Russian security.

The imperial structure of the USSR will impact post-breakup relations between the constituent parts of the former Soviet multi-ethnic state in a way that is distinct from that of other multi-ethnic but non-imperial states which have dissolved. As a historical bureaucratic empire,[53] which survived a revolution, two world wars, the creation of the United Nations, and decolonization, the Soviet Union (heir to the tsarist imperial legacy) dissolved abruptly, quickly, and in the absence of war. Furthermore, the dissolution of the Soviet Union led to the creation of 15 new states that gained sovereignty by default after the Soviet regime relinquished control over the Republics. Before the twentieth century they most certainly would have been swallowed up and conquered by adjacent powers.

But two features distinguish the Soviet case. First, the center of any empire usually has continued interests in the affairs of its former territories. Britain has the Commonwealth and France has its "special" relationship with the francophone countries of West Africa and the Middle East. Since the Soviet Union was a territorially contiguous empire, Russia can be expected to have an even greater interest in its former territories as these territories are regarded as intrinsic to Russian national security. In combination with considerable power vis-à-vis the Successor States, this interest translates into the exercise of political and economic control and influence in the near abroad.

Second, the Successor States, as the former periphery, though nominally independent, continue to be largely dependent on the center for economic and military security. In Eurasia the old political, economic, and military structures continue to predominate, a fact that hampers national and state development to varying degrees in the Successor States. For example, most of the Successor States still depend on Russia for petroleum and natural gas because they are unable to afford them on the open world market. Likewise, Turkmenistan and Kyrgyzstan early on signed security arrangements with Russia whereby the Russian military would maintain its presence in these countries for the purpose of defending the southern borders of the former Soviet Union. Belarus has a customs and military arrangement with Russia and is the only former Republic to remain within the ruble zone. Georgia has capitulated to President Putin's demands that Russian troops patrol Georgia's border with Chechnya, ostensibly to prevent reinforcements from reaching the Chechen rebels. Such bilateral arrangements allow for continued Russian influence in the areas of its former periphery.

However, there are differences among the Successor States in individual potential for successful nation and state building. Despite their shared imperial history, they differ widely from each other in their strategies in dealing with Russia. These differences are most clear if the Successor States are considered on a regional basis; accordingly the Successor States examined in this study are divided into three categories—the Slavic, Central Asian, and Baltic states. All were a part of the same system for most of the twentieth century, and all under went modernization while a part of the Soviet system. There existed a certain political and economic homogeneity as a result of an overarching administrative and bureaucratic apparatus.

But with the dissolution of the Soviet Union, it was clear institutionalization and political integration had failed;[54] the empire became a series of states by virtue of the political age in which it dissolved, that is, the age of the nation-state. And their efforts to establish themselves as sovereign states are vulnerable to changing conditions in Russia; that is, all are dependent on their giant neighbor for a variety of necessities: political good will (necessary for avoiding confrontations), material resources, markets for goods, and security arrangements.

Still it is clear that the different regions face vastly different prospects in the wake of the breakup. In order to examine these divergent outcomes more closely, one must begin by defining more precisely what is meant when it is said that the Soviet Union was an "empire" and Russia the "imperial" nationality.

The Political and Economic Administrative Apparatus of the Soviet Union

The Soviet system combined traditional and modern features that served as the basis for later contradictions and inefficiencies that emerged in the Soviet system. On the one hand traditional features as holdovers from the Tsarist empire represented continuity and provided structure for the new Soviet regime that was attempting to engineer from the ground up a revolutionary political, economic, and social order based on an abstract, utopian ideology. On the other hand the introduction of certain modern features created basic contradictions within the empire.[55]

The traditional features include those aspects of the Soviet system that have their origins in the Tsarist empire: territory, patrimonialism, and bureaucracy. The Soviet State is in this sense the direct heir to the Tsarist Empire. In fact after WWII the amount of territory under Moscow's control *exceeded* the boundaries of the Tsarist Empire. The Soviet Union retained an authoritarian mode of governance that stressed citizens' duties to the state and it even expanded the state's sphere of control to include the personal lives of its citizens and central control over the economy. A highly centralized bureaucracy that was accountable to the central government in Moscow administered the Soviet Union. Despite its federal structure, the Soviet Union was administered as a centralized polity.

But the perpetuation of a historic bureaucratic empire depends on the political apathy and noninvolvement of most of the population, a fact at variance with the modern aspects of the Soviet Union. The mass mobilization of the population into the political system is a modern concept, one that upsets the delicate balance in center/periphery relations necessary for the maintenance of historic bureaucratic empires.[56] Popular participation in the political process is generally associated with some variant of democracy, but in the Soviet case, political participation was a compulsory and meaningless ritual. The legitimatizing of the Soviet Union rested on Marxist-Leninist ideology that in the Soviet interpretation, demanded complete state control of every aspect of society.

Here it is useful to recall how authoritarian and totalitarian regimes differ. An authoritarian regime is concerned with controlling the government; to that end it excludes out-groups from the political process and suppresses only those elements that actively oppose it. A totalitarian regime by contrast seeks to control all aspects of not only political life, but economic and social life as well. All aspects of life become "politicized," including the private thoughts of individuals. All groups—interest, ethnic, class, and so on—are therefore co-opted into the state system according to parameters defined by the state.[57] Accordingly the state demanded the political mobilization and compulsory participation of its citizens.

In the realm of center/periphery relations, Moscow mobilized Republican leaders and sought their support for the Union; at the same time Moscow attempted to tightly control all aspects of civil society in the Republics. Mass mobilization and the notion of popular participation in the political process, however nominal, clashed with the totalitarian mode of governance. Let us in turn consider the center and periphery of the Soviet Union in the context of the broader concept of empires.

The Center: Russia

If the Soviet Union can be characterized as an empire, then Russia, or more precisely, the RSFSR (the Russian Soviet Federal Socialist Republic), can be regarded as its imperial center. The most obvious manifestation of this is the location of the administrative apparatus of the Soviet Union. The All-Union Party and state structures of the Soviet Union were located in Moscow. Political (including the economic and social spheres) power was concentrated in the center, Moscow. Gosplan, the organ responsible for setting the manufacturing quotas and prices for all manner of goods produced in the Soviet Union, was based in Moscow; hence economic planning and investment policies for the Republics were made in Moscow. Government at all levels was merely an extension of the central government and they were not, as in federated democracies, autonomous from the central government.

The various theories of empires stress the dominance of the center over the periphery, and if the center is represented by a particular nation, then it follows that this nation occupies a privileged position within the empire. The concept of nationality is implicit in most discourses on imperialism. As Hobson noted, imperialism occurs when one nationality exceeds its own "natural" boundaries and expands to include territories of neighboring nations. Russian expansion into the Republics fits this pattern. A large number of Russians had relocated to areas of the periphery during the Soviet period, and retained their privileged position because ignorance of the local language was not an impediment to employment or advancement.[58]

Russia at the center of the Soviet Empire placed Russia in a dominant position vis-à-vis the Republics. This fact indicates that the impetus for imperial expansion originated in Russia, with all that implies about national will and grandiose ideologies. If Russia is the center of the Soviet Empire, then Russia can be considered the dominant, or imperial, nation. The Russian language was the *lingua franca* of the Soviet Union, used in all spheres of government, education, and media. Although titular languages were sometimes used on television, radio, or local newspapers and journals, the geographic range of titular language broadcasting on television or radio was limited to local areas. Naturally this placed non-Russian speakers at a disadvantage socially and professionally, particularly if they lived outside their titular Republic or were of an ethnicity not represented territorially.

There are several reasons to assume the dominance of the Russian nationality in the Soviet Union. These include the following: ethnic makeup of the leadership, the Russian presence in the Republics, and the fact that Moscow managed the economy which created the perception among the Republics that investment decisions were detrimental to their interests.

Most of the top party leadership positions, those in the Politburo and the Secretariat, went to ethnic Russians. Though other nationalities were represented in the All-Union structures, their numbers never came close to their respective percentages of the Soviet population. Ethnic Russians have always been over represented in the party apparatus of the Soviet Union. The percentage of ethnic Russians as members and candidates for membership for the Central Committee ranged from 55 percent to 71.5 percent from 1939–1981. Corresponding percentages for members and candidates for membership in the Politburo range from 61.9 percent–81 percent during the same period.[59] Ethnic Russians comprised 64.9 percent of membership in the Communist Party of the Soviet Union in 1927, 67.8 percent in 1946, 63.5 percent in 1961, and 59.8 percent in 1982. When taken together with other Slavs—Ukrainians and Belarusians—these numbers swell to 79.6 percent, 82 percent, 81.2 percent, and 79.6 percent respectively.[60]

Second, a substantial Russian presence in the Republics developed over the years. Numerically Russians dominated not only at the All-Union level, but also frequently at the Republican level as well. Russians formed a substantial portion of party membership and party government positions in the various Republics. This was true at the inception of the Soviet Union when there was a dearth of local cadres, and it was true on the eve of the dissolution, though the overall percentages of non-Russian cadres did increase over time. In general the lower the levels of government, the higher the percentage of native representation. Hence at the Soviet Union's inception, Ukrainians accounted for only 36.2 percent of the party at the Republican level, but 75.9 percent at the All-Union level. In Turkmenistan the numbers were 8.4 percent and 24.1 percent respectively. Only in Armenia and Georgia was the titular share of the party apparatus high, 93.5 percent and 94.6 percent, and 74.1 percent and 80.9 percent respectively.[61] While native representation increased over time, Russians continued to be over represented in party structures (in relation to their proportion) of the local population at all levels.

Russian influence in the Republics was further enhanced by the Soviet pattern of governing. In the Republics a local cadre, the First Secretary, headed the governing body of the Central Committee, or bureau. The First Secretary was the "boss" in the Republics. An unspoken agreement between the center and the Republics maintained the loyalty of the Republican cadres who were given carte blanche in governing in return for their support. Nonetheless, the Second Secretary was almost invariably a Russian who was the "eyes and ears" of Moscow.[62] These were among the empire's "agents" in the field.

In addition to the pervasive Russian presence in the government evident in party membership and political appointments, there was a substantial number of Russians living in all the Republics except those in the Caucasus. In some Republics such as Estonia, Latvia, and Kazakhstan, the percentage of Russians threatened to exceed that of the titular nations. This fact underscored the privileged status of Russians in a variety of ways.

First, Russians did not feel the need to learn the titular language because obtaining work was not hindered by this lack of knowledge. That is not to say that Russians living in the Republics were never bilingual, only that their job, housing, and advancement opportunities did not depend on it. In ranking the important reasons for learning the titular language, "interaction and contact with coworkers," not "the fulfillment of official duties," ranked the highest among intellectuals and workers at 70 percent and 64 percent of Russian respondents in Estonia respectively.[63] Even higher education was generally in Russian, though there were some colleges that taught primarily in the titular language, most notably in Georgia. But the Georgian case was the exception; Russian language schools and universities were the norm. Russian speakers always had a choice whereas most non-Russian minorities did not.

In matters of language policy Russians in the periphery could count on support from the Russian center. The non-Russians had no such recourse for arbitration. Even emphasizing the use and study of the titular language of a Republic serves to reinforce the use of Russian by making it a mandatory second language in every Republic. In practice, Russian remained the *lingua franca*—the "language of inter-ethnic communication."[64]

Second, the Russians in many Republics, with a few notable exceptions, formed a significant share of the skilled, technical workforce and the intelligentsia. They also tended to be urban dwellers. These two facts combined serve to place the Russian population in a higher socio-economic position vis-à-vis the native population. Since urban areas generally received the bulk of resources distributed through economic planning, superior living conditions made city life more attractive. Urban dwellers have access to housing, transportation, employment, and other amenities not found in the country. In general urbanites enjoy a higher standard of living than do the people living in the countryside. Since Russians living in the Republics were mostly urban, they formed a significant percentage of the privileged class of the Republics, especially taking into account that Soviet authorities strictly controlled internal migration.

Only in northern Kazakhstan did the Russian population, who migrated there in large numbers during Khrushchev's "virgin lands" scheme, settle rural areas in large numbers.

Third, economic problems were blamed on Russia, as it was Moscow that managed every aspect of the economy through Gosplan's five-year plans. Decisions about investment (the allocation of resources to manufacturers), production (where, by whom, and how much), and consumption (distribution) were made in Moscow. Whether or not Russians were actually favored in these arrangements was immaterial; that was the perception of the Republics and in politics, perception matters more than reality. Discontent over central management of Republican economies was directed against Russia. The Baltic Republics for example, while being the most well-off in terms of standard of living indices, felt they were being held back economically with economic decisions made in Moscow instead of Tallinn, Riga, or Vilnius. Similarly the Central Asian states, being the poorest by the same measure, regarded central planning, especially the introduction of the cotton monoculture at the expense of cereal production and the lack of investment in industry, as the reason for economic ills and poor living conditions. Endemic unemployment and underdevelopment in Central Asia is widely blamed on Moscow.[65] Moldova, Ukraine, and Belarus could point to central planning as the main reasons behind ecological disasters: in the case of Moldova, the pollution of rivers through over-fertilization and waste dumping; in the case of Ukraine and Belarus, the explosion at Chernobyl.

Notoriously inefficient centrally planned economies naturally provided a continual impetus for discontent. By the 1980s the economy of the Soviet Union was in crisis. GNP was falling, growth in the economy virtually ceased and may have even declined, and productivity was at a low, as were capital investments.[66] Even the Soviet regime admitted there was a problem; after all, it was the economic crisis that originally motivated Gorbachev to reform the system. The economic crisis was also instrumental in the nationalist mobilization that took place in varying degrees in virtually every Republic in the latter half of the 1980s.

Korenizatsiia in the Republics and Political Oppression

The identification of Russians as the imperial nationality must be subject to some qualification. First, the Soviet Union was not a democracy and Russians too were victimized by the system. They died in large numbers during Stalin's purges and they were subject to the same repression by security organs. In a similar vein it can be argued that the nomenclature, the ruling elite of the Soviet Union, had no nationality nor did ordinary Russians, by virtue of their ethnicity, share in its wealth and privilege. An ordinary Russian worker would hardly have viewed himself as "privileged" compared to non-Russian members of the nomenclature.

Second, Russians did not enjoy significantly higher standards of living compared to non-Russians. Indeed the Baltic Republics had, and still have, higher standards of living than the RSFSR. The same was frequently cited for Georgia.

Third, the policy of *korenizatsiia,* or "indigenization of the Republican ruling elite," encouraged national differentiation which effectively reinforced national identity in the Republics. Because the Bolsheviks were essentially Russian, they originally found it necessary to make concessions to non-Russians living on the periphery in order to secure their allegiance and extend Soviet rule into these areas.[67] As originally conceived, *korenizatsiia* was implemented for the purpose of extending the Soviet state apparatus into non-Russian areas of the Soviet Union by co-opting local cadres. By developing national intelligentsia in the Republics, it was hoped that Republican leaders would be socialized to support Soviet rule and encourage the masses to do likewise. While that hope was substantially realized, it was also true that ethnic and cultural differences between Russians and non-Russians were reinforced.[68] At the same time *korenizatsiia* was initiated, Russian nationalism itself was harshly repressed as a challenge to Soviet rule.

Korenizatsiia directly affected Russians living in the Republics. The implementation of this policy was in effect affirmative action favoring the titular nationality of the Republics. In areas such as university admissions, government jobs and so forth, the titular nationality was favored. Ironically while *korenizatsiia* applied to the Republics, it did not apply to the RSFSR. For example, through indigenization, the titular nationalities had their own academies of sciences, writers' unions, and various cultural facilities while there were no comparable Russian institutions apart from the All-Union "Soviet" ones. There was not even a Russian Party apparatus for the RSFSR, a courtesy afforded the rest of the Union Republics.

The above caveats do not abrogate the fact of Russian central control of the Soviet Empire. There is a difference between the situation of individual Russians and the reality of the administrative structure of the Soviet Union. The Republican governments were simply organs of the central government. Implementing policies favorable to local leaders if the purpose of such policies is to strengthen the center's control over the periphery does not alter the power balance between the center and periphery. The Soviet regime early on made certain conscious decisions that encouraged Republican cadres to find it in their individual self-interest to support the empire.

Nor are higher living standards among some minorities necessarily indicative of equality between Russia and the Republics. Living standards are a measure of economic well-being, but not necessarily of political power. And in a totalitarian political system, such disparities in living standards are an acceptable price to pay for political control. Maintaining an empire is an expensive enterprise that is made easier with the support or at least acceptance of the peripheral nations. Attempts by the center to level disparities of living standards would be more costly in terms of implementing such polices in the face of stiff resistance than leaving well-enough alone.

The effects of *korenizatsiia* were felt primarily in the Republics. Should titular minorities (i.e., minorities represented territorially in the Soviet federal structure) move from their respective homelands, their social situation would change drastically for the worse (just how much worse depends on the nationality of the minority in question as well as individual career choices). An Uzbek is in a far better position, all things being equal, living in Uzbekistan that if he moved to Russia.

The Periphery: The Non-Russian Republics

While the impulse from the center provides the initial impetus for imperial expansion, conditions in the periphery determine the success and durability of the center's efforts. What conditions make possible imperial conquest? How and why did Russian expansion into these areas become possible?

The conditions that made conquest possible include the following: low levels of economic development; low levels of national consciousness that might otherwise provide an incentive to ward off invasion; the small size of some nations which makes self-defense impossible despite national cohesiveness; general political and economic instability stemming from underdevelopment and/or fighting between ethnic or clan groups; and international conditions that favor or reject imperial conquest.

The Slavic Successor States of Ukraine and Belarus are characterized by low levels of national consciousness and a general uncertainty regarding national affiliation, which is complicated by their close historic, ethnic, and linguistic connection to Russia. The exception to this is the Ukrainian nationalism that emanates primarily from the far-western part of Ukraine, Galicia and Ruthenia, which had been added to the Soviet Union relatively soon after WWII. It is an area known for its resistance, especially instances of armed resistance, to the imposition of communist rule. Neither Belarus nor Ukraine has a history of independence and that also complicates matters.[69]

In Central Asia the problems of underdevelopment, the persistence of traditional social structures such as clan and tribe, combined with low levels of national consciousness and persistent instability due to fighting between factions created conditions of vulnerability to conquest. Low levels of nationalism stem from the artificial creation of the Republics from what was previously one region. The region of Central Asia was originally called Turkestan, with the people speaking various Turkic dialects that in some cases were not even written languages. When the Republics of Kazakhstan, Kyrgyzstan, Turkmenistan, Uzbekistan, and Tajikistan were created in 1925 after resistance to incorporation into the Soviet Union was quelled, dialects were codified in a manner designed to obscure their common origins. In addition, borders divided nations.[70] For example Osh, located in Kyrgyzstan, is largely an Uzbek city.

In the case of the Baltic States, their small size meant that throughout history these territories have succumbed to larger political entities (e.g., Prussia, Sweden, Poland, and Russia) despite relatively higher levels of development and high levels of national consciousness. International conditions contributed to the annexation of the Baltic States to the Soviet Union. The incorporation of the Baltic States into the Soviet Union was the result of the Molotov-Ribbentrop pact between Nazi Germany and the Soviet Union, two larger powers concerned with augmenting their own positions and undermining those of their respective opponents.

COMPARING THREE REGIONS

Different Regions; Similar Difficulties vis-à-vis Russia

This study highlights the different strategies that the Successor States of each region are using to cope with independence and state-building. The imperial structure of the Soviet Union and the abruptness of its demise complicate post-Soviet relations among the constituent parts of the former empire. Russia has a continued interest in the former Republics and uses its power to influence events in what it terms as the "near abroad" (*blizhnee zarubezhe*). But the strategies of the Successor States in dealing with this lingering dependence have varied, despite the fact that Russia remains the common security concern for all of the Successor States.

The chapters will focus on the following criteria for comparisons: (1) historical relationship to Russia, (2) nationalism and national consciousness, in particular the nationalist revivals of the late 1980s, (3) post-independence political and economic strategies with an emphasis on the impact of these on the relationship with Russia, and (4) international conditions as they might affect state-building and economic development. The above criteria highlight the historical role of Russia as well as the role Russia is likely to play in the future development of the Successor States in the post-Soviet era. They also demonstrate the differences of the regions in regard to one another while highlighting the similar dilemmas they all face.

The history of Russian dominance in these regions underscores the vulnerability of the former Soviet Republics. The topography of Ukraine and Belarus offers no resistance to conquering armies. Ukraine and Belarus experienced continual warfare and changed hands often. This historical experience contributed to the development, or lack of, a distinct national identity. The historical experience of Central Asia served to keep that region underdeveloped and fractured. Constant warring among indigenous political factions made the establishment and maintenance of a unified political system difficult. Continued feuding and persistent economic underdevelopment meant the lack of a coherent, coordinated national resistance to Russian coercion. In the case of the Baltic States, they were simply small states that, due to their size, were easily swallowed up by larger powers.

To understand the nationalist movements that emerged to challenge Soviet rule in the mid-1980s, a brief look at how each region developed during the Soviet period becomes informative. A look at the Soviet period makes clear that nationality was reinforced due to the nationality policies of the center that vacillated between promotion and repression of the indigenous cultures of the Union Republics. It was during the Soviet period that the vertical pattern of interaction between the center and each of the Union Republics was established. This pattern of interaction included political and economic control of the Republics directly by Moscow, a development that precluded the establishment of horizontal linkages among the Republics themselves. This has direct implications for the post-Soviet period as the imperial links to the Moscow endured while the lack of linkages among the former Republics weakened the bargaining power of the governments of the new states after independence. Horizontal links among the former Republics might have made them less dependent on Russia for trade and energy supplies. They might also have collectively faced and prevailed over Russian political pressures.

The events of the Soviet period also highlight variations in economic development. The Soviet command economy dictated different economic roles for the regions. In Ukraine and Belarus, industrial development was combined with agricultural development. Under Soviet rule, Ukraine and Belarus were nominally able to establish and reassert their own separate national identities. At the same time, russification was largely successful due to cultural and linguistic similarities and the practical advantages and opportunities to be had through a Russian education. Both conditions explain why Belarusians and Ukrainians did not suffer ethnic discrimination since they were not recognized as significantly different than Russians. It is true that the languages of both were repressed and considered unfit for literary and scientific expression.

Nationalists were not so much discriminated against because of their ethnicity; rather their nationalist tendencies were viewed as a *political* challenge to the center and were repressed for political reasons. The Central Asian Republics were kept underdeveloped in the scheme of Soviet central planners. Infrastructure built in Central Asia was to support mining and other extractive industries, and agriculture. Central Asia was relegated to supplying the union with raw materials that were processed in other areas of the Soviet Union. The Baltic States were heavily industrialized and militarized. They also produced agricultural commodities such as dairy products. Their economic development was successful enough to make them an attractive place to settle for Russians. The militarization and industrialization of the Baltic States facilitated the movement of large numbers of Russians into the Baltic States.

Finally, the post-Soviet period is characterized first and foremost by the *endurance* of imperial ties between Russia and the former Republics. Continuing dependence on Russia and Moscow's continued interference in the domestic and foreign policies of the former Republics is very much in evidence. In the absence of any external aid or alternative foreign trading partners, old imperial links with Russia have become the principal means of salvaging interstate trade and to countering deteriorating economic conditions. Thus is the situation in the Slavic and Central Asian Successor States. The Baltic States by contrast have chosen to eschew old imperial links and replace them with expanded relations with European, especially Scandinavian, countries.

The remaining chapters are organized as follows. The third and fourth chapters deal with Russian nationalism and Russian intentions in the near abroad as well as Moscow's capabilities and limitations in influencing events in the near abroad. Any attempt to gauge the potential of the Successor States to establish viable states must begin with examining Russian intentions toward its former borderlands.

Chapters 5, 6, and 7 deal with the three regions: the Slavic, Central Asian, and the Baltic States. The basis for categorizing the Successor States into different regions stems from the need to concentrate on the larger issue of the breakup of empires and to avoid redundancies. Outstanding exceptions to the regions will be noted, for example Kazakhstan's geographic and demographic schism between Russians and Kazakhs.

NOTES

1. A. P. Thornton, *Imperialism in the Twentieth Century* (Minneapolis: University of Minnesota Press, 1977) pp. 3–6.

2. See for example Helene Carrere d'Encausse, *Decline of an Empire* (New York: Newsweek Books, 1979) and *The End of the Soviet Empire: The Triumph of the Nations* (New York: Basic Books, 1993); Robert Conquest (ed.), *The Last Empire* (Stanford: Hoover Institution Press, 1986); and Alexander Motyl, "From Imperial Decay to Imperial Collapse: The Fall of the Soviet Empire in Comparative Perspective," in *Nationalism and Empire* (New York: St. Martin's Press, 1992). These are only a few of the works by specialists in the field which refer to the Soviet Union as an empire.

3. Joseph Schumpeter, *Imperialism and Social Classes* (New York: Meridian Books, 1951), p. 65–67.

4. S. N. Eisenstadt, *The Political Systems of Empires* (New York: The Free Press of Glencoe, 1963) p. 11.

5. Monte Palmer, *Dilemmas of Political Development: An Introduction to the Politics of Developing Areas*, 4th ed. (Itasca: F. E. Peacock Publishers, 1989) p. 72.

6. Eisenstadt, *The Political Systems of Empires*, p. 116.

7. Ibid., p. 118.

8. Ibid., p. 117.

9. Ibid., p. 118.

10. S. N. Eisenstadt, "Introduction," in *The Decline of Empires* (ed.) S. N. Eisenstadt (New Jersey: Prentice-Hall, 1967), p. 4.

11. Ibid., p. 120.

12. J. A. Hobson, *Imperialism* (Ann Arbor: reprinted by the University of Michigan, 1965), p. v; V. I. Lenin, *Imperialism: The Highest Stage of Capitalism* (New York: reprinted by International Publishers, 1939) p. 15.

13. Hobson, *Imperialism*, p. 220.

14. Ibid., pp. 15–27.

15. Ibid., p. 6.

16. Ibid., pp. 221–222.

17. Ibid., p. 211.

18. Ibid.

19. Ibid., pp. 206–207.

20. Vladimir I. Lenin, *Imperialism: The Highest Stage of Capitalism*, pp. 62–64.

21. Immanuel Wallerstein, *The Capitalist World-Economy* (Cambridge: Cambridge University Press, 1979) p. 162.

22. Ibid., p. 133.

23. Ibid., p. 21.

24. Johan Galtung, "A Structural Theory of Imperialism," *Journal of Peace Research*, no. 2 (1971) p. 83.

25. Michael W. Doyle, *Empires* (Ithaca: Cornell University Press, 1986) p. 33.

26. Ibid., p. 12.

27. Ibid., p. 45.

28. Alexander J. Motyl, "From Imperial Decay to Imperial Collapse: The Fall of the Soviet Empire in Comparative Perspective," in *Nationalism and Empire: The Hapsburg Monarchy and the Soviet Union* (ed.) Richard L. Rudolph and David F. Good (Minnesota: St. Martin's Press, 1992) p. 18.

29. Ibid., pp. 24–25.

30. Johan Galtung, "A Structural Theory of Imperialism," p. 83.

31. Ibid.

32. Fernando Cardoso and Enzo Faletto, *Dependency and Development in Latin America* (Berkeley: University of California Press, 1979) ch. 6.

33. Johan Galtung, "A Structural Theory of Imperialism," p. 83.

34. Doyle, *Empires*, p. 30.

35. Ibid., p. 33.

36. Herbert Kaufman, "The Collapse of Ancient States and Civilizations as an Organizational Problem," in *The Collapse of Ancient States and Civilizations* (ed.) Norman Yoffee and George L. Cowgill (Tucson: The University of Arizona Press, 1988) p. 227.

37. Doyle, *Empires*, p. 30.

38. Kaufman, "The Collapse of Ancient States and Civilizations as an Organizational Problem," p. 223.

39. Doyle, *Empires*, pp. 43–44.

40. Eisenstadt, *The Political Systems of Empires*, p. 358.

41. Hobson, *Imperialism*, p. 6.

42. Norman Yoffee, "Orienting Collapse," in *The Collapse of Ancient States and Civilizations*, p. 11.

43. Kaufman, "The Collapse of Ancient States and Civilizations as an Organizational Problem," p. 219.

44. Yoffee, "Orienting Collapse," p. 13.

45. Norman Yoffee, "The Collapse of the Ancient Mesopotamian States and Civilization," in *The Collapse of Ancient States and Civilizations*, p. 45.

46. Rice Odell cited by Yoffee, "Orienting Collapse," p. 5.

47. Kaufman, "The Collapse of Ancient States and Civilizations as an Organizational Problem," pp. 220–224.

48. Cho-yun Hsu, "The Roles of the Literati and of Regionalism in the Fall of the Han Dynasty," in *The Collapse of Ancient States and Civilizations*, p. 176.

49. Bruce Parrot, "Analyzing the Transformation of the Soviet Union in Comparative Perspective," in *The End of Empire? The Transformation of the USSR in Comparative Perspective* (ed.) Karen Dawisha and Bruce Parrott (New York: M. E. Sharpe, 1997) p. 19.

50. Eisenstadt, "Introduction," in *The Decline of Empires*, p. 6.

51. Vladislav Krasnov, "Russian National Feeling: An Informal Poll," in *The Last Empire* (ed.) Robert Conquest (Stanford: Hoover Institution Press, 1986) pp. 109–111 and Vladislav Krasnov, *Russia Beyond Communism: A Chronicle of National Rebirth* (Boulder: Westview, 1991) pp. 61; 233–237.

52. Anatol Lieven, "Russia's Military Nadir," *The National Interest*, Summer (1996), p. 25.

53. The term "historic bureaucratic empire" is S.N. Eisenstadt's conception of empires as pre-modern, centralized political orders, see S.N. Eisenstadt, *The Political Systems of Empires* (New York: The Free Press of Glencoe, 1963) pp. 10–12.

54. Samual P. Huntington, "Political Development and Political Decay," *World Politics*, vol. 17, no. 3 (1965), pp. 395–403. Huntington equates political development with high levels of institutionalization. He measures the level of institutionalization using four criteria: adaptability, complexity, autonomy, and coherence of organizations and procedures.

55. S.N. Eisenstadt, "The Breakdown of Communist Regimes and the Vicissitudes of Modernity," pp. 28–29.

56. S.N. Eisenstadt, "Center-Periphery Relations in the Soviet Empire: Some Interpretive Observations," in *Thinking Theoretically About Soviet Nationalities* (ed) by Alexander J. Motyl (New York: Columbia University Press, 1992) pp. 205–206.

57. For more on the differences between authoritarian and totalitarian regimes, see Juan Linz, "Totalitarianism and Authoritarian Regimes, in *Handbook of Political Science: vol. 3, Macropolitical Theory*, (ed.) Fred Greenstein and Nelson Polsby (Reading, Mass.: Addison-Wesley Press, 1975) pp. 175–411, and Giovanni Sartori, "Totalitarianism, Model Mania and Learning From Error," *Journal of Theoretical Politics*, vol. 5, no. 1 (1993) pp. 5–22.

58. Rasma Karklins, *Ethnic Relations in the USSR: The Perspective from Below* (Boston: Allen and Unwin, 1986) p. 58.

59. Gerhard Simon, *Nationalism and Policy Toward the Nationalities in the Soviet Union: From Totalitarian Dictatorship to Post-Stalinist Society* (Boulder: Westview Press, 1991) pp. 418–419.

60. Ibid., p. 415.

61. Ibid., p. 37.

62. Georgiy I. Mirsky, *On the Ruins of Empire: Ethnicity and Nationalism in the Former Soviet Union* (Westport: Greenwood Press, 1997) pp. 3–5.

63. Karklins, *Ethnic Relations in the USSR: The Perspective from Below*, p. 58.

64. Ibid., p. 61.

65. Martha Brill Olcott, "Youth and Nationality in the USSR," *Journal of Soviet Nationalities*, vol. 1, no. 1 (1990) p. 137.

66. Alexander J. Motyl, *Will the Non-Russians Rebel?* (Ithaca: Cornell University Press, 1987) pp. 155–156.

67. Paul Kolstoe, *Russians in the Former Soviet Republics* (Bloomington: Indiana University Press, 1995) pp. 73, 76–77.

68. Ibid., pp. 104–105.

69. Evgenii Golovakha, Natalia Panina, and Nikolai Churilov, "Russians in the Ukraine," in *The New Russian Diaspora*, (ed.) Vladimir Shlapentokh, Munir Sendich, and Emil Payin (New York: M. E. Sharpe, 1994) pp. 59–61.

70. Robin Wright, "Report from Turkestan," *The New Yorker*, April 6 (1992) p. 55.

Chapter 3

The Historical Origins
of the Russian Nation

Russian national identity is being redefined. There is no agreement among Russians regarding whether Russia's future should include formal and/or informal control over the former republics of what was the Soviet periphery. The history of the Russian nation and nationalist thought is important in understanding the current debates and general confusion regarding Russian national identity and the future of Russia. In short the relationship between the Russian nation and the state in which it occupied has been a contentious one throughout Russian history. There was seldom a perfect "fit" between nation and state, the state typically including many non-Russians. Despite this reality, Russian political actors tended to fuse ideas of *Russian* nationhood with imperial expansion that ultimately became state expansion.

This chapter examines the origins of Russian nationalism by exploring the foundations of the Russian nation and the subsequent development of Russian nationalist thought in the context of the general theoretical literature on nationalism. The Russian minorities who settled in other republics in the Soviet era are a holdover from the old Soviet order and are necessarily the focus of any debate over Russia's great power status. The link between Russian nationalism, particularly as displayed through the policies and rhetoric of the Russian government and its political rivals, and the Russian minorities in the former Republics are of particular interest.

The Russian minority issue is sometimes presented as the result of Russian nationalist sentiments and primordial feelings of attachment to their "co-nationals" living in the near abroad.[1] Indeed if one were to take the rhetoric of political leaders at face value, then not only is the issue one of the most pressing, but the political elite feels so strongly about it that the use of military force for the protection of the Russian minority is distinctly possible. Former Vice

President Alexander Rutskoy has proposed the shelling of Tblisi, Georgia for the ostensible purpose of protecting Russian speakers.[2] Colonel General Vladimir Churanov, Deputy Defense Minister, told the Russian press that he did not rule out the use of military force to protect interests of ethnic Russians in the former Soviet republics.[3] Even moderates, such as former Foreign Minister Andrei Kozyrev, were forced to take a stand on the issue. He spoke of the issue in the context of protecting the rights of all minorities. "I am convinced that it is precisely in confirming Russia's right as any state to protect its interests and *its compatriots and citizens* within the country and *abroad* . . . we have a military doctrine that also stipulates the use of the Armed Forces to protect our interests."[4]

Despite this emotive rhetoric, the issue of the Russian minority is based on an instrumentalist, rather than primordial, nationalism, particularly for the Russian government and policy makers. A primordialist view of nationalism contends that nationalism is biologically based; emotions and feelings, however irrational, characterize the response of members. The primordial school of nationalism arose from anthropological studies of ethnic groups. By contrast an instrumentalist nationalism refers to a nationalism that is learned through socialization; the national consciousness of nations is not biologically based but is based on specific political circumstances. Nationalism therefore is not a "natural" phenomenon but an artificial one that emerges within a particular political context.

It is not deep feelings of brotherhood that prompt such reactions in the Russian leadership and political opposition. Rather, the Russian minorities in the near abroad provide Moscow the opportunity and the justification to retain a presence in the countries of the near abroad in order to preserve the option of possible intervention in the former Soviet empire. And President Vladimir Putin has added another justification for intervention, that of containing terrorism. An instrumentalist conception of nationalism requires the existence of certain criteria beyond common cultural/kinship ties, such as territory and a sense of a common future. In this instance, the *territory* of the former republics plays a role in Russian national identity and the Russian minorities are a means for retaining some influence in these areas.

In the context of nationalism the connection between the Russian minorities and Russia stems not so much from ethnic affiliation (the phrase "Russian minorities" includes not only ethnic Russians, but also russified non-Russians, for example), but from the link between the Russian minorities and the old Union. More than anyone else, they identified their country as the "Soviet Union" rather than "Russia" or the titular republic in which they live.[5] Russia, as the successor state to the Soviet Union, has also assumed the responsibility for the Russian minority and any other former Soviet citizens who do not wish to assume the citizenship of the non-Russian Successor States in which they reside. The Russian citizenship law, adopted in February of 1992, made it possible for citizens of the former USSR, who did not have citizenship of another state, to acquire Russian citizenship. A subsequent amendment made it possible for those who did have citizenship of another successor state to also hold Russian citizenship. This potentially gives Russia an added justification to protect the rights of Russian minorities, that of protecting the rights of *Russian citizens.*[6]

In order to understand the current debate over Russian policy regarding the Russian minorities, the basis of Russian nationalism and the Russian State will be examined. In the context of nationalism and nation-building, an elite/mass distinction characterizes Russian nationalism; elite and mass perceptions of Russian nationalism, the Russian nation-state, and the national future differ.[7] The phrase elite/mass is used here though neither can lay claim to having an exclusive "elite" or "mass" support base. "Elite" refers to the politics of government and the concerns of those in power; generally these concerns go hand in hand with an interventionist attitude toward the near abroad which is closely linked with great power ambitions. In contrast "mass" reflects the common concerns of ordinary people including general feelings about language, culture, and their government. While mass notions of nationalism are associated with emotive sentiments toward Russians in the near abroad, the Russian public is by and large apolitical and isolationist in outlook. However the mass position, like the elite, has been articulated by scholars and literary figures. They nonetheless represent a popular viewpoint because they verbalize emotions and reactions and do not attempt the logical argumentation usually associated with politicians and intellectuals.

Elite perceptions of Russian nationalism differ widely among individuals, but all tackle the question of Russia's imperial past, especially the Soviet era, and the character of relations between the state and society. The prominent view which increasingly dominates discussions of Russia's future and in particular Russia's relations with the near abroad can be termed "imperial" in that the Soviet Union's superpower status, and Tsarist Russia's great power status before that, is at the crux of Russian identity. Accordingly, the dissolution of the Soviet Union was particularly painful and disparate Russian voices speak of the breakup of the Soviet Union as Russia's humiliation.[8]

Mass perceptions of Russian identity and Russia's future, by contrast, are more isolationist and narrow. Much more emphasis is placed on domestic issues rather than Russia's status in the world or even foreign policy in the near abroad. Talk of rebuilding Russia, reforming the economy and expressing national repentance for the past are common themes. The most famous proponent of the latter theme is Alexander Solzhenitsyn, and "village writers" or *derevenshchiki* such as Vladimir Soloukhin and Valentin Rasputin focus on the preservation of rural tradition, villages, and the environment (a subject which became a politically explosive issue in the waning years of the Soviet Union).[9] Insofar as feelings about the Russian minorities are concerned, there is much more concern about economic dislocation and job shortages associated with Russian immigration to Russia from the near abroad than with the plight of their compatriots still living there. Among these concerns are direct and indirect costs to the citizens of the Russian Federation such as the exacerbation of the housing and job shortage, and the dearth of public funds for schools and hospitals.[10]

The mass perception of what is Russia does not encompass the entire territory of the former Soviet Union. Ukraine and Belarus, owing to their close cultural and historical relationship to Russia, are considered part of Russia, while regions such as Central Asia (excluding northern Kazakhstan) are not. Still, most Russians oppose military intervention in the areas of the former Soviet Union. According to a poll taken in 1992 and again in 1994, while most Russians felt that Russia should " . . . protect the rights of Russians . . ." living in the near abroad, only 6.8 percent polled in 1992 supported military intervention in support of this objective; that number dropped to 2 percent in 1994.[11] When asked in another poll the question "Is your own personal life today linked with other republics of the former Union" 59.2 percent answered "virtually not at all" while an additional 17.8 percent answered "yes to an insignificant degree" and 6.3 percent didn't know.[12]

What are the consequences of this divergence of elite/mass perceptions of Russian policy vis-à-vis the near abroad? In essence, the lack of popular enthusiasm for military solutions either in the protection of the Russian minorities or in the forcible annexation of portions of the near abroad effectively acts as a constraint on the Russian regime. Despite the political rhetoric of many of Russia's politicians, the use of military force to re-annex the former Republics in the near abroad is not likely. Though it remains to be seen what Putin will do. He has certainly been much more bellicose than Yeltsin. But Putin's anti-Western, militaristic posturing was part of the Russian reaction to the NATO bombing of Serbia and U.S. intransigence over Iraq.

Under Yeltsin, Russia made the choice to relinquish formal control, but retain informal control over the former Republics. It can be argued that the actual control need not be achieved militarily (indeed it probably could not); in fact economic and political leverage has been far more effective and is the likely course of action for future Russian policy. If this continues to be the case, elite and mass conceptions of Russian nationalism will not likely conflict. And in foreign policy, elite conceptions will predominate.

"Nation" and "nationalism," especially their political usage, need to be defined. The chapter will outline the evolution of the Russian nation and the origins of what we are calling elite and mass conceptions of Russian nationalism. The dissolution of the Soviet Union and its impact on Russian nationalism will be addressed, with some mention of the national debate in Russia.

NATION, NATIONALISM, AND THE STATE

Much of the literature on nationalism has regarded the establishment of the state as the ultimate manifestation of nationalism that in turn reflects group consciousness of nationhood. The concepts of nation, nationalism, and state have generally been treated as separate, if related entities. That is, nations have been said to exist without nationalism (i.e., those ethnic groups with common cultural, linguistic, geographical attributes but without politically relevant group consciousness), nations without states, and even states without nations (Jordan, Saudi Arabia). In part the bewildering jumble of definitions, arguments, and assumptions surrounding the terms "nation" and "nationalism" is a consequence of the interdisciplinary nature of the literature, drawn as it is from anthropology, history, sociology, and political science. It is the latter, the political facets of nations, nationalism, and states with which this chapter is concerned.

A "nation" is typically understood as a group of people who share a common ancestry, culture, history, language, and so on. Clifford Geertz enumerates the traits that form a nation including a common biological ancestry, race, language, region, religion, and custom. Primordial ties such as biological, racial, and kinship ties occupy a pivotal position in Geertz's conception of nations.[13] He stresses that the importance of such individual attributes varies from case to case. For instance, religion plays the definitive role in defining the Sikh nation while being largely marginal in delineating the German nation. Adding to this definition, Karl Deutsch stresses communication among members that give the nation a group consciousness, that is an awareness among members that they in fact form a group.[14] Seton-Watson likewise stresses the necessity of a "national" consciousness in the formation of nations.[15]

Anthony Smith distinguishes between ethnic groups and nations. Geertz's method of defining nations (according to common cultural attributes) corresponds to Smith's definition of an *ethnie* or ethnic group. He regards the nation as those ethnic groups that seek *nationhood* that includes territorial claims and a civic model, the precursors to achieving sovereignty. An *ethnie* becomes a nation through a conscious effort to gain territory and recognition as a nation.[16] Hence a nation is a social group defined by certain cultural characteristics and which possesses a national consciousness and an attachment to a specific piece of territory.

In the creation of nations, the elite/mass distinction is a vital one. Before mass participation in politics and mass literacy, the creation and assemblage of culture attributes such as a written language, literature, and history which contribute to the creation of a nation are largely the product and work of the literate who have a monopoly on information. Seminal national works on linguistics, literature and historiography were the province of the literate few in society. For instance, in Europe, the religious doctrine of Catholicism, as well as that of the Reformation that followed, was originally defined and/or interpreted by the clerics. If the development of language, history, religion, and so on, occurred before the advent of mass literacy or mass communications (which was in fact the case in Russia before the twentieth century), then national consciousness was generally confined to the educated few. National consciousness spread to the masses only with the advent of mass literacy and communication.

If an elite/mass distinction is taken into account, it then becomes possible to conceive of nations existing before nationalism. Seton-Watson refers to such nations in Europe including Russia—the existence of a national consciousness among the elite classes that by and large excluded the masses—as "historic" nations. Discourses on nineteenth-century national movements for sovereignty (e.g., Hungarians) and earlier crusades for unity among members of a nation (e.g., Germany, Italy) naturally focused on the role of prominent individuals who were invariably from the ruling classes or the cultural elite (artists, writers, etc.).[17] In the case of Russia, parallel discourses centered over a debate over the legitimacy of state-society relations and the autocratic nature of the Russian government. While there was a national consciousness among Russian intellectuals and political leaders, this consciousness was not provoked by external events, such as ideas of independence or unification, but by domestic affairs, especially the policies of the Russian Tsarist government. As in the rest of Europe, such debates by and large excluded the masses.

Ernest Gellner identifies the progression from elite to mass national consciousness with the transition from agrarian to industrial societies. Nationalism becomes a force only with the advent of industrial society and mass literacy. High culture, which Gellner links with literacy, was limited to a small minority who comprised the elite in agrarian societies. Print capitalism, to use Benedict Anderson's term, contributed to mass national consciousness by raising vernacular languages to the level of administrative languages and by standardizing languages and so providing a sense of historical continuity.[18]

The shift from societies based on agrarian production to those based on industrial production (the division of labor its hallmark) coincides with a similar shift in social order.[19] In agrarian societies, one's social position and occupation were largely hereditary which meant that social order was contextual in nature: grounded in kinship and patron-client ties. Industrial social relations in contrast were more impersonal, requiring standardization of communication and therefore language. Increasingly literacy became a necessary skill in industrial societies. Education rather than heredity became the vehicle for socialization and the procurement of a profession. In short, mass literacy becomes a necessity for industrial production and social relations within an industrial society. With mass literacy comes the age of universal high culture. Loyalties in industrial society lie not in kinship ties, but in cultural ties. The education system of industrial societies becomes a force that standardizes culture and transmits it in a systematic way to entire generations and ultimately provides the underlying foundation for industrial society.[20]

What then is the relationship between nations and nationalism? When speaking of nations, feelings among members of solidarity and fervent devotion to one's customs, religion, territory, and so on, such sentiments are not in and of themselves manifestations of nationalism, but are "natural" feelings which involve cultural attachments which also happen to be present in nation-alism. According to Hans Kohn, *"They are the natural elements out of which na-tionalism is formed; but nationalism is not a natural phenomenon . . . it is a product of the growth of social and intellectual factors at a certain stage of his-tory."*[21] In fact nationalism as a political phenomenon cannot be conceived of before the " . . . idea of popular sovereignty," in other words the participation, or at least the consideration, of the masses in the political process.

The notion that the masses should have a say in choosing those who would rule over them was the outgrowth of natural law as first articulated by Hobbes and Locke (the first rule of nature being self-preservation). Natural law was revolutionary in that it was universal (applying to everyone regardless of class) and transcended the authority of autocrats who professed to rule by divine right. The acceptance of the idea of popular political participation meant that the legitimacy of government rule came from the people, not God. People cannot be expected to follow a ruler who does not protect them, or who him-self threatens their lives. Rulers began to appeal to the masses by stressing their common connection to the people and did so on the basis of nationalism. Kohn defines nationalism as the "process of integration of the masses into a common political form. Nationalism is unthinkable before the emergence of the modern state . . ."[22] Nationalism as a mentality or even an ideology seeks the establishment of a state. The state becomes the highest form or organiza-tion for the nation.

Thus far nationalism has been identified as a mentality that is mass-based and which has as its principal aim the creation of a state with the nation at its core. What then is the significance of nationalism once the state has been cre-ated? In short, it becomes a modus operandi. John Breuilly defines nationalism in ideological terms. Nationalist doctrine is based on three fundamental asser-tions: the existence of the nation with exclusive traits; the priority of national interests and values over all others; and the sovereignty, if not independence, of the nation.[23] The key to understanding the continuation of nationalism after the establishment of the state lies with the second assertion. Nationalism, as it is used here, is defined using a simple, functional meaning proposed by Seton-Watson that excludes the negative normative bias often associated with the term. Nationalism is *"a doctrine about political organization that puts the per-ceived interests of the nation above . . . everything else, and a movement (usually a political party or several parties) whose professed aim is to promote the interests of the nation."*[24]

If the political manifestation of the nation is its organization into a state, then the state can said to be based, at least in theory, on a particular nation. Na-tionalists claim that the nation should have a state and that the state should be based on a particular nation. Nationalism as a modus operandi of an estab-lished state and as it relates to the establishment of state institutions seeks to shape the state so that it conforms to the political, cultural, and social charac-teristics of the dominant nationality *to the greatest extent possible*. Gellner regards nationalism as a political principle. Ideally the political boundaries of the state should correspond to those of the nation. National sentiments and nationalist movements are manifestations of the violation of this principle.[25] That is, they arise when the state in question has significant minority populations or when some members of one nation live in adjacent state(s).

This drive towards the homogenization (standardization of language and communication for example) of culture within states is necessary for the state to maintain its rationale for its own existence. High culture exemplifies a nation, and the nation is the justification for the state. Hence Gellner argues that the demand for homogeneity of culture in a state is not generated by nationalism as such, but rather by the entity of the state that requires such homogeneity in order to exist.[26]

This principle of nationalism that demands congruence between national and political boundaries is a prime motivation behind the nation-state building endeavors of several of the former republics of the Soviet Union. These actions in the former Republics could be said to have generated a similar reaction in Russia. Yet how would the nationalist principle be applied in Russia now that Communist ideology has largely been discredited? What is Russia and what does it mean to be Russian? Because of the uncertain relationship between Russian nationalism and the former Tsarist, and later Soviet, state, many different notions of Russian nationalism compete with one another.

The current ambiguity of Russian nationalism stems from the circumstances of its development. Its development is inseparable from the imperial legacy of Tsarist Russia with its expansionist foreign policies and multi-ethnic character, and the Soviet period with its Communist ideology, centralized political structure, nationalities' policies, and the introduction of mass education.

THE DEVELOPMENT OF RUSSIAN NATIONALISM AND THE STATE

Nation and state building in Russia were two parallel processes occurring simultaneously. The development of the Russian nation took place before the advent of nationalism, giving Russia the stamp of a historic nation as defined by Seton-Watson. As in the case of most European historic nations, the Russian nation was originally based on an elite high-culture. The development of the Russian nation began after the establishment of the state. During the middle ages that state was Old Muscovy which included Moscow and surrounding territories.

Though Muscovy expanded after the end of Mongol rule under Ivan III (the Great) (1462–1505) and Ivan IV (the Terrible) (1533–1584), a Russian "state" as such could not have been said to have been the result. Russia's history of imperial expansion is sometimes linked to this time period, but since these developments were ultimately and quickly reversed, I place the birth of the modern Russian State with the advent of the Romanov dynasty. The violent excesses of Ivan the Terrible's *Oprichnina*, bad harvests, widespread and severe famine, plague, and finally the massive depopulation of towns and farmland due to death and migration, weakened the Muscovite State economically and politically.[27] Along with internal chaos, Muscovy faced periodic raids by roving bands from the Caucasus and the Ottoman Empire that it was powerless to prevent. The death of Ivan the Terrible and the feeble-minded son who succeeded him created a power vacuum and a political crisis during which nothing was done to alleviate the terrible condition of the country. Though Muscovy expanded through conquest under Ivan the Terrible, those conquests had not been fully consolidated, and in subsequent years, Muscovy was unable to protect its borders from raids and invasions. Because of its internal chaos and lack of a defensive military capability, Muscovy has not been regarded as an empire. The establishment of the Romanov dynasty and the reign of Peter the Great mark the beginning of the Russian empire.

The Romanov dynasty ushered in Russia's imperial age in 1613 and marked an end to the Time of Troubles by inaugurating a new imperial lineage, thus resolving the issue of succession. Still, the lack of a military force for even minimal border defense, a condition stemming from a weak central government, plagued the nascent Russian state until the advent of Peter I who established Russia's first modern army and navy along Western lines. Peter even revised the workings of civil government through the introduction of a table of ranks modeled after those in Europe. The table of ranks codified a standard promotion process of military and civilian bureaucracies which was based on merit and seniority.

The subordination of the Russian Orthodox Church to the state, the strengthening of a centralized government, the consolidation of an empire through the expansion of Russia's frontiers at the expense of Sweden and the Ottoman Empire, and the effective defense of Russia's borders were Peter's primary legacies. The break with the past was so extensive that the period before Peter's reign is referred to as pre-Petrine Russia. Peter's reforms were numerous; only those reforms affecting the state and the parameters of the empire are of concern here. Catherine the Great (1762–1796) essentially continued the policies begun by Peter. Under Catherine the empire expanded southward to the Black Sea and the Caucasus.

It should be noted that the state, which later became the Russian Empire, was not an ethnically-based Russian state. The tsar or tsaritsa was considered a servant of God to which all subjects, regardless of ethnicity, owed allegiance. Initially, non-Russians were not discriminated against on the basis of ethnicity nor were there any attempts to russify them. And although there were efforts to convert non-Russian Orthodox believers, Muslims and other non-Russian Orthodox religions nonetheless endured and faced serious oppression only in the Soviet period.

Russification as a policy did not appear until the reign of Alexander III (1881–1894), around the same time that Russian nationalism and revolutionary ideas were gaining prominence. The policy of russification was based on the notion that all citizens of the empire should consider themselves Russians, and Russian language and culture should take priority over their own indigenous ones. In practice this meant the imposition of the Russian language, and to a lesser extent culture, to the detriment of non-Russian languages.[28] During the reign of Alexander III, Russian was made the primary language of instruction in secondary and higher education in the Baltic region as well as the language of the courts.[29] The imposition of Russian in public life—becoming as it did, the language in schools, government, and courts of law—forced non-Russians to become bilingual and placed limits to social advancement on those who were not conversant in Russian.

It was during the Imperial period that the Russian nation took shape. The development of the Russian nation began with the establishment of institutions of higher learning, such as universities, academic institutes, scientific and literary academies, and so on. These institutions provided the training and recruitment of an indigenous, Russian educated class to serve as the basis for a Russian intelligentsia. The attributes of national identity—for example, a standard, literary language, literature, history, science, and so on—led to the development of a national awareness among the intelligentsia.

The Intelligentsia and the Formation of Russian Nationalist Thought

In addition to territorial conquests, Peter and Catherine sought to form organizations of higher learning in order to provide for the advancement of arts and sciences in Russia. Though Kievian scholars had founded the Slavo-Greek-Latin Academy in Moscow in 1687, Peter proposed an academy of sciences modeled on the French academy of sciences. He first established a university and gymnasium, the former to provide academic positions to teach university students and the latter to provide the university with appropriately educated recruits.[30]

The establishment of universities and academic institutes in Moscow and St. Petersburg facilitated the development of an indigenous intelligentsia that would form the basis of the Russian nation. From their ranks emerged writers, linguists, scientists and artists who produced works on language (dictionaries, standardization of grammar, etc.), literature and historiography.

This was significant because the period of imperial Russia—the reign of Peter the Great up until the twentieth century—was one of considerable foreign influence in the cultural sphere. First German, then French, became the language of the Russian royal court. Reforms in civil government, the military, and education were inspired by and modeled on corresponding institutions in Europe. Heavy foreign influence in cultural and scientific spheres highlighted the distinctiveness of Russia, which in turn, inspired Russian intellectuals such as Mikhail Vasilievich Lomonosov and Nikolai Mikhailovich Karamzin to develop Russia's scientific base, Russian historiography, and to establish the fundamentals of the Russian language in grammar texts and dictionaries. Lomonosov, one of the first Russian scholars to emerge from the newly created system of higher education, pioneered work on the Russian language, especially providing general principles for Russian scientific and literary language. Scientific terms in German and Dutch, for example, were given Russian names. Lomonosov also did groundbreaking work in the hard sciences, especially physics, chemistry, and astronomy, and he began work in writing Russian history. His works in this area include *Short Russian Chronicle* and *Ancient Russian History*.[31] Karamzin's *History of the Russian State* was a seminal twelve-volume work in Russian historiography that inspired future generations of Russian historiographers. Karamzin also reformed the Russian literary language, alleviating the dependency on Church Slavonic and Latin, and it became the literary style for Pushkin.[32] Other prominent Russian scholars continued the work begun by the Russian Academy of Sciences.

As these efforts progressed, a Russian intelligentsia formed and began to show signs of political awareness and a desire for political reform including reforming and/or abolishing absolute rule and eliminating serfdom. The intelligentsia as a group did not agree on what types of reforms should be implemented or how they should be implemented. Some wanted to abolish absolutism while others thought that the Russian autocracy should be strengthened. Most agreed that serfdom should be abolished, either because the institution itself was morally despicable or because it was an anachronism that would eventually be abolished from below if it were not abolished from above. From the latter half of the eighteenth century until the turn of the twentieth century, Russian national culture expanded, especially in the literary sphere, and so did a national consciousness among the intelligentsia. However, the development of Russian nationalism was hampered by the wide gap between the intelligentsia and the masses, or *narod*.

National ideas are transformed into nationalism with the transmittal of these ideas to the masses, a condition generally preceded by political ideas of popular sovereignty and popular participation in politics according to Kohn. The majority of people were serfs who were legally regarded as property and were not considered citizens. Most of the rural population—estimated to have been 94.3 percent of the population as of 1858—were serfs or state peasants.[33] Serfs were bound to individual owners while state peasants were bound to the land.

Serfdom, not abolished until 1861 and then only incrementally, obstructed real political reform, industrialization, and thus more generally, modernization. *Ulozhenie*, the law code of 1649 that marked the legal beginnings of serfdom as it was practiced until its formal abolition, exercised considerable constraints on industrialization. First, it eliminated freedom of movement among the peasantry which had the detrimental effect of keeping the rural population at artificially high levels, impeding urbanization, and making them economically dependent on their lords and hence impoverished. Without rural migration to cities, industries faced labor shortages. Second, it eliminated economic differentiation and created a mono-culture because it prohibited the peasants from engaging in any occupations considered "urban" such as trade and the manufacturing of goods.[34] This system lasted over two centuries and in fact came into being in Russian long after it was abolished in Western Europe. As a result, the prerequisites for the development of a mass nationalism were absent from Russia.

Not surprisingly, the intelligentsia pushed for its abolition. The Decembrist uprising of 1825 was the first organized push for political reforms that included ending autocracy and serfdom, among other aims. Its failure radicalized the intelligentsia, and it was during this time that revolutionary ideas became prominent. The plethora of groups, ideologies, movements, and ideas had implications for the Russian revolution (after all, the Bolsheviks and other socialist movements came from the intelligentsia and had their origins in the latter half of the nineteenth century). This turbulent period is the source for the ideological schisms that have cropped up since the dissolution of the Soviet Union. Its manifestations are found in debates between Westernizers/Reformers and Slavophiles/Eurasianists. If the Decembrists had succeeded, modernization might have come sooner to Russia. Russian nationalism might not have been tinged with an enduring bitterness between the state and intelligentsia, and among the various groups of radicals that emerged following the abortive uprising.

What are the implications of these ideological divisions among the intelligentsia for the development of Russian nationalism? The answer can be found by taking a closer look at the relationship between the Russian intelligentsia and the state in the latter half of the nineteenth century. Some identified with the state; others were alienated from it. It is in this early schism that the roots of elite/mass perceptions of Russian nationalism lie.

The intelligentsia as a class was over-educated for Russian society. Furthermore, that education was a Western one with the recipient having become more familiar with Europe than with Russia.[35] The combination of over-education and economic backwardness in Russia created a class that had few career opportunities outside the civil service and the state bureaucracy. Part of the intelligentsia formed the bureaucratic and managerial oligarchy closely linked to the state, while the remainder was completely alienated from both Russian society and the state.[36] The latter group included regional governors and marginal government officials who had administrative responsibilities as well as various aimless, alienated individuals, the "superfluous person" (*lishnii chelovek*), who figured prominently in eighteenth-century Russian literature. As a result, the bureaucratic intelligentsia tended to be pro-state and it is among this group that Russian nationalism became closely associated with the state. This was the segment of Russian society that took pride in Russia's military achievements and territorial expansion. Tsar Alexander III, who was imbued with ideas of ethnic purity, exemplifies this national pride. Under him, non-Russian citizens were pressured to become "Russian" through the adoption of the Russian language and conversion to the Russian Orthodox faith.[37]

The alienated intelligentsia by contrast was very hostile to the state, and it was among this group that radical political ideas, including variants of socialism and communism which influenced the Russian Revolution, took hold. The complete alienation from the state and society made extreme political ideas such as abolishing the state and devising a whole new social order attractive.

The origins of current debates can be traced back to this period. Here, three main strains of thought have relevance to current national debates. They include the positions of the Westernizers, the Slavophiles, and the Populists. Westernizers regarded Europe as the center of Western civilization and Russia as being part of Europe as opposed to Asia. Peter's reforms marked the beginning of rapprochement with the West.[38] Westernizers gained inspiration from Western philosophy, science, and politics. From among the Westernizers emerged what are generally termed "liberals" and "socialists." The liberal tradition among the Russian intelligentsia includes ideas of popular, constitutional democracy, positive law, and natural rights. The socialist tradition was derived primarily from the philosophies of Hegel and Marx (though utopian socialists such as Saint Simon and Fourier had their adherents). The socialist tradition spawned many movements in pre-revolutionary Russia including the Mensheviks and Socialist Revolutionaries as well as, of course, the Bolsheviks.

The Slavophiles by contrast eschewed Europe and the West, especially capitalism and industrialization. They were reactionary in that they sought a return to the ideal past of pre-Petrine Russia; Slavophiles regarded Peter's reforms as an abomination to Russian values and way of life. They regarded the peasants as the savior of modern Russia and even of the West. The Slavophile "felt that the integral Christian civilization of pre-Petrine Russia had been partially preserved—and in a largely unselfconscious way—in the Russian Peasant."[39] Hence the Slavophile reverence of the peasant and of peasant traditions, especially the peasant commune or village, have religious, Orthodox overtones.

The Populists borrowed from both Western and Slavophile traditions. The Populists adopted the Slavophile notion of the peasant as the source of inspiration for Russia. It was thought that neither the government nor the intelligentsia should dictate to the peasant; rather the intelligentsia had much to learn from the peasant.[40] Unlike the Slavophiles, who regarded the peasantry as a reactionary, inert, spiritual if not religious body, the Populists observed the peasantry as an activist force that could and would act in a revolutionary way when the timing was ripe. But rather than a return to an idealized past, the activism of the peasantry would lead to socialism.[41] The socialist aspect to the Populist vision of revolutionary change reflects the Westernizer's influence on the Populists.

Though historians have tended, for conceptual clarity, to categorize the various movements and ideologies of this period, it must be pointed out that the ideas of various groups frequently overlapped. For example, in the writings of Alexander Herzen, a Russian radical who is regarded as a "liberal," one can find elements of Slavophile and even Populist thinking. For instance Herzen spoke passionately of "the equal right of every peasant to land . . ." and called on the younger generation to preserve the "communal principle."[42] The sanctity of the peasant commune is a dominant theme among Slavophiles. Writers and historians have long debated the parameters of ideologies that differentiate Populists and Slavophiles. But in reality, writers, scholars, and journalists alternately advocated Western ideas of positive law and human rights, and such home-grown institutions as the peasant commune and Russian orthodoxy.[43]

Despite the development of a distinct Russian nation, transference of a national idea to the masses was delayed by the late arrival of the industrial revolution. The delay of industrialization in Russia and the corresponding transformation of political and social relations meant the delay of mass education. Serfdom retarded industrialization by constraining population movement, obstructing the growth of towns, and restricting trade and other non-agricultural trades among the peasantry. Illiteracy characterized Russian agrarian society, and social relations were based, not on the rule of law, but on kinship ties and patron-client relations. The rule of law, rudimentary to the extent it existed, did not govern the relationship between Boyars and peasants. After the radicalization of the intelligentsia, the state itself came under attack from claims that it ruled only for the sake of its own preservation and for no higher value. It repressed ideas and only took from the *narod*.

Hence Russia has a long intellectual tradition of both strong identification with the state and strong opposition to it. Much in the same way that Nicholas I preserved a bureaucratic oligarchy which supported the imperial government, while simultaneously generating opposition to its rule among the intelligentsia who did not have direct access to power, the Soviet Union generated its own loyal and dissident intelligentsia groups. It was the alienated intelligentsia of the imperial period that provided the revolutionary fervor that made the Russian revolution. After the advent of the Soviet Union, another bureaucratic oligarchy and a dissident intelligentsia in opposition to the Soviet State was generated.

Soviet dissident thought bore a strong resemblance to the radical thought of the late nineteenth century. Dissidents like Roy Medvedev who criticized the Soviet regime on the basis of its distortion of Marxism and hence can be considered a Westernizer and a Socialist. Solzhenitsyn favored a return to the monarchy and idealized the peasant commune as the only uncorrupted indigenous form of political organization. The *derevenshchiki*, though not strictly dissident, were nevertheless critical of Soviet policies that destroyed villages and led to ecological disasters. For instance in Rasputin's *Farewell to Matyora* an old village is purposely flooded as the result of a gigantic hydroelectric project.[44] They also took up the themes of forced collectivization and the devastation to the countryside wrought by WWII. Both the village writers and

Solzhenitsyn could be categorized as Slavophile. The dissidents and critics of the Soviet State are a part of the Russian intellectual tradition of criticizing the state. When one hears Russian leaders or writers today speak of a distinctly *Russian* path as an alternative to Western models, one is hearing the voice of Russian nationalism.

The Rise of the Soviet Union and the Growth of Russian Nationalism

Kohn argued that nationalism "is the process of integrating the masses into a common political form," and that the idea of nationalism is inherently linked to ideas of popular sovereignty. In Russia this process began in the Soviet era. The transference of the national idea to the masses began in the revolutionary period when various groups of Communists and Socialists made efforts at mass recruitment. The legitimacy of their ideologies was mass-based in that all claimed to act in the interests of the people, and they competed with one another for popular support. After the Bolsheviks prevailed over the Mensheviks and Socialist Revolutionaries with the creation of the Soviet state, the government set about encouraging, and in fact making compulsory, popular political participation. Concurrently, mass education and mass communications, including print media as well as TV and radio, served to spread political ideas of the state.

From the very beginning there was an alliance of interest between the ruling Bolsheviks and Russian nationalists. The Russian nationalists of this period included members of the old regime such as government functionaries and military officers who, though not Communist, nonetheless joined the new government for the purpose of re-establishing law and order, strengthening the state, and preventing the disintegration of what was the Russian empire.[45] The new Bolshevik government headed by Lenin needed to put an end to the chaos and to establish state institutions. To this end, there was a recognized need for the experience and expertise of these relics of the previous government. The "nationalists" for their part saw their role as crucial in preserving the Russian Empire and serving their country. They were motivated by a desire to see their country strong again and this included retaining control over the peripheral territories of the former Russian Empire.[46]

In this alliance between Communist and Great Russian nationalists, it was the Communists who held power, and their attitude toward Russian nationalism was ambivalent. At various times during Soviet history, manifestations of Russian nationalism were alternatively repressed and encouraged. Of the former, one could point to the suppression of authors who, while very pro-Russian, expounded views which directly challenged Soviet rule such as Solzhenitsyn and many of the village writers. A classic example of the latter is Stalin's revival of the Russian Orthodox Church, and his (Russian) nationalistic political speeches during WWII.

In understanding the contradictory official attitudes toward Russian nationalism, Alain Besancon found it useful to distinguish between Russian pa-
triotism and Russian nationalism. The former represents the individual's ties
to the community, and included elements that were under attack by the Communists such as the Church, traditional social classes, and the family.[47] By contrast nationalism consisted of xenophobic feelings and resentment of state
weakness, sentiments that appealed to the Communist's own disposition of
"Us vs. Them," and supported the autarkic policies of the Communist government as exemplified by Stalin's "Socialism in One Country."[48]

Mikhail Agursky, rather than referring to an alliance between Communism
and Russian nationalism, emphasizes the complementary goals of each and
how they were fused in an ideological tendency he terms "National Bolshevism."
National Bolshevism is defined as "the ideology of a political current that legit-
imizes the existing Soviet political system from a Russian national point of
view."[49] He stresses that the two do not contradict, but complement each
other and argues that the aim of Communism, the creation of a world communist system, became the National Bolshevik goal of establishing Russia as a superpower and an international order in which Russia is the dominant power.[50]
Though Agursky wrote before the formal dissolution of the Soviet Union, elements of this mentality abound in the post-Soviet period. They are manifest in
the desire of Russia to assume the role as the successor state to the Soviet Union, in spite of the practical drawbacks this entailed. As a result of this fusion of
Communist ideology and Russian Nationalism, the distinction between "Russian" and "Soviet" became blurred.

NATIONALISM, THE SOVIET UNION, AND
POST-IMPERIAL RELATIONSHIPS

How does nationalism carry through to the development of relations in the
post-Soviet period? Nationalism, as it developed in the Soviet republics and
Russia, has implications for the post-Soviet environment. Nationalism as a
process develops in conjunction with the general process of modernization.
This process took place during the Soviet era and affected, to varying degrees,
the titular republics including the RSFSR. Nationalism emerged or
re-emerged as a mass political movement in the Slavic, Central Asian, and Baltic States during Perestroika.

Qualitative differences in national movements centered over the level of
popular participation in these movements and the extent to which these movements were organized. In the Baltic States there are high levels of mass participation in and support of nationalist movements. In Ukraine, popular reaction
to the nationalist movement was mixed, with the far-western region of Ukraine
registering the highest level of support. In Belarus as in Central Asia, the level
of popular participation in and support of nationalist movements was rather
low. In Central Asia, the movements themselves were not highly organized or

coordinated; nationalism made itself felt primarily through riots and mob behavior toward "enemy" ethnic groups rather than any coordinated, political
effort vis-à-vis the central government.

In Russia itself, nationalism has led to the questioning of Russia's relationship to the Soviet periphery. This question has direct implications for Russia's
policies toward the Slavic, Central Asian, and Baltic regions.

The Dissolution of the Soviet Union and the
Former Republics

To understand contemporary Russian nationalism it is necessary to examine
it in the context of the breakup of an empire and the re-emergence of a distinctly *Russian* State. According to Ronald Suny an empire is "made up of diverse peoples in which one group is privileged in its relationship with the
central authority and other subordinate peoples."[51] With the classification of
the Soviet Union as an empire based on the Russian nationality, Russian nationalism becomes inextricably linked to the former Republics of the Soviet
Union. It fuels contemporary debates over the authenticity of current borders
and the role Russia should adopt in the affairs of the Successor States. Russia's
continued involvement in the affairs of the Successor States of the former periphery is driven by an elite conception of Russian nationalism. The unexpected loss of the Soviet empire and accompanying economic morass has
meant the loss of international prestige and superpower status for Russia and
the sudden elevation of the former republics to the level of independent states.

But the imperial relationship between Russia and subject nations of the former republics will not be banished as easily or as quickly as the old union. Even
in its weakened condition, Russia dominates the territory of the former Soviet
Union. Residual ties to the old Soviet order are manifest in the continuing economic dependence of the Successor States on Russia and Russia's lingering
presence and influence in the internal affairs of the Successor States.

Continued Russian dominance reflects the imperial ambition of segments
of the Russian political elite and their political rivals (and of certain parts of the
intelligentsia) and their difficulties in reconciling themselves with the loss of
the Soviet Union. This feeling that Russia somehow lost, while everyone else
gained (i.e., independence for the Republics), is directly related to the rise in
Russian nationalism that views Russian control (formal or informal) over these
areas as essential to Russian national interests.

The following summarizes this conception of Russian nationalism: the Russian nation is inseparable from a Russian state; the dissolution of the Soviet
Union threatened the Russian state and hence the Russian nation; and the
newly created states of the former republics are artificial and therefore illegiti-
mate. The stress placed on the entity of the state has its origins in Russian history that has been characterized by continual warfare; only with the rise of an

imperial Russian state was Russia able to defend itself from invaders and later conquer and settle the large expanses of Asia.

The issue of Russian involvement in areas of the former empire was, and continues to be, motivated by a concern for Russia's perceived national interests. This was true of Yeltsin's administration and is doubly the case under President Putin. Putin has taken an increasing hard-line toward the former Republics and has already demonstrated a willingness to intervene militarily as seen in the resumption of the war in Chechnya, the ruthless destruction of Grozny, and the strong-armed tactics in coercing Georgia into agreeing to Russian border patrols along its border.

The present debate over Russia's national interests is a part of the larger debate over the search for a national identity in replacement of the former Soviet one. From where does the concern over the legitimate boundaries of a future Russia stem? An obvious answer would seem to lie in Russian nationalism as embodied in a Russian political elite which is seeking to reestablish hegemony over areas of the former Soviet Union, a union dominated by Russia.

But this simplistic answer is problematic. For one thing, it is vague. Russian nationalism has become a catchall phrase used to describe everything from Russian spirituality to anti-Semitism. First, the "rise in Russian nationalism" has been employed in a wide range of discussions on Russian culture and literature, Russian Orthodoxy, and political parties representing such extremes as the Liberal Democratic Party of Zhirinovsky, hard-line communist groups such as Edinstvo, and the monarchist and anti-Semitic Black Hundreds.[52] In the political sphere are exhortations of extremist groups such as Pamyat on a par with the more prosaic debate over Russian political interests in the near abroad? Are they both manifestations of Russian nationalism? If so, then the term 'nationalism' as applied to Russia is essentially meaningless.

Second, the indiscriminate usage of the term Russian nationalism blurs the distinction between Tsarist Russia and the Soviet Union. Much of the literature on nationalism attributes significance to the origins of the nation and nationalism. In the case of Russia, nationalism as a mass ideology gathered strength in the turbulent period preceding the Communist Revolution though it did not gain widespread resonance until the establishment of a system of mass education and communication following the consolidation of the Soviet regime. As a consequence, the Soviet period would have had a profound impact on Russian national identity. This influence became evident in the inconsistent usage of the terms "Russian" and "soviet."

With the dissolution of the Soviet Union, the debate over what is "Russian" as well as the location of the borders of the Russian "homeland" have become areas of contention among Russians themselves. As for politicians, when did this transformation from Soviet to Russian nationalism take place? Given the abruptness of the dissolution of the Soviet Union and Marxist-Leninist ideology, at what point did Russian nationalism replace loyalty to the Soviet State? Or were they really one and the same?

NOTES

1. Paul Kolstoe's interview with Vladimir Kuznechevskii of Russia's daily *Rossiiskaia Gazeta* illustrates this view and is cited in Paul Kolstoe *Russians in the Former Soviet Republics* (Bloomington: Indiana University Press, 1995) pp. 266–267.

2. "Kozyrev Explains Remarks on Russians abroad," *FBIS-SOV,* 21 April (1995) p. 8.

3. "Deputy Defense Minister Backs Kozyrev Warning on Ethnic Russians," *FBIS-SOV,* 24 April (1995), p. 6.

4. "Kozyrev: Work Needed on Issues in 'Near Abroad,'" *FBIS-SOV,* 24 April (1995) p. 6; quote from "Kozyrev Explains Remarks on Russians Abroad," p. 8.

5. Emil Payin, "The Disintegration of the Empire and the Fate of the 'Imperial Minority,'" in *The New Russian Diaspora,* Vladimir Shlapentokh, Munir Sendich, and Emil Payin (ed.) (New York: M. E. Sharpe, 1994) p. 22.

6. Lowell Barrington, "Citizenship in the Soviet Successor States," *Europe-Asia Studies*, vol. 47, no. 5, July (1995) pp. 739–740.

7. Cynthia Enloe, *Ethnic Conflict and Political Development* (Boston: Little, Brown and Company, 1973) p. 18.

8. Gregory Guroff and Alexander Guroff, "The Paradox of Russian National Identity," in *National Identity and Ethnicity in Russia and the New States of Eurasia,* ed. by Roman Szporluk (New York: M. E. Sharpe, 1994), pp. 90–91.

9. Vladislav Krasnov, *Russia Beyond Communism* (Boulder: Westview Press, 1991) pp. 43–55; Stephen Carter, *Russian Nationalism: Yesterday, Today, Tomorrow* (New York: St. Martin's Press, 1990) pp. 92–97.

10. Vladimir Terekhon, "Bezhentsy i emigranty kak predotvratit' katastro," *Izvestia,* 11 August (1992) p. 3; Arnold Pushkar, "Sed'maia volna emigratsii mozhet stat' samoi moshchnoi v istorii Rossii," *Nezavisimaya Gazeta,* 12 January (1994) p. 6.

11. The Current Digest of the Post-Soviet Press, vol. XLVI, no. 30 (1994) p.13.

12. Emil Payin, *Sevodnya,* 22 July (1994) p. 9.

13. Clifford Geertz, "The Integrative Revolution: Primordial Sentiments and Civil Politics in the New States," in Clifford Geertz (ed.) *Old Societies and New States: The Quest for Modernity in Asia and Africa* (New York: Free Press, 1963) pp. 107–13, reprinted in John Hutchinson and Anthony D. Smith (ed.), *Nationalism* (Oxford: Oxford University Press, 1994).

14. Karl Deutsch, *Nationalism and Social Communication,* 2nd ed. (Cambridge: the Massachusetts Institute of Technology, 1953) p. 91.

15. Hugh Seton-Watson, *Nations and States* (Boulder: Westview Press, 1977) pp. 1–2.

16. Anthony Smith, *The Ethnic Origins of Nations* (London: Basil Blackwell, 1986) p. 154.

17. Hugh Seton-Watson, "Russian Nationalism in Historical Perspective," in *The Last Empire,* ed. Robert Conquest (Stanford, California: Hoover Institution Press, 1986) p. 21.

18. Ernest Gellner, *Nations and Nationalism* (London: Basil Blackwell, 1983) p. 44.

19. Ibid., p. 49.

20. Ibid., pp. 50–51.

21. Hans Kohn, *The Idea of Nationalism* (New York: Collier Books, 1948) p. 3.

22. Ibid., p. 4.

23. John Breuilly, *Nationalism and the State*, 2nd ed.(Manchester: Manchester University Press, 1994) p. 2.

24. Hugh Seton-Watson, "Russian Nationalism in Historical Perspective," in *The Last Empire*, p. 14.

25. Gellner, p. 1.

26. Ibid., p. 39.

27. E. I. Kolycheva, *Agrarnyui stroi Rossii XVI veka* (Moskva: Nauka, 1987) pp. 178–179.

28. Seton-Watson, *Nations and States*, p. 85.

29. Ibid., p. 86.

30. George Vernadsky, *Russian Historiography: A History* (Massachusetts: Nordland Publishing Company, 1978) pp. 1–3.

31. Ibid., pp. 8–19.

32. Ibid., pp. 49, 51–54.

33. Abbott Gleason, *Young Russia* (Chicago: University of Chicago Press, 1980), p. 3.

34. Richard Hellie, *Enserfment and Military Change in Muscovy* (Chicago: University of Chicago Press, 1971) p. 142.

35. Gleason, p. 25.

36. Isaiah Berlin, *Russian Thinkers* (New York: Viking Press, 1978) p. 117.

37. Seton-Watson, *Nations and States*, pp. 84–85.

38. Gleason, p. 38.

39. Ibid., p. 37.

40. Ibid., p. 33.

41. Ibid., p. 41.

42. Ibid., p. 98.

43. Ibid., pp. 180–185.

44. Carter, p. 97.

45. Alain Besancon, "Nationalism and Bolshevism in the USSR," in *The Last Empire: Nationality and the Soviet Future*, ed. by Robert Conquest (Stanford: Hoover Institution Press, 1986) pp. 3–4.

46. Ibid.

47. Ibid., pp. 4–5.

48. Ibid., p. 5.

49. Mikhail Agursky, "The Prospects of National Bolshevism," in *The Last Empire: Nationality and the Soviet Future*, ed. by Robert Conquest (Stanford: Hoover Institution Press, 1986) p. 87.

50. Ibid.

51. Ronald Grigor Suny, *The Revenge of the Past* (Stanford, California: Stanford University Press, 1993), pp. 128–129.

52. For a list of various extremist Russian political parties see Vladimir Pribylovsky, "A Survey of Radical Right-Wing Groups in Russia," *RFE/RL Research Report*, vol. 3, no. 16 (1994) pp. 28–37.

Chapter 4

Russia: National Interests and the Near Abroad

The rise of nationalism and related attempts to define national identity have been integral in the process of establishing statehood in the Successor States after the breakup of the Soviet Union. No where has this process been more difficult than in Russia. The question as to how the Russians view themselves will influence Russian foreign policy in the near abroad. Despite Russia's pro-Western orientation in the early part of the 1990s, there has been, since 1993 or so, an emerging consensus regarding the importance to Russia of the territories of the former Soviet Union, or what the Russian press and politicians refer to as the "near abroad." This consensus is manifest in an increasing belligerence towards the former republics and a rising sensitivity over the growing foreign presence. And with the election of Vladimir Putin, an individual who has already demonstrated a willingness to use military force as seen in Chechnya, this belligerence will only increase.

Key to Russian national identity is territory. Notions about which territories should be included in Russia range from all of the near abroad to just the "Slavic lands" (Ukraine and Belarus), to only the territory of the RSFSR. National identity is not static: how members perceive themselves and their nation's place in the world changes over time, particularly in the wake of a national disaster. Prominent Russian sociologist Vladimir Shlapentokh has noted the re-evaluation of the Russian national idea that followed Russia's losses in the Crimean and Russo-Japanese Wars, both of which ushered in monumental reforms transforming the relationship between state and society.[1]

National self-identification involves, among other things, perceptions of a territorial homeland that may or may not correspond to political borders. Even when the sovereignty of states is formally recognized, powerful states ex-

ert influence over less powerful ones (especially in the absence of transnational
organizations such as economic unions or political alliances which might mitigate such behavior), and in fact may consider such exercise of influence as vital
to national interests. It is a truism that relations between states are not relations between equals; relations typically reflect another's "national interests."
The ensuing debate over how the former Republics fit into Russia's national
interests is indicative of a nation attempting to adjust to the loss of its state.

THE DEBATE FRAMED: WESTERN VERSUS EURASIAN

The broad categories of Western and Eurasian positions are a way in which
to conceptualize the debate over Russian nationalism by representing two
opposing positions of a spectrum. They do not represent an exclusive ei-
ther/or position taken on this issue, nor are the views of political leaders and
intellectuals easily pigeonholed. This dichotomy does not reflect changes in
individual beliefs over the course of the ten years since the breakup of the Union. Nevertheless, it is possible to identify the general political leanings of individuals, not to mention Russia's foreign policies, as tending toward one or
another pole.

The Western position holds that Russia should accept the dissolution of the
Soviet Union and define a new role for Russia within the borders of the former
RSFSR. In this endeavor Russia should concentrate on improving the quality
of day-to-day life rather than restoring the empire. A preoccupation with Russia's historical past as a great power only leads to the adoption of inappropriate
and/or harmful polices.[2] In fact, Russian intellectuals initially viewed the dissolution of the Soviet Union and the creation of the Commonwealth of Independent States (CIS) as a positive development because it signaled the orderly
demise of a defunct system. Proponents of the Western position (also labeled
Liberals) greeted the establishment of the CIS with enthusiasm, because it ostensibly provided a non-compulsory forum for the continued economic and
political cooperation between Russia and the former Republics (excluding the
Baltic States).[3] Former President's Yeltsin's adviser, the late Galina
Starovoitova, spoke of the CIS in terms of a "future confederation," while the
head of Russian Television's First Channel, Egor Yakovlev, referred to the CIS
as representing the beginning of a new Union.[4] In this arrangement, the coercive, ideological underpinnings of the old system were replaced with a legal,
voluntary organization in which the sovereignty of member states would be
recognized.

The Western position repudiates the Soviet era. But since there is no historical precedent for the current borders of the Russian Federation, Westernizers
are left to argue that Russia, great power pretensions aside, simply cannot afford, materially or spiritually, to forcibly re-establish formal political control
over the peripheral territories of the former Union.[5] The tenets of liberalism—
democracy, human rights, free trade, rule of law— are incompatible with au-

thoritarianism, the command economy, and coercion as was practiced against the Soviet Republics and the Eastern bloc countries. The Western position advocated a new role for Russia based on the political and economic institutions of the West.[6]

In this vein, the West is considered to be a natural ally of Russia in the post-Cold War era, especially because both share the same security threats, for example, immigration, terrorism, militant Islam, and so forth.[7] Andrei Kozyrev, Russian foreign minister until his replacement in 1996, was the chief proponent of a foreign policy oriented toward the West. Kozyrev viewed Russia as belonging to the advanced industrialized states of the North and saw the eventual inclusion of Russia in the Group of Seven industrialized countries as the ultimate goal of Russian economic reforms.[8]

In contrast, the Eurasian position stresses Russia's connection not only with Europe but also with Asia. Russia has a special historical role and therefore needs to follow its own path, a path determined indigenously and not through imitating the West. While Westernizers emphasize Russia's connection and commonalties with the West, Eurasianists stress the differences between the two and the uniqueness of Russia's Asian tradition.

Eurasianists regard the borders of the Russian Federation as artificial. There are differing opinions over the Soviet era. Some accept it and consequently call for recreating the Union while others, such as monarchists who view Orthodoxy as the path to national salvation, reject the Soviet legacy. Yet the latter can be considered Eurasian in outlook due to their belief that certain areas of the near abroad are Russian lands, and any notion of Russian statehood is incomplete without their inclusion. Though there are variations as to how the borders should be redrawn, the following generalization can be made: that the former territories of the Soviet Union are areas in which Russia should and must exert informal, if not outright formal control.

In the sphere of foreign policy, this position is manifest in declarations that the near abroad, rather than Europe, should be the highest priority of Russian foreign policy. Neither is the West viewed as an unconditional ally of Russia. Russia, owing to its unique geographic position, had national interests apart from, and in some instances in opposition to, those of European countries. Despite the end of the Cold War, the United States would continue to be the principal rival (though not necessarily enemy) of Russia.

Eurasianists point to the lack of historical precedent for current borders and the independence of the former peripheral territories. Furthermore, Russian withdrawal from the near abroad is more in the interests of the West than of Russia. In repudiating Russia's past (including the Soviet period) and looking to the West to provide the model for Russian statehood, Westernizers are regarded as rejecting Russian values and denying Russia a national identity, patriotic pride, and the right to protect its national interests.[9]

Westernizers, Eurasianists and Russian Foreign Policy in the Near Abroad

In the sphere of foreign policy, Westernizers prevailed in the initial period following the August coup attempt in 1991 under President Boris Yeltsin. Then Russian Foreign Minister Andrei Kozyrev directed a foreign policy aimed at cooperation with the West. To this end Russia accepted the reunification of Germany and its admittance to NATO and voted in the UN Security Council for the use of force against Iraq in the Gulf war without attempting to extract concessions from the West. As evidence of the success of their pro-Western foreign policy, Kozyrev and Yeltsin have pointed to the West's recognition of Russia as the legal successor state to the Soviet Union, a fact that carried with it the retention for Russia of the Soviet Union's permanent seat in the UN Security Council. Most importantly, in accepting without resistance the independence of the former Eastern bloc countries and formally renouncing the coercive elements of Soviet foreign policy (Kozyrev used the word imperialistic), Russia has managed to avoid the tragic fate of Yugoslavia.[10] Furthermore, Kozyrev viewed the creation of the CIS as the beginning for the creation of a common post-Soviet space on the territory of the former Soviet Union. Within the framework of the CIS and without using intimidation tactics, Kozyrev expected the CIS to provide a forum for greater economic and political integration.

The Westernizers' influence, although the prevailing force in Russian foreign policy from 1991 to mid-1992, began to decline after 1992. For one thing, Russian foreign policy drew considerable criticism from the political opposition. Even Yeltsin began to distance himself from the controversy surrounding Kozyrev's foreign policy. Among the policies criticized were his emphasis on cooperation with the West and the lack of a coherent policy towards the near abroad. He was accused of acting contrary to Russia's national interests by neglecting the near abroad and the situation of the 25 million Russians living there. As early as October 1992, only a little over a year since the coup attempt, Yeltsin publicly blamed the Foreign Ministry for not having a distinct, consistent policy towards the near abroad, especially in the defense of the Russian minorities.[11]

Russia's national interests, as defined by Kozyrev in a Foreign Ministry document submitted to parliament in response to this criticism, included the following objectives: economic recovery, observance of human rights, democracy, and integration into the world economy. To this end, Russia welcomed multilateral diplomacy within such transnational organizations as the Organization on Security and Cooperation in Europe (OSCE), the European Union (EU), and the Western European Union (WEU), among others.[12]

The reference to maintaining ties with the Russian minorities living in the near abroad was vague. Kozyrev had stressed the need for the general adoption by CIS member states of a human rights treaty based on internationally recognized standards endorsed by the United Nations and the OSCE which would apply to all minority groups including the Russian ones.[13] In fact Russia spearheaded this effort and is largely responsible for its expanded role in the post-Soviet era. This universal approach to the Russian minority issue was generally considered ineffectual. Its perceived failure (as witnessed by the restrictive citizenship laws of the Baltic States and the conflicts in Moldova, Georgia, and Tajikistan, and the clashes between Russians and Kazakhs in northern Kazakhstan), provoked criticism not just from the political opposition, but from members of Yeltsin's government as well.

Andranik Migranyan, a former member of the Presidential Council of Experts and a well-known political scientist who is currently vice president of the Reform Foundation, summed up Russia's national interests as centrally including the near abroad. The reason for the incoherent policy towards the near abroad stemmed from the lack of experience and tradition of establishing formal, interstate bilateral relations with these areas.[14] For this reason, according to Migranyan, it was wrong to expect the CIS to be able to preserve the economic and political space previously maintained by the Soviet Union.

Similarly it was erroneous for Russia to turn inward within the political borders of the Russian Federation, renounce any special position in the near abroad, and to withdraw from there. Even if Russia were inclined to do so it cannot for at least three reasons. First, Russia cannot ignore events taking place in the near abroad because of its central role in these conflicts. Second, the international community was not about to take on the task of resolving/containing these conflicts. And third, events, whether open fighting or political and economic strife, impact to varying degrees the domestic situation in Russia.[15] An obvious example of this is the migration to Russia of refugees from conflict areas in the near abroad. Uncontrolled mass movements of people strain limited government resources and provoke popular resentment as migrants are generally regarded as competition for scarce jobs, housing, government benefits, and so on.[16]

The Eurasian position on Russia's national interests differed sharply from those enumerated by Kozyrev in the Foreign Ministry document. The document was rejected by the Russian parliament on several grounds. First it ignored the state of Russia's bilateral relations with non-Western states and did not take into account those states with strong bilateral ties to Russia, which deserve special attention. Second, the document was vague in its references to the near abroad and that vagueness has complicated relations with the Successor States. Negotiations with the Baltic States over troop removal, borders, and the Russian minorities are cases in point.[17] Third, such notions of Russian national interest ignore the multinational character of the Russian Federation itself. Here Eurasianists draw a long-standing distinction between *Russkii* and *Rossiisky*. The first means "ethnically Russian" while the second refers to all inhabitants who call Russia their home. Eurasianists recognize Russia as the product of centuries of combined Slavic and Turkic cultural traditions. In fact many non-ethnic Russian traditions contributed to the development of what later became Russia. What all Russians and non-Russians have in common is a "Eurasian geographical and cultural space."[18]

CONSENSUS OVER RUSSIA'S NATIONAL INTERESTS IN THE NEAR ABROAD

The shift towards a Eurasian conception of Russia's national interests was not the result of one group prevailing over another, nor can it be entirely attributed to political grandstanding. Rather it was the result of Westernizers changing their own positions, as economic difficulties from market reforms became evident. Disillusionment was compounded by the inadequacy of Western assistance and political support for the success of Russian reforms. Intellectuals and academics in Russia, formerly the most vocal proponents of liberal, Western values, have increasingly shifted to a more conservative, Eurasian orientation. Journalist and political commentator Vladimir Razuvaev noted this marked defection to the Eurasian camp during a conference on Russian Foreign Policy held by the Russian Foreign Ministry in 1992.[19] But the rift between Russia and the West became a chasm, beginning with the 1996 war in Chechnya, and ending with the NATO campaign in Kosovo and the renewal of military intervention in Chechnya toward the end of the millennia. The Westernizers in the Russian government were among the casualties of these events.

The growing criticism of the Foreign Ministry's pro-West orientation had two results: the increasing conservatism of the Foreign Ministry and the increasing activism of other organizations in the sphere of foreign policy. As early as 1992, opposition leaders and even members of Yeltsin's government criticized the Foreign Ministry's policy of pursuing Russian integration into Western political and economic organizations at the expense of neglecting the former Republics. In response Kozyrev appointed Fedor Shelov-Kovedyaev as First Deputy Foreign Minister whose chief task was engaging the near abroad.

But after Shelov-Kovedyaev presented to Yeltsin a report advocating a restrained policy vis-à-vis the near abroad which included "gradual integration taking into account the interests of other [CIS] states," he resigned from the post, apparently due to concern over Yeltsin's own shift to the right.[20] To demonstrate his support for renewed activism in the near abroad, the new deputy foreign minister, Boris Pastukhov, pledged to increase the level of performance at Russian consulates. They were established in the countries of the near abroad in order to serve the visa needs of the Russian minorities, and to generally act as a go-between between them and the Russian government.[21]

In the midst of this criticism of the Foreign Ministry, Kozyrev began to advocate a more activist policy in the near abroad. He toured the near abroad for the first time in April 1992, after he had made several tours to Western countries. Though originally hoping to promote greater integration within the structure of the CIS, Kozyrev began to rely more on bilateral arrangements between Russia and respective CIS members. This shift is significant because it mirrors the vertical pattern of center-periphery interaction during the Soviet era and can be viewed as a continuation of Soviet-era center-periphery relations.

Kozyrev also began to adopt a tougher line on protecting the Russian minorities in the near abroad. He stated that protection of the Russian minorities in the near abroad was Russia's duty, and that the use of force under certain circumstances could not be ruled out. He noted that the existence of a "wide range of options to defend compatriots living abroad, beginning from expression of a slight dissatisfaction by an anonymous representative of the Russian Foreign Ministry and ending with sanctions of a political economic nature." He went on to name as an option the use "of a direct armed force in some cases."[22]

This remark provoked a storm of protest in Western governments as well as the governments of the Successor States, generating fear that this statement marked the beginnings of a more aggressive foreign policy.[23] It strained relations with the Baltic States, especially Estonia and Lithuania. Estonian Foreign Ministry Press Secretary Mari-Ann Kelam indicated that such statements hinder the normalization of Estonian-Russian relations and made clear that the Estonian government regarded the statement as threatening. Lithuania, which had expressed a concern for being surrounded by a heavily militarized Kaliningrad Oblast and Belarus, was similarly critical and noted Russia's penchant for threats that were "incompatible with norms of international law."[24] His statement elicited similar negative responses from Tashkent and Dushanbe.[25] However, Latvian Foreign Minister Valdis Birkavs and the chairman of the Saeima Commission on Foreign Affairs basically viewed Kozyrev's statement as political rhetoric to satisfy the more chauvinist elements in Russia, which had been critical of his policies.[26] Likewise, Kazakhstan's President Nursultan Nazarbayev dismissed Kozyrev's comments as electoral rhetoric.[27] It is notable that the speaker of the Crimean parliament, Serhiy Tsekov, publicly applauded Kozyrev's statement and furthermore appealed to the Russian president to "adopt measures according to international commitments, protecting the rights of compatriots living on the territory of the Crimea and representing a national minority in Ukraine."[28]

Despite the hardening line of the Foreign Ministry, Kozyrev was still drawing criticism. His tough rhetoric on defending the rights of the Russian minorities and not ruling out the use of force as an option, though welcome to some such as General Alexander Lebed, seemed by others to be motivated by electoral politics rather than a sincere change of heart.[29] Domestic skepticism is not surprising considering the similarly sanguine reaction of some successor state leaders. Shortly after Kozyrev's statement, Grigory Karasin, an official spokesman for the Russian Foreign Ministry is quoted as saying that the Ministry has "so far failed to considerably improve the situation with ethnic Russian's rights in the CIS and the Baltic States." A collegium in the Foreign Ministry attributed this failure to inadequate staffing of the Russian consulates.[30] In a long awaited move, Yeltsin relieved Kozyrev of his position as Foreign Minister in January of 1996.[31]

At the same time the Foreign Ministry began adopting a more aggressive stance towards the near abroad, at least rhetorically, other organizations began to exert growing influence over foreign policy. Parliamentarians such as Speaker Ruslan Khasbulatov and Alexander Rutskoi have been outspoken on the need to protect Russians in the near abroad. Others, such as Nikolay Ryzhkov, openly advocated re-unification with Ukraine.[32]

The individual voices of politicians aside, other government bodies such as the Defense Ministry, the Presidential Council of Experts, and the Security Council have become more involved with Russian foreign policy. The Ministry of Defense, and more specifically former Defense Minister Pavel Grachev, in a speech given in a meeting with Tajik representatives addressing the dangerous situation of Russian servicemen there, took a hardline position towards the near abroad about the protection of the Russian minorities.[33] Andranik Migranian, member of the Presidential Council of Experts, has written several influential articles on Russian national interests in the near abroad and the need of greater Russian activism in protecting the rights of Russians. Even more significant was the appointment of Sergei Stankevich to the position of political advisor to the president. Stankevich has been outspoken in his views on Russian policy in the near abroad and in the need of concrete measures for the protection of the Russian minorities.[34]

While the above actors certainly have considerable influence over Yeltsin and others involved in formulating foreign policy, their role was more informal than that of the Security Council. In fact their influence was directly related to the ambiguous position of the Foreign Ministry over policy towards the near abroad. The Security Council, which encompasses intelligence and security agencies, has gained greater powers at the expense of the Foreign Ministry and has, in specific cases, taken over substantial areas formerly relegated to the Foreign Ministry.

In July 1996, Alexander Lebed, well known for his uncompromising stance vis-à-vis the near abroad, became the secretary of the Security Council. After Lebed took the post, the Council was given expanded power. Among its duties are the following: defining state and societal interests (national interests); identifying internal and external threats to security; constructing strategies to deal with national security threats (including the imposition of states of emergency); authorizing the use of the military in times of crises; and submitting recommendations to the president on the above matters as well as on domestic and foreign policies which impact Russian security. A subsequent statute on the expanded powers of the Security Council omitted mention of the participation of Security Council members, especially in the submission to the Council of alternative proposals, provoking some to question the boundaries of the secretary's powers.[35] The Security Council's broadened powers in all areas of national security have clear implications for policy in the near abroad since by any measure, the near abroad falls within the sphere of Russia's national interest. Indeed, the Foreign Ministry's ambiguous role in constructing policy towards the near abroad was noted obliquely by Lebed in his reply to a question about the expanded Security Council powers. When asked "at the expense of which government structures [the Foreign Ministry?]" did the expansion of powers take place, Lebed answered that the Security Council was filling a vacuum.[36]

After Lebed's appointment, the Security Council officially condemned Latvia's declaration of its own occupation during the Soviet period, viewing the declaration as a potential threat to Russia's territorial integrity. The Council has also taken over the issue of control over the Black Sea Fleet in negotiations with Ukraine. The significance of both issues lies in questions of national security. In the Latvian case, accusations of occupation are potential preludes to territorial demands and border adjustments, while in the Ukrainian case, the key to the issue of the Black Sea Fleet is the joint defense of the Caspian-Black Sea region.[37] Having primary jurisdiction over national security issues, the Security Council exerts significant power over Russian foreign policy in the near abroad.

The term nationalism implies emotive reactions to events, reactions that vary widely among Russians, especially Russian politicians. But the existence of a Russian nation implies underlying commonalties apart from the differences in opinions as reflected by the current nationalist debate. What do the proponents of various visions of Russia's future have in common? Despite their differences, they are united by the belief that Russia's "objective" security interests include maintaining dominance over the former Republics. Following Kozyrev's removal and Russia's shift to the right, a more coherent set of security priorities became evident.

RUSSIAN SECURITY CONCERNS

The dissolution of the Soviet Union created numerous security considerations for Russia, many of which are recognized by assorted Russian politicians and high-ranking military personal. Broadly outlined, these include some of the following: forestalling the fragmentation of the Russian Federation; redefining relations with the former Republics in light of Russia's diminished power both in Central Eurasia and the international political arena; managing threats stemming from conflicts in areas of the former Republics; and finding ways to mitigate discriminatory practices against the Russian minorities in the former Republics so as to lessen immigration and its resultant hardships. To this end, Russia has pursued, however inconsistently, policies that would promote the establishment of a single economic and security region under Russian hegemony.

Any future Russian government, whatever its political ideology, wants to avoid fragmentation of the Russian federation. Nationalism played a large part in the breakup of the Soviet Union at a time when state borders were considered inviolable and states as political organizations were thought to be permanent. It is significant that the Republics seceded along established Soviet republican borders. Yeltsin and/or his close advisors in the government feared the possibility that the Republics and Regions of the Russian Federation, which are also nationality-based territories, might follow the separatist example set by the former Republics. The constitutional wrangle with Tatarstan and the armed rebellion in Chechnya are two outstanding cases of Regions exercising autonomy. Other Republics have taken control over the big extractive industries located in their districts, withheld taxes from the center, and have even negotiated deals directly with foreign firms.

Following the breakup, the Yeltsin administration set about reforming the federal structure of the former Soviet Union which included a hierarchical order among territories established ostensibly on the basis of ethnicity. The Autonomous Regions assumed the status of Republics while the Autonomous Oblasts rose to the status of Regions. The original plan of the constitutional assembly of 1990 was to make all territories of equal status. This created such resistance among the Republics, especially Tatarstan, Sakha, and Chechnya, that the idea was dropped, to the anger of the regional governments who disavowed their secondary status.[38]

Leaving aside the problem of Republics versus Regions, the Yeltsin administration sought to define powers between the Federal and the Republics/Regions constitutionally through the 1992 Federal Treaty. Although the treaty was signed by all except Tatarstan and Chechnya, which refused to enter into an unequal arrangement with Moscow, they did so only with many reservations and conditions. While the Republics wanted equal status vis-à-vis the Federal government, the Regions protested their diminutive status vis-à-vis the Republics, regarded as unfair since the Regions were more populous and paid more taxes than the Republics.[39] In the end, three treaties were drafted, one each for the Republics, Regions and Oblasts.[40]

Both the Republics and the Regions had been acting with increasing autonomy vis-à-vis the center, mostly because the Central government had abrogated its power to appoint regional governors after 1991. Instead, their constituents would elect regional governors for the first time. The behavior of the regional governors shifted accordingly. In 1992, in reaction to the crash privatization policies and the move to float prices, regional officials took control of food and industrial supplies. The outflow of agricultural goods was halted and kept within the Regions for local consumption. In this way, regional governments managed to stave off unrest, unemployment, and food shortages. They also took control of local banks and law enforcement agencies.[41] When the Federal government, in an attempt to reign in the budget and bring down inflation, shifted the burden of financing social services and price subsidies onto local governments, many Republican and regional governments withheld taxes from the Federal government. They argued that they needed the money because the Federal government neither allocated sufficient resources nor gave them the power to levy taxes at the local level.[42] In addition, there is ample evidence that the Republics are conducting foreign policy by taking the lead in developing foreign contacts and conducting trade with foreign countries that bypasses Moscow.[43]

There are indications that Putin is attempting to reign in the Republics and Regions. In the first place, Putin has introduced legislation aimed at curtailing the independence of the Republics and Regions. One piece of legislation passed by the Duma (the Lower House) June 30, 2000 was a bill giving the Russian president the right to dismiss governors or regional leaders who "violate federal laws." Under this law, Regional legislatures can also be dissolved. Currently the bill is stalled in the Upper House which after all is comprised of those very Republican and regional leaders.[44]

He has also demonstrated his willingness to use military force to maintain Moscow's control over recalcitrant Republics. His policies in Chechnya reflect the determination of Moscow to retain its territorial integrity. The total destruction of Grozny (the Russian military had a difficult time finding an undamaged building appropriate for setting up headquarters) in the name of "combating terrorism" seems a high price to pay for keeping Chechnya within the Federation. And with Putin's offensive in Chechnya, with its indiscriminate bombing of villages and attacks on civilians, the designation of all Chechen males ages 10 to 65 as guerrilla terrorists, and the retreat of most Chechen fighters to the mountains south of Grozny, terrorist activity is only going to increase.

Of course an even bigger incentive is driving Putin; retaining control in the Caucasus is essential if Moscow is to capitalize on the exploitation of Caspian Sea oil and subsequent oil pipeline projects. Russia has been trying, so far unsuccessfully, to push through the construction of a pipeline that goes through Russia. The current pipeline from Baku to the port at Novorossiysk runs through Chechnya. Even before the 1994 war in Chechnya, the theft of oil from this pipeline was a problem that the Dudayev government was unable to control.[45] From the Russian view, an enormous amount of revenue was being lost.

A hostile and unstable Chechnya hurts Russia's bargaining position in the Caspian Sea oil debates because without Chechnya, Russia will have a difficult time achieving its primary goal: to control the flow of Caspian Sea oil. Achieving that goal means increasing the capacity of both the Baku-Chechnya-Novorossiysk and Tengiz-Novorossiysk pipelines. Either by itself is currently insufficient to handle the projected outflow of the Caspian deposits. The mess in Chechnya also complicates Russia's battle to resolve the Caspian Sea's legal status in its favor.

Second, the loss of superpower status prompted the Yeltsin government to pursue policies aimed at maintaining a presence in the former Republics. This trend will only increase under Putin. All of the former Republics have significant minority populations, and the largest minority group are Russians, a fact which is significant because they represent the imperial minority of the former empire and because the capabilities of Russia still far outweigh those of the former Republics. And the reaction of the Russian government to issues affecting the Russian minorities in the former Republics is unpredictable since official pronouncements on this issue in the past have ranged from indifference to chauvinism.

In the midst of economic and political turmoil, Russia is struggling to establish its own state institutions. On what should the Russian state be based? Some think it should be based on the *Russkii*, that is ethnic Russian, nation while others believe that it should be based on a broader *Rossiisky identity*, a term that refers to all inhabitants who call Russia their home. A *Rossiisky* identity underscores the fact that Russia is the product of centuries of combined Slavic and Turkic cultural traditions. Many non-ethnic Russian traditions have contributed to the development of what later became Russia. What all Russian and non-Russians have in common is a "Eurasian geographical and cultural space."[46] Despite the internal debate over what it means to be Russian, general feelings of national humiliation over the loss of the "empire" and of superpower status have given voice to the idea of restoring Russian influence in the near abroad as a part of a larger attempt to regain great power status, if not in the world, then at least on the Eurasian landmass.

Third, political turmoil in the areas of the former Soviet Union has obvious security implications for Russia. Armed conflicts in Tajikistan, Georgia, Moldova, Chechnya, and the conflict between Armenia and Azerbaijan, have a direct impact on the Russian Federation. They generate population movements and refugees, they provoke the interference of outside regional actors such as Iran, Turkey, and Afghanistan, and they cost the Russian government by increasing the need for military defense spending and the rebuilding of damaged infrastructure. These conflicts hinder the development of normal political and economic structures, laws, and institutions.

The Yeltsin government was forced to contend with the security dilemma wrought by the dissolution of the Soviet Union and has viewed the support of key allies as an important part of boosting security at home. Putin has bolstered this part of Yeltsin's security agenda. Russia has been, and remains, the main source of logistical support of the Rahmanov government in Dushambe, which has been fighting anti-government groups. Intermittent fighting has plagued Tajikistan for most of the last decade since independence. Russia sees it in its own interests to support the secular, Soviet-styled Rahmanov regime. Similarly, Russia supported Abkhazi separatists in Georgia in order to pressure Georgia into joining the CIS. Moscow has also been the primary arbitrator in the Armenian/Azerbaijani crisis and the chief source of support for the pro-Russian, breakaway government in Tiraspol. Lastly, the Yeltsin regime fought an unpopular and unsuccessful war in Chechnya that lasted from 1994–1996 and ended with a Russian retreat following a failed attempt to capture the Chechen capital of Grozny. The resumption of hostilities under Putin beginning in the latter part of 1999 has been similarly troubled though Putin, unlike Yeltsin, has controlled to a greater extent media coverage of the fighting which in general has cast the conflict as a success for the Russian military. The campaign in Chechnya was so dubbed because of the capture of Grozny. But those who tout the military success in Chechnya ignore the rules of guerrilla warfare; the Chechen fighters retreated from Grozny not in defeat, but to re-group and redirect their assaults on Russian forces. By any measure, the Chechen conflict has cost Russia tremendously in terms of lives, morale among military personnel, and military hardware.

Another security concern has to do with the influence of outside powers in the territories of the former Republics. Moscow is interested in the sources of foreign investment as well as more overt manifestations of foreign influence, which might dilute its own influence. The Russian government faces increased Western leverage in the Baltic States and has found it difficult to woo or even influence the policy direction of the pro-Western governments of the Baltic States who defiantly and loudly proclaim their desire to join the EU and NATO. In the area of the Caspian Sea basin, there are several interested for-eign parties, including states and foreign firms, who all want a piece of the oil wealth of the Caspian. The activities of Muslim states such as Iran and Pakistan in Central Asia and the Caucasus,[47] and Japan's growing economic prestige in the Russian Far East, especially in the Kurile Islands, are the results of Yeltsin's negligence, inability, or unwillingness to maintain a strong presence in these areas.

Putin's own rhetoric indicates his intent to reverse this trend. Foreign Min-ister Igor Ivanov publicly stated the unlikelyhood that Russia and Japan would conclude a peace treaty this year according to Japan's Kyodo news agency. [48] This stance is a departure from the more conciliatory posture of the Yeltsin gov-ernment. However, events beyond Putin's control may serve to push the former Republics closer to Moscow. The 1998 financial crisis revealed how tightly bound many of the Successor State economies are to the Russian economy.

In addition, outside influences may push the former Republics toward Rus-sia. Increasingly the former Republics are finding it too difficult and expensive to join the ranks of free-market, Western democracies. Western assistance is contingent on the adoption of certain economic policies such as the privatiza-tion of government enterprises, maintaining strict control over the money supply so as not to fuel inflation, and especially upholding strict guidelines for government spending. This last policy has proved to be the most painful for it has meant reductions in social services and wage/pension payments. At the same time, budgetary funds are allotted to payback IMF (International Mone-tary Fund) and World Bank loans. It is a thorny issue with voters who have not seen any improvement in their lives (unless one is a part of the "Mafia," the standard of living actually declined in most of the former Republics including Russia) since the dissolution of the Soviet Union. People are faced with governments unable or unwilling to pay wages/pensions owed to them; however, funds are found to pay back loans to foreigners that had no tangible results other than to enrich a few people lucky or corrupt enough to profit from them. Now that voters elect governments, the latter need to consider the impact of their policies on voter behavior, at least to some extent. An inability to pay wages coupled with declining health care, education, and public transport just might spur the public to vote against an incumbent government.

Moldova's parliament voted to accept the resignation of reformist Prime Minister Ion Sturza after the latter threatened to resign upon parliament's refusal to adopt bills privatizing the country's tobacco and wine industries. These industries are two of Moldova's three moneymaking industries. The reformists were ousted and a coalition comprised of the Communists and the Popular Front emerged to choose a new government.[49] Lithuania's government faced a similar spit when many parliamentarians balked at spending $350 million to modernize the state-owned oil refinery Mazeikiu Nafta. The American company Williams International has been negotiating the privatization of Mazeikiu Nafta. On October 19 the Lithuanian Cabinet of Ministers voted in favor of signing an agreement that would grant Williams controlling stock in the company. Prime Minister Rolandas Paksas, Finance Minister Jonas Lionginas and Economics Minister Eugenijus Maldeikis were the primary voices of opposition and voted against the deal. They have subsequently resigned in protest. Spending $350 million to modernize the refinery meant risking economic ruin for unspecified and uncertain returns. The conclusion of a business deal is not viewed in the West as a precursor to broader political guarantees. By contrast Russia viewed this buy-out in political terms and turned up the heat by threatening to shut off the oil unless they were given a chance to match the Williams bid.[50] If Lithuania, the most pro-Western of the Successor States, can decide that integration into Western security and economic structures is not worth the risk, then it follows that this sort of resistance will likely crop up in other areas of the former Soviet Union.

Finally, the Successor States of the former Republics are busily engaged in the construction of indigenous political and economic institutions based on the titular nationality of each state. A growing influence of the indigenous, titular cultures and languages of the former Republics in public life may impact Russian security; the expansion of titular culture may lead to overt discrimination of Russian minorities and signal the decline of Moscow's influence over these territories. The importance of nationalism in the Successor States in this endeavor can be gleaned from measures these states have taken to bolster their statehood. These include the adoption of language laws replacing Russian as the official language; establishing strict citizenship requirements; citizenship laws banning non-indigenous groups from participating in the political process; and making elementary social services such as housing, education, and health care difficult if not impossible for non-titular minorities to obtain. The disenfranchisement of minority populations could possibly lead to political unrest, and in extreme cases, mass movements of populations, all of which would directly impact Russia. The Russian government is concerned with the treatment of Russian minorities because population movements mean refugees and the high financial and political costs associated with repatriating Russian minorities. If, either as the result of conflict or of discrimination, conditions deteriorate to the point where the Russian minorities migrate in large numbers to the Russian Federation, this would cause innumerable difficulties from the standpoint of the Russian government. The Russian minorities—especially those from areas which are expected to generate the greatest number of forced migrants such as Chechnya, Moldova, Dagestan, and Central Asia—are mostly urban dwellers and therefore would compete with Russian citizens for jobs rather than fill vacant rural areas.[51] And there is growing evidence that Russian citizens do not want these refugees. In a survey of 1,600 teenagers at schools in Moscow, the number of teenagers who believe that Russia should be open to refugees was zero.[52]

Finally, the Russian government has to be concerned with maintaining the area of the former Soviet Union as a single economic and security zone. In short, economic integration has become a priority because it is viewed as bolstering Russia's ties to the Successor States as well as preventing unwanted foreign involvement by foreign countries. Russia still has considerable influence in the economic and security spheres. The Successor States are dependent to a considerable degree on Russia for raw materials and especially natural gas and petroleum. Unable to pay for these in hard currency, the Successor States must continually negotiate with Russia regarding the terms of payment and the rescheduling of debts. This dependence has given Russia considerable leverage in extracting political and military concessions from the Successor States.[53] Similarly, Russia has concluded security pacts with several of the Successor States including Turkmenistan, Belarus, Kyrgyzstan, Kazakhstan, and it is in the process of negotiating with Lithuania matter of overland passage to Kaliningrad Oblast. Kazakhstan pulled out of the ruble zone in November of 1993 after Russia demanded that the gold reserves of participating countries be deposited in Russia and has since introduced the tenge as legal tender.[54] In contrast, Belarus has signed military and customs agreements in return for retaining the use of the Russian ruble.

STRENGTHS AND LIMITATIONS: RUSSIAN ACTIVISM IN THE NEAR ABROAD

What are the implications of the political consensus on the importance of the near abroad to Russian national interests for Russian policy in the near abroad? The answer lies in Russia's capacity to influence events in the near abroad and domestic limitations on the implementation of certain policies. The strengths and limitations of Russian foreign policy towards the near abroad are evident in the actual strategies Russia has employed in its relations vis-à-vis the former Republics.

Economically, Russia easily dominates Central Eurasia. Despite economic difficulties, Russia is in a far more advantageous position than most other Successor States for several reasons. First, the countries of the near abroad are trade-dependent on Russia and each other. Despite a decline in inter-republican trade following the collapse of the ruble zone in 1993, a considerable percentage of successor state exports go to Russia which is also the primary source for raw materials and inputs for local industries. Even in the Baltic countries, where progress away from dependence from the former Soviet Republics is most advanced, Russia continues to be the single largest trade partner, though in the case of Estonia, Finland became an equally important trade partner.[55]

The dependence on Russia and the former Republics for export market and imports is much higher in Central Asia, though accurate statistics are not always available. For example the trade statistics complied for the Kyrgyz Republic show that in 1992, trade with former Soviet Republics totaled 87.8 percent of exports and 95.5 percent of imports, while in 1991, the numbers for Turkmenistan were 85.8 percent and 83.8 percent respectively.[56] In 1994, Tajikistan, the most dependent on Russia due to the civil war, exported 77.6 percent of its products to the former Republics while 54.6 percent of total imports came from them.[57] Comparative numbers for Uzbekistan in 1995 were 49.5 percent and 44.4 percent respectively.[58] And though the level of trade has since declined, and while these statistics cover trade with all the former Republics, Russia continues to be the dominant trade partner. Residual inter-republican trade in the region is by and large restricted to other Central Asian states. While not strictly comparable due to annual changes and availability of recent data, the statistics on Central Asia illustrate the general decline in the percentage of trade with former Soviet Republics, but they do not take into account unregulated cross-border trade.

In Kazakhstan dependence on trade with Successor States other than Russia declined while trade with Russia increased from 37.7 percent in 1994 to 43.9 percent in 1995.[59] In 1998, 76.62 percent of Kazakhstan's exports to CIS countries went to Russia. Russia remained the primary source of Kazakhstan's imports, accounting for 39.4 percent of all imports.[60] The level of dependence on Russia for both export markets and imports is especially high for Ukraine and Belarus, both of which have instituted only minimal market reforms.[61] Belarusian trade with Russia totaled 47.8 percent of total exports and 59.7 percent of total imports in 1995.[62] In 1998, these figures were 65.5 percent and 53.8 percent respectively.[63] In 1998, the corresponding figures for Ukraine were 48.13 percent and 23 percent respectively.[64] These are conservative estimates however since they do not include unregulated and thus untabulated cross-border trade.

Second, the countries of the near abroad are still dependent on Russia for energy resources, especially petroleum. Even for the Baltic States, it is easier and less expensive to buy petroleum from Russia via existing pipelines than to build new pipelines to alternative sources. Although Turkmenistan is becoming a source of natural gas and exports it to other former Republics such as Uzbekistan, Kyrgyzstan, and Ukraine, Russian remains the principal source for fuel. Furthermore, energy resources extracted from Central Asia must be sent to Russia for refinement and export, as the pipelines go through Russian territory and the Central Asian states are land-locked countries.[65] Lithuania and Belarus receive virtually all of their gas and oil from Russia, Latvia gets all of its natural gas from Russia, and Ukraine receives an estimated 86 percent of its oil and 52 percent of its gas from Russia.[66]

Apart from trade, most of the near abroad cannot afford to pay for fuel in hard currency, which Russia now demands for these exports. As a result, many of these countries are indebted to Russia. Debt rescheduling and negotiations over energy deliveries give Russia considerable political leverage over the near abroad which has been used to extract political concessions. Ukraine's acceptance in 1994 of the provisions of the START Treaty in exchange for, among other things, the cancellation of Ukraine's fuel debt to Russia is a case in point.

And current trends indicate that Russia's influence will increase in the future. After the fall of communism and independence, many of the new governments held an idealized image of the West and sought ways to transform their economies and societies according to the Western model. To become a part of the West, the Baltic States, Ukraine, and Moldova all proclaimed their objective to join Western economic and political organizations such as the EU, NATO, and also international organizations such as GATT (General Agreement on Tariffs and Trade) and the WTO (World Trade Organization). The governments of the former Republics expected the transformation of their economies to be supported and subsidized by Western governments. But when Western assistance failed to be sufficient and effective in offsetting the high social and political costs, governments began to back away from reforms or institute them piecemeal and half-heartedly. The result was a general disillusionment with reforms and a continuing dependence on Russia.

Third, the Russian ruble, while weak compared to European currencies, is much stronger than those introduced by the countries of the near abroad, with the exception of those of the Baltic States, following the collapse of the ruble zone. Russia refused to underwrite the old Soviet rubles of the former Republics. Russia instituted central control (by the Central Bank of Russia) over money supply and demanded all gold reserves be deposited in Russia. These measures effectively drove all the CIS countries, with the exception of Belarus and Tajikistan, out of the ruble zone (See Table 4.1). Provisions for a ruble zone, whereby a single currency would be used to conduct trade on the territory of the former Soviet Union, were originally established under CIS agreements. However, conducting trade in rubles meant that the Republics (especially Russia) were exporting goods at below market prices, prompting

Table 4.1
Currency Table of the Successor States

Country	Currency	Date of Intro	Exchange Rate $ (as of 1/98)
Russia	Ruble	1993	5,972.00 : $1
Belarus	Ruble	June 1992	30,830.00 : $1
Ukraine	Hryvnya	Sept 1996	1.90 : $1
Estonia	Kroon	June 1992	14.50 : $1
Latvia	Lat	June 1993	.60 : $1
Lithuania	Litas	July 1993	4.00 : $1
Moldova	Leu	November 1993	4.66 : $1
Kazakhstan	Tenge	November 1993	75.60 : $1
Kyrgyz Republic	Som	May 1993	17.40 : $1
Tajikistan	Tajik Ruble	May 1995	748.00 : $1
Turkmenistan	Manat	November 1993	4,165.00 : $1
Uzbekistan	Som	July 1994	80.40 : $1

Source: *The Economist Intelligence Unit Country Report, 1st quarter: Belarus* (London: The Economist Intelligence Unit Limited, 1998), p. 6.

the re-export by the Successor States of such goods to far abroad countries at a profit.[67]

Such practices persuaded Russia to tighten monetary policy and stabilize the ruble. The Successor States have since established their own currencies. Although Belarus has established its own ruble and Tajikistan has done likewise, they are parallel currencies, tied to the Russian ruble.[68] Thus detached from the former Republics, Russia refused payments in rubles and instead demanded payment in hard currency. These tightened monetary policies bolstered the Russian ruble; Russia is in an advantageous position vis-à-vis other CIS states in the strength of its currency as determined by the purchasing power of each of the currencies.[69]

Last, the sheer size of the Russian economy as compared to those of the former Republics makes Russia a formidable economic power (See Table 4.2). The gross domestic product of Russia in 1995 totaled $677.7 billion. The second largest economy of the near abroad, Ukraine, had a gross domestic product during the same period totaling approximately $150 billion, less than a fourth of Russia's Gross Domestic Product (GDP).[70] After Ukraine came Uzbekistan, Kazakhstan, Belarus, Azerbaijan, and Moldova, with GDPs of approximately $58 billion, $55 billion, $45 billion, $17 billion, and $15 billion respectively.[71] The remaining Successor States have still smaller economies. This disparity remained even after the 1998 finiancial crisis. Though the Russian economy shrank by more than half, the economies of the former Republics likewise shrank (See Table 4.2).

THE 1998 SUMMER FINANCIAL CRISIS AND ITS AFTEREFFECTS

Though Russia has weathered many economic crises, the 1998 summer crisis was the worst since independence. It also graphically demonstrated the interdependence of the post-Soviet economies as well as the central position of the Russian economy; Russia's financial stability remains a precondition for the economic recovery of the former Republics.

To understand the impact of the crisis, a few points need to be made regarding the implications of unreformed enterprises of Russia and the former Republics. The first point to be made is what is meant by "reformed." Here they are considered unreformed because day-to-day operations have not changed, privatization notwithstanding. Privatization amounted to the wholesale transfer of state enterprises (only the desirable ones of course) into the hands of a few individuals, or oligarchs as they are called. Only now profits go into the pockets of the oligarchs rather than into state coffers, and wage payments to workers are sporadic. In theory privatization should have eliminated wage arrears. In reality however workers of both "privatized" and state enterprises often go under or unpaid.

Ultimately it is the Russian government that bares the cost of keeping large, inefficient enterprises afloat. Unprofitable enterprises drain rather than add to government coffers. They are "unprofitable" because unscrupulous individuals have no vested interest in their success. By hiding profits to show that an enterprise is losing money, oligarchs avoid paying taxes and pocket the profits via overseas bank accounts. Maintaining industries means among other things paying workers' wages and pensions. So financial crises have devastating consequences for the economy. Workers don't get paid, and industrial output declines precipitously (See Table 4.2). Why? The lack of reforms means that industries by and large continue to function the way they did during Soviet times. Rather than buying industrial inputs and calculating their cost into the final cost of the product, enterprises are forced to barter with one another for

Table 4.2
Gross Domestic Product of Successor States (in billions $)*

Country	1996	After August 1998
Russia	667.7	191
Ukraine	150	32
Uzbekistan	58	12
Kazakhstan	55	17
Belarus	45	10
Moldova	15	1
Lithuania	13	9.5
Turkmenistan	12	6
Latvia	10	9
Estonia	9.5	8
Kyrgyz Republic	9	1.5
Tajikistan	5	1

Source: *The Economist Intelligence Unit Country Report: Ukraine 1996–97 Annual Reportt*
(London: The Economist Intelligence Unit, 1996); *The Economist Intelligence Unit Country
Profile: Estonia* (London: The Economist Intelligence Unit Limited, 2000).

*Numerical values are approximations except the value given for Russia.

needed supplies. In a command economy industries must scrounge for materials. Besides being inefficient, this system is inadequate. Frequently enterprises are unable to obtain necessary materials in sufficient quantities. Quality control was, and still is, practically non-existent. This reliance on barter is indicative of a weak and unstable currency.

Supplies that enterprises are required to buy, such as energy, also generate problems. Enterprises face huge budget problems due to arrears owed to energy suppliers. This triggers a domino effect: enterprises are not able to pay for supplies with money, the supply sources cannot make money (because their clients cannot pay them), they therefore cannot continue to supply because they become unable to produce. The only way both can stay afloat is by government bailouts. But government bailouts ensure that enterprises will not reform. Yet enterprises cannot make profits when they are forced to barter due to the instability of the ruble. And their closure would mean mass layoffs and unemployment.

Low tax revenues exacerbate fiscal problems. Estimates have placed tax revenues (collected taxes) as comprising only 10 percent of the Gross Domestic Product![72] Tax collection has been poor, true. But even if tax-collecting methods improved, revenues would still be low for two simple reasons. State sector enterprises running at a loss do not generate taxable profits. As for those that do make profits, well, the current tax system so penalizes businesses that it forces the economy underground as industries conspire to avoid them. Currently an estimated 14,000 Russian companies are registered in Cyprus. Interenterprise payments are done offshore in Cyprus to avoid taxes. Taxes that come from taxable personal income are likewise insufficient when workers are not paid for months or years at a time. Furthermore, individuals are more likely to make money through the informal or underground economy, which is beyond the reach of the tax collectors. Working in the informal economy is frequently the only source of reliable income for ordinary Russians.

Since independence, the government has had a continuing crisis regarding back wages for workers. Wage arrears are bad in all sectors of the economy. Needless to say, irregular paychecks are extremely deleterious to work performance. Workers live by getting other forms of payment. In Soviet times, different regions specialized in producing certain products. In Yaroslav, that product was automobile tires. Yaroslav still makes tires and frequently workers get paid in kind. One librarian I interviewed received payment in tires! As in Soviet times, people barter with one another for needed items.

The agricultural sector similarly suffers from the lack of reforms. So now we see low output without the Soviet-style work brigades whereby people were forced to help bring in the harvest by picking potatoes on the local collective farm. Still, land reforms may not sufficiently boost production because many farmers do not trust that property laws would be binding and furthermore have been raised in a system that demonized the idea of private property. Land ownership is at best a calculated risk for farmers. Looking back on recent Soviet history—for example, the "kulak" purges, forced collectivization, forced grain requisitions, famines—one can understand their reluctance.

The summer financial crisis of 1998 was triggered by chronic federal deficits and an increasing reliance on external borrowing from the IMF and World Bank, and from the issuing of GKOs, Short-term Government Securities (similar to U.S. government bonds). GKOs required high-interest rates, which added to the government debt (as the government must pay out interest payments), and fueled the need to issue more treasury bills. GKOs were an IMF insistence because they help generate the revenue necessary to pay back IMF loans. But when Russia and the IMF could not agree on a 1998 austerity plan, the IMF delayed disbursement of a 3-year, $9 billion IMF loan. Investors then sold off en masse Russian stocks and GKOs (fearing Russia would default on the securities).

As a result, the Russian government did not have enough foreign reserves to back up the ruble. The Russian government announced that revenues would be less than predicted (revenues = estimated tax collection). Investors sold Russian stocks for fear of a mass devaluation of the ruble. In the end, the G–7 refused to bail out Russia in spite of the fact that the GKOs were an IMF requirement. Russia was forced to devalue the ruble. The lack of a stable currency exacerbated the previously mentioned problems in industry and agricultural production. The ruble fell by 30 percent. Prices rose sharply; wholesale prices rose by about 30 percent. The cost of food imports increased 100–150 percent! The cost of Russian-made products rose by 50–100 percent. In some places, increases were even greater. This was even true for basics like butter, sugar and salt. In response, Regions imposed price controls and prohibited the export of certain goods outside the region.

While industries in the former Republics (with the exception of the Baltic States) depend on Russia for inputs and markets, the reverse is not true. State-owned businesses and collective/state farms are still the norm in the near abroad (excluding the Baltic States). This is not to suggest however that privatization and Western style reforms would solve the problem of dependency. As demonstrated in Russia, privatization has not solved the operational problems of Soviet-built industries. It is difficult enough for Russian firms to obtain supplies needed for production. It is even more difficult for industries in the former Republics that depend on their unstable Russian counterparts for supplies. Russia remains the primary market for goods that are otherwise uncompetitive on the world market.

The 1998 summer crisis demonstrated how the economies of the Successor States were dependent on the performance of the Russian economy. Devaluation of the ruble was followed by a fall in demand. The collapse of the export market in Russia hit the CIS states hardest. Exports from Russia to the former Republics fell because Russian enterprises became less inclined to except barter arrangements, which had been commonplace. Most of CIS trade arrangements were in the form of barter. The crisis did not affect exports to non-CIS countries because the CIS currencies did not appreciate against the dollar. And though they appreciated against the ruble after the ruble itself was devalued, the appreciation was only temporary. CIS state governments quickly devalued their own currencies. Since CIS countries are competing with one another for the same export market, that is, Russia, then one country's devaluation puts the others at a competitive disadvantage.[73] The rash of devaluations combined with the collapse of the Russian export market and inter-CIS trade, demonstrated the interconnected character of the economies of Central Eurasia much more clearly than simple trade statistics ever could.

THE DOMINANCE OF RUSSIA IN THE POLITICAL SPHERE

Politically Russia is considerably more powerful than its neighbors. Internationally Russia was recognized as the Successor State of the Soviet Union, and as previously mentioned, took the place of the Soviet Union in the UN Security Council. As a result of this recognition, the international community has tended to pay Russia far more attention than the former Republics in several ways.

First, Russia receives the lion's share of foreign investment. Kazakhstan does not fare too badly in the area of foreign investment, though most of it is in extractive industries and has run into numerous administrative difficulties stemming from unclear and ill-defined state business and investment procedures.[74] Turkmenistan and Azerbaijan have also attracted some foreign investment, largely as a result of their petroleum and natural gas reserves. CIS countries without substantial mineral and energy reserves have not attracted significant foreign investment. Foreign investors tend to be cautious about investing in countries that lack political and economic stability and clearly established laws and procedures in matters of investment, taxation, and property ownership. Russia too has its own problems in the area of stability, but relative to the other countries of the near abroad, it does comparatively well.

Second, despite rhetoric from Europe and the United States in support of Successor States' sovereignty, there has been very little tangible support for the Successor States, with the exception of the Baltic States. As noted, most foreign investment (with the exception of oil and mining industries) is concentrated in Russia. Furthermore, Western countries often deal with countries in the near abroad, especially Ukraine, through Russia on issues of critical importance. For example, on the issue of nuclear weapons, the United States has made clear its preference for dealing with only one nuclear power on the territory of the former Soviet Union, namely Russia. To this end, negotiations have centered on moving nuclear missiles from Ukraine and Belarus to Russia, and dismantling those forces, which cannot be moved, like ICBM silos in Kazakhstan.[75] United States' determination to consolidate Soviet nuclear forces within the borders of the Russian Federation was evident in promises to Ukraine of developmental aid in return for relinquishing its nuclear weapons to Russia.[76] As for Belarus, the need to remove nuclear weapons to Russia was made redundant by the security union between Minsk and Moscow, which placed Belarusian military security, including the nuclear weapons located in Belarus, under Russian control.

Third, Russia enjoys the political advantage of being a power broker in Central Eurasia. The reasons for this lie in Russia's relative strength vis-à-vis the former Republics and the inability of the Successor States to present a unified front in dealings with Russia. This is due to the lack of horizontal links among the Successor States. Linkages generally run through Moscow, as they did during the Soviet period. The CIS has by and large failed, and bilateral agreements between Russia and individual Successor States on trade, quotas, and licensing have become the modus operandi.[77] Political agreements, such as the establishment of consulates and accords guaranteeing protection of the rights of Russian minorities, have similarly been concluded bilaterally.[78]

Where horizontal linkages among the Successor States do exist, they are usually regionally based (as among the countries of the Baltic, the Caucasus, and Central Asia) and are contentious at best and hostile at worst. Furthermore, many of the Successor States—Georgia, Kazakhstan, Tajikistan, Moldova—face internal threats to unity all of which weakens their position vis-à-vis Russia. It can further be argued that Estonia, Ukraine, and Kyrgyzstan also face potential threats to unity as in the case of the Russian minorities in Narva, Crimea, and the North/South divide respectively. Such political weaknesses provide Russia opportunities to intervene, as it has in Moldova, Tajikistan, and the Caucasus.

Russia faces certain limitations in the strategies it employs towards the Successor States. For one thing, a willingness to provide economic assistance to the countries on its periphery would substantially enhance Russia's position in the near abroad, especially in Central Asia. However there is little domestic support for providing such assistance in light of Russia's own financial problems. Another perception hindering Russian involvement in the near abroad involves the widespread belief that Russia is much better off on its own. The belief was shared by international financial institutions, which advised Russia to stabilize and privatize its own economy without the cooperation of its CIS partners.[79] Since the independence of the Successor States, Russia is no longer responsible for subsidizing industrial development in the form of free energy supplies and raw materials.

The most notable limitation on Russian policy in the near abroad is widespread public resistance to the use of military force. Despite rising Russian nationalism and an increasing interest in expanding Russian involvement in the near abroad, support stops short of outright military intervention. Moldova and the Caucasus are not exceptions: the conflicts in these areas are holdovers from the Soviet days. The 14th Army in Moldova was already stationed in Moldova at the time of independence. When fighting broke out after breakup of the Soviet Union between the self-proclaimed Dneistr Republic (Tiraspol) and Moldova proper (Chisinau), the 14th Army fought on the side of Tiraspol. However, their ranks were not recruited from Russia. And before Lebed intervened, the 14th Army acted independently of Moscow. Russian intervention in the Caucasus, both in the Georgian Civil war and the Armenian/Azerbaijani conflict, was more covert and involved large numbers of renegade soldiers and mercenaries whose ties to Moscow were vague and difficult to substantiate.[80]

Throughout the 1990s, the public by and large did not support large-scale military intervention. According to a poll taken in 1992 and again in 1994, most Russians felt that Russia should be active in protecting the rights of Russians living in the near abroad. Yet only 6.8 percent polled in 1992 supported military intervention in support of this objective; that number dropped to 2 percent in 1994.[81] Even more telling, 65.2 percent in another poll answered that the only way Russia can regain its former great power status is through the successful development of the Russian economy.[82] As of 1996, the most pressing problems faced by Russia today, according to polls, did not include matters of foreign policy or the near abroad. Sixty-three percent of Russians and 72 percent of Muscovites cited rising crime as among the most disturbing problems Russia faces. Rising prices and the economic crisis (low agricultural and industrial production) were among the top three concerns of both Russians and Muscovites with percentages of 74 percent and 70 percent, and 50 percent and 52 percent respectively.[83]

The renewed invasion of Chechnya in the latter half of 1999s garnered popular support in large part due to the "invasion" of Dagestan, supposedly by Islamic extremists (the Wahhabi), and the September 1999 apartment bombings in Moscow and Volgodonsk. The Kremlin/Putin propaganda machine labeled this war as a war against terrorism. In this vein the "public support" was more for the tough stance against a group most Russians are anyway prejudiced against, rather than active support for military ventures. Despite claims by various foreign and Russian media, anecdotal evidence strongly suggests public resistance to military ventures. The most compelling, albeit unscientific, evidence is simply the lengths Russians go to avoid military service, as seen by the organized efforts of the Soldiers' Mothers Committee which is an advocacy group that holds open meetings about legal means mothers can employ to keep their sons out of the military.

Regardless of public opinion regarding Chechnya, wars cannot be fought without armies. And armies cannot be maintained without recruits. Anatol Lieven labeled those that loudly advocate Russian dominance over the territories of the near abroad "cheap hawks" because of their unwillingness to back up their words with deeds. They want to see Russia as a great military power but they avoid military service (or help their sons to avoid military service). Moreover, the desire to see Russia strong again is influenced more by nostalgia for the Soviet Union, and the order and stability it represents, rather than by nationalist fervor.[84] Russians have repeatedly demonstrated that they are more concerned with crime and the non-payment of wages than they are with any nationalist/imperialist foreign policy agenda.

As for the rationale behind the renewal of hostilities, it is widely believed that Putin and/or his sponsors, that is, Boris Berezovsky, staged the raid into Dagestan and were responsible for the Moscow apartment bombings. According to *Novaya gazeta*, and reported by *The Exile*, an alternative newspaper for expatriates, and the *Moscow Times* among others, FSB (Federal Security Service) agents where caught planting hexagen bombs in the basement of an apartment building in Ryazan, a sizeable city located southwest of Moscow. Residents called local authorities who apprehended the suspects.[85] Hexagen bombs had been used in the previous bombings. After their identities became known, the FSB agents claimed to be conducting an exercise for preparedness and that the "explosive" substance planted was in fact sugar. Putin's party, Unity, voted in the Duma to kill the investigation into this incident which occurred September 16, 1999, just after the four apartment bombings.[86]

Novaya gazeta, which has aggressively investigated FSB claims of Chechen involvement, reported allegations that the government was responsible for the bombings. They have also become a part of the Moscow rumor mill. The veracity of these claims was strengthened after someone broke into *Novaya gazeta*'s computer system and deleted the issue that was dated March 20. The issue detailed the story of a soldier who discovered hexagen in sacks that were labeled "sugar." According to *Novaya gazeta*, he and another soldier were guarding a storehouse and opened one of the sacks with thoughts of sweetening their tea. The funny taste prompted their superiors to test the substance that was subsequently identified as hexagen. *Novaya gazeta* openly expressed the view that the government planted the Moscow bombs. They also reported that Ryazan residents and local authorities believed the bombs were real.[87]

The credibility of the allegation lies in the fact that only Putin and his sponsors benefited from the bombings and the Dagestan raids. They provided a rationale for retaking Chechnya which stands between Russia and the pipeline routes of the yet-to-be-exploited Caspian Sea oil. They also provided patriot appeal to voters on the eve of the 2000 presidential elections. They presented the Russian military an opportunity for vindication and revenge for their defeat/withdrawal in 1996, and gave Putin a justification for significantly increasing military spending (which in turn guarantees Putin's support among the military establishment). For the Chechen side, a renewal of hostilities was not in their interests.

CONCLUSION

The leverage that Russia has over the Successor States stems from the power that Russia wielded in the Soviet Union. The imperial structure of the Soviet Union has meant a vertical pattern of interaction whereby economic and political links were with Russia; at the same time links among the Republics themselves were largely absent. Following the dissolution of the Soviet Union and the failure of multilateral diplomacy in the form of the CIS, the prominence of bilateral relations with Russia was the result. Given that Russia is larger and more powerful than all of the other Successor States combined, the institution of the CIS was not likely to constrain Russia in the near abroad. However in bilateral diplomacy, Russia remains in an advantageous position vis-à-vis individual Successor States.

After neglecting the near abroad during Yeltsin's tenure, the Russian government is demonstrating a renewed activism in the near abroad. On numerous occasions and in many forums the Russian government, especially after the election of Putin, declared the territories of the former Soviet Union to be within its sphere of influence. Foreign policy strategies have differed according to region. In the Baltic States, Russia linked troop withdrawal with concessions on the issue of the local Russian minorities. The withholding of energy deliveries had periodically been used against the Baltic States as well as Ukraine, Belarus, and Moldova. Russia was able to call on the OSCE to condemn Estonian citizenship laws. In the Caucasus, the military option has been used in the Armenia/Azerbaijan conflict and in the Abkhazi separatist movement that eventually pressured Georgia to join the CIS. In Central Asia security agreements concluded between Moscow and the individual states have meant in effect that Moscow will continue to provide for the security of the southern border dividing the former Soviet Union from Iran, Afghanistan, and China. The specifics of these strategies are detailed in the following chapters.

NOTES

1. Vladimir Shlapentokh, *How Russians See Themselves Now: In the Aftermath of the Defeat in Chechnya*, Michigan State University, unpublished manuscript; available on "Johnson's Russia List, 11 January (1997), djohnson@cdi.org.

2. Vera Tolz, "Russia: Westernizers Continue to Challenge National Patriots," *RFE/RL Research Report*, vol. 1, no. 49, 11 December (1992) p. 3.

3. Vera Tolz and Elizabeth Teague, "Russian Intellectuals Adjust to Loss of Empire," *RFE/RL Research Report*, vol. 1, no. 8, 21 February (1992) pp. 4–5.

4. Ibid., p. 4.

5. Tolz, "Russia: Westernizers Continue to Challenge National Patriots," pp. 1–3.

6. Stephen D. Shenfield, "Post-Soviet Russia in Search of Identity," in *Russia's Future: Consolidation or Disintegration*, ed. Douglas W. Blum (Westview: Boulder, 1994) p. 10.

7. Alexander Rahr, " '*Atlanticists*' *versus* '*Eurasians*' *in Russian Foreign Policy*," *RFE/RL Research Report*, vol. 1, no. 22, 29 May (1992) p. 18.

8. Ibid., p. 19; *FBIS-SOV*, 4 March (1992), p. 31.

9. *FBIS-SOV*, 13 April (1995) p. 20.

10. Andrei Kozyrev, "Ne partiinye a natsionalnye interesy," *Rossiiskaya gazeta*, 2 February (1994) p. 1.

11. John Lough, "Defining Russia's Relations with Neighboring States," *RFE/RL Research Report*, vol. 2, no. 20, 14 May (1993), p. 54.

12. Suzanne Crow, "Russia Debates Its National Interests," *RFE/RL Research Report*, vol. 1, no. 28, 10 July (1992) p. 44.

13. Kozyrev, " Ne partiinye a natsionalnye interesy," p. 6.

14. Andranik Migranyan, "Rossiia i Blizhnee Zarubezhye," *Nezavisimaya gazeta*, 12 January (1994) p. 1.

15. Ibid., p. 4.

16. Yuri Kobishchanov, "Kto budet zhit' v Rossii XXI veka," *Nezavisimaya gazeta*, 10 February (1995) p. 2.

17. Crow, "Russia Debates National Interests," p. 44.

18. Elena Chinyaeva, "A Eurasianist Model of Interethnic Relations Could Help Russia Find Harmony," *Transition*, 1 November (1996) p. 34.

19. Crow, "Russia Debates Its National Interests," p. 46.

20. Lough, "Defining Russia's Relations with Neighboring States," pp. 56–57.

21. Igor Andreyev, "Mid Nameren Aktivnee Zashchishchat' prava Russkikh za Granitsei," *Izvestiia*, 30 April (1994), p. 4.

22. *FBIS-SOV*, 20 April (1995) p. 72.

23. *FBIS-SOV*, 21 April (1995) p. 8.

24. *FBIS-SOV*, 20 April (1995) p. 74.

25. *FBIS-SOV*, 20, April (1995) p. 62; *FBIS-SOV*, 20 April (1995) p. 14.

26. *FBIS-SOV*, 20 April (1995) p. 73.

27. *FBIS-SOV*, 21 April (1995) p. 59.

28. *FBIS-SOV*, 21 April (1995) pp. 45–46.

29. *FBIS-SOV*, 20 April (1995) p. 15.

30. *FBIS-SOV*, 31 May (1995) p. 12.

31. Dmitrii Gornostaev, "Andrei Kozyrev predpochel deputatshii mandat ministerskomy portfeliu," *Nezavisimaya gazeta*, 6 January (1996) p. 1.

32. *FBIS-SOV*, 20 November (1995) p. 4.

33. *FBIS-SOV*, 25 April (1995) p. 18.

34. Neil Melvin, *Forging the New Russian Nation* (London: The Royal Institute of International Affairs, 1994) p. 38; Suzanne Crow, "Russia Prepares to Take a Hard Line on 'Near Abroad,' " *RFE/RL Research Report*, vol. 1, no. 32, 14 August (1992) p. 22.

35. Tat'iana Malkina, Anton Trofimov, and Dmitrii Volkov, "Alexander Lebed' 'zapolniaet vakuum,' " *Segodnya*, 12 July (1996) p. 1.

36. Ibid.

37. *FBIS-SOV*, 6 September (1996) p. 5; *FBIS-SOV*, 9 September (1996) p. 11.

38. Elizabeth Teague, "Center-Periphery Relations in Russia," in *National Identity and Ethnicity in Russian and the New States of Eurasia* ed. by Roman Szporluk (London: M.E. Sharpe, 1994) p. 31.

39. Ibid., pp. 32, 34–35

40. Ibid.

41. Ibid., pp. 39–40.

42. Ibid., pp. 41–42.

43. Neil Melvin, *Regional Foreign Policies in the Russian Federation* (London: The Royal Institute of International Affairs, 1995) p. 11.

44. Radio Free Europe/Radio Liberty, "Duma Delivers Putin Another Victory," *RFE/RL Newsline*, Vol. 4, No. 127, Part I, June 30, 2000.

45. Lieven, Anatol, *Chechnya: Tombstone of Russian Power* (New Haven: Yale University Press, 1998) pp. 74–77.

46. Elena Chinyaeva, "A Eurasianist Model of Interethnic Relations Could Help Russia Find Harmony," *Transition*, 1 November (1996) p. 34.

47. Irina Zviagelskaia, *The Russian Policy Debate on Central Asia* (London: The Royal Institute of International Affairs, 1995) pp. 8, 10–12.

48. Radio Free Europe/Radio Liberty, "Moscow says signing of peace treaty with Japan this year Unlikely" *RFE/RL Newsline*, vol.4, no. 29, part I, February 10, 2000.

49. Stratfor Global Intelligence Update, "Moldova Calls the IMF's Bluff," *Stratfor. com*, November 10, 1999 [see http://www.stratfor.com/SERVICES/GIU/ 1110.99.ASP].

50. Stratfor Global Intelligence Update, "Lithuania Faces Political Split Over Oil Deal," *Stratfor.com*, October 22, 1999 [see http://www.stratfor.com/SERVICES/ GIU/102299.ASP].

51. *Nezavisimaya gazeta*, 12 January (1994) p. 6.

52. Radio Free Europe/Radio Liberty, "Russian teens like Empires, Dollars, Closed Borders," *RFE/RL Newsline*, Vol. 4, No. 72, Part I, April 11, 2000.

53. Chauncy D. Harris, "Ethnic Tensions in the Successor Republics in 1993 and Early 1994," *Post-Soviet Geography*, vol. XXXV, no. 4 (1994) p. 186.

54. Martha Brill Olcott, "Kazakhstan: Pushing for Eurasia," in *New States, New Politics: Building the Post-Soviet Nations*, ed. by Ian Bremmer and Ray Taras (Cambridge: Cambridge University Press, 1997) p. 559.

55. *The Economist Intelligence Unit Country Report: Estonia, Latvia, Lithuania, 1st quarter* (London: The Economist Intelligence Unit, 1998) pp. 6, 21, 34.

56. *The Economist Intelligence Unit Country Report: Kyrgyz Republic, Tajikistan, Turkmenistan, Uzbekistan, 4th quarter* (London: The Economist Intelligence Unit, 1996) pp. 6, 29.

57. Ibid., p. 19.

58. Ibid., p. 58.

59. *The Economist Intelligence Unit Country Report: Kazakhstan, Annual Report*, (London: The Economic Intelligence Unit, 1996) p. 46.

60. *The Economist Intelligence Unit Country Report: Kazakhstan, Country Report 1st quarter* (London: The Economic Intelligence Unit, 2000), pp. 44, 45.

61. Helen Boss and Peter Havlik, "Slavic (dis)union: Consequences for Russia, Belarus, and Ukraine," *Economics of Transition*, vol. 2, no. 2, June (1994) pp. 239–240.

62. *The Economist Intelligence Unit Country Report: Belarus, Moldova, 4th quarter* (London: The Economist Intelligence Unit, 1996) p. 6.

63. *The Economist Intelligence Unit Country Report: Belarus, Moldova, 1st quarter* (London: The Economist Intelligence Unit, 2000) p. 6.

64. *The Economist Intelligence Unit Country Report: Ukraine, 1st quarter* (London: The Economist Intelligence Unit, 2000) p. 38.

65. "News and Comments," *Central Asia Monitor*, no. 5 (1996), p. 1.

66. Lidiya Kosikova and Anna Mikhalskaya, "Problems of State Regulation of Trade Between Russia and the Near Abroad Countries," *Foreign Trade*, 11–12 (1992) p. 40.

67. Ibid., p. 41.

68. *The Economist Intelligence Unit Country Report: Russia, 4th quarter* (London: The Economist Intelligence Unit, 1996) p. 36.

69. *The Economist Intelligence Unit Country Report: Kyrgyz Republic, Tajikistan, Turkmenistan, Uzbekistan, 4th quarter 1996* (London: The Economic Intelligence Unit, 1996) pp. 66–67.

70. *The Economist Intelligence Unit Country Report: Ukraine, 1996–97 Annual Report* (London: The Economic Intelligence Unit, 1996) p. 20.

71. Ibid.

72. Radoslav K. Petkov, "Farewell to the Orthodox Market Transition," *Transitions Country Files: Russia, Annual Report 1998*, http://www.tol.cz/countries/rusar983.html.

73. Peter Westin, "The Domino Effect of the Russian Crisis," *Russian Economic Trends*, vol. 4, no. 8 (1999) pp. 46–47.

74. Georgie Ann Geyer, *Waiting For Winter to End: An Extraordinary Journey Through Central Asia* (Washington-London: Brassey's, 1994) pp. 59–60, 65–72.

75. *FBIS-SOV*, 12 September (1996), pp. 3–4.

76. Susanne M. Birgerson and Roger E. Kanet, "East-Central Europe and the Russian Federation," *Problems of Post-Communism*, vol. 42, no. 4, July–August (1995) p. 34.

77. Kosikova and Mikhalskaya, p. 40.

78. *FBIS-SOV*, 30 March (1994) p. 10.

79. Boss and Havlik, p. 243.

80. See Thomas Goltz, "Letter From Eurasia: The Hidden Russian Hand," *Foreign Policy*, no. 92, Fall (1993).

81. *The Current Digest of the Post-Soviet Press*, vol. XLVI, no. 30 (1994) p. 13.

82. Emil Payin, "konsolidatsiia Rossii ili vosstanovlenie soiuza," *Segodnya*, 22 July (1994) p. 9.

83. Oleg Savelyev, "Rossiian kusaiut tseny Moskvichei dostali vgolovniki," *Segodnya*, 23 February (1996) p. 12.

84. Lieven, Anatol, *Chechnya: Tombstone of Russian Power* (New Haven: Yale University Press, 1998) pp. 200–206.

85. Borisova, Yevgenia, "No Proof Chechens Blew Up Buildings," *Moscow Times*, 17 March (2000); Borisova, Yevgenia, "Duma Rejects Move to Probe Ryazan Apartment Bomb," *Moscow Times*, 21 March (2000).

86. Afanas'eva, Elena, "Obstoiatel'stva i FSB im istiny dorozhe . . . " *Novaya gazeta*, 20 March (2000).

87. Karush, Sarah, "Hackers Attack Novaya Gazeta," *Moscow Times*, 16 March (2000).

Chapter 5

The Slavic Successor States: Belarus and Ukraine

INTRODUCTION: CENTER AND PERIPHERY, PAST AND PRESENT

Before considering the specifics of the regions under study, some general comments about Russian relations with the former Republics are in order. Comments about generalities common to all the former Republics would eliminate the need to reiterate the same facts for subsequent chapters. Likewise the former Republics have in common shared Soviet experiences. All have undergone the following processes: russification, sovietization, and modernization.

In spite of the changing-of-the-guard from Yeltsin to Putin, the climate in Russia is not conducive to empire restoration. Russian nationalism as an idea has not been a unifying force among the Russian political elite nor among ordinary Russians. To the contrary, the issue has ideologically divided Russians. Under Yeltsin, Russia lacked a unified national policy. The Yeltsin leadership lacked the willingness to retake its former periphery and a general malaise among the population at large matched their indifference. The revival of the Chechen conflict under Putin has changed the public's apathy toward the near abroad.

This lack of a unified sense of national identity is reflected in the ideological fragmentation of the Russian government. As a result of political infighting, Russia's foreign policy became disjointed and confused in such a way as to work against continued Russian hegemony. The Russian daily *Nezavisimaya gazeta* published a report from the Institute of CIS countries that objected to Zbigniew Brzezinski's concept of geopolitical pluralism and multiculturalism in the post-Soviet space. The report objected to alternative groupings within the CIS that did not include Russia as the central actor. The report alleged that with the aid of Western countries, the CIS was being undermined by those who wish to see the post-Soviet space fractured into competing geographical and cultural regions.[1] Not only did this report provoke outrage among CIS leaders, but surprisingly it also irked the Russian Ministry of Foreign Affairs that was quick to issue a public condemnation of the report. The Union of Russia and Belarus was another issue that was effectively sabotaged due to political infighting among Russian politicians.

Even if the Russian government had the will to restore the empire along with popular support (or at least in the absence of popular opposition) for a serious military undertaking, it is doubtful that the Russian military would be prepared to carry out military operations necessary for the restoration of the empire. The state of the Russian military is in shambles. Salaries to officers are not being paid, promised housing is not being provided, and a new provision to the law that allows officers to resign if the state violates its contract will make it easier and lawful for officers to leave the army.[2] Russia has proved with the disaster in Chechnya that its military is in an advance state of decline, particularly in the conventional field. For one thing a career in the military is not an attractive option for Russians due to low pay, poor conditions and low morale. A reduced military budget has meant deep cuts in equipment procurement and maintenance and inadequate training for infantry, artillery and pilots.[3] Putin's attempts to reinvigorate the military through mandated increases in military spending have not reversed this trend. Also, it is unclear as to whether actual increases will be realized due to uncertain budget revenues. Actual revenues may not support increases in military spending.

Though prospects for the restoration of the former empire are remote, this does not mean that the center has relinquished its interests in the former Republics. Russia regards them as comprising its sphere of influence. In fact Russia has used its advantage in various ways to influence political outcomes in the near abroad. This holds true for all three regions discussed in subsequent chapters.

And what of the former Republics? Their historic conquest and inclusion into the Russian and later Soviet empires suggest that past conditions on balance still do not favor independence from Russian domination. The ability to withstand pressures from Russia depends in large part on the unifying force of nationalism. In the past, nationalism among the masses simply did not exist because people identified themselves in terms of family ties, religion and perhaps by village or town.

Nationalism really became a force in the Republics only during the Soviet era. Soviet nationality policies served to reinforce rather than eradicate national differences. As discussed in some detail in chapter 3, the idea of nationalism among the masses cannot really be said to exist before ideas of mass participation in politics. According to Hans Kohn, the idea that political systems exist because of the people and that people have a stake in their (the political system's) future generates the feeling of belonging to something greater than themselves.

Ideas of mass political participation were a part of the greater process of modernization. Modernization in the Soviet context includes the twin processes of russification and sovietization. Russification generally refers to the imposition of the Russian language as the main language of education, publication, and political administration. In the case of Ukraine and Belarus, russification culminated in the banning of the use of Ukrainian and Belarusian at the height of Stalin's reign.[4] The process of sovietization can be said to include the political, economic and social subordination of the non-Russian periphery to Russia. It represents the consolidation of the new Soviet regime. This process included the collectivization of agriculture; rapid industrialization and proletarianization of labor; and the use of purges in the Communist Party and the population at large to rid the Soviet leadership of any potential opposition. Politically, it meant the introduction of the party apparatus into the country and cities of these areas. Political control was established through Communist administrators who were directly accountable to Moscow. These administrators include party members who served in a variety of offices, from factory managers to committee chairs on collective farms. For the implementation of some of the more brutal Soviet policies under Stalin, these administrators were deliberately brought in from outside of whatever region to which they were assigned so as to ensure their exclusive loyalty to Moscow. Those who had any local ties were either purged or avoided.[5]

The political and the economic were fused in the Soviet system, and it is impossible to discuss one without reference to the other. Economically the Republics were purged of capitalist elements including business owners and managers as well as any individuals who were even modestly prosperous. Agriculture was collectivized, that is small farms were confiscated from peasants and consolidated to form large farms belonging to the state. Collectivization induced peasants to either join the collective farms or move to the cities where labor was in short supply. The latter contributed to rapid urbanization and provided much needed labor to nascent industries. Mass movements of people were the result of warfare, rapid urbanization, political purges and the migration of Russian settlers into Belarus, Ukraine, Baltic, and Central Asian Republics.

In the Soviet Union the process of modernization was imposed from above. Modernization typically began with economic development such as industrialization. During the 1920s, Lenin's New Economic Policy (NEP) facilitated industrial development. After NEP was scrapped by Stalin, the industrialization drive continued under the direction of the central government.

With economic development came social and political development. As is well known, the Soviets made mass education a priority. Russian and minority languages were standardized and written down. Many minority languages had not been written languages before the Soviet period. Mass education favored the widespread use of Russian. Political development in the Soviet Union consisted of the forced participation of the people in political activities such as voting and attending political meetings. Giving political speeches and doing political work similar to that of a civil servant working for a U.S. city political machine was a prerequisite for career advancement. Mass political participation became compulsory and ritualistic.

Though this political activity was symbolic (some would say meaningless), it did introduce the *idea* of government accountability to the people while at the same time *made people aware of their own powerlessness.* People who might otherwise remain apathetic became openly cynical of the system. This cynicism eventually undermined the Soviet system and contributes to the current apathy of the former Soviet peoples.

Russia and the Slavic Periphery

Conditions in the Slavic periphery are not on balance conducive to independence from the former center, due mainly to the ambivalence among the populations in Ukraine and Belarus regarding national identity. This ambivalence is indicative of the close historical and cultural links among the peoples of Russia, Ukraine, and Belarus. Besides a shared history with common national origins, the three Slavic languages are mutually intelligible. The Russian Revolution that ushered in the Soviet period involved the active participation of Ukrainians and Belarusians. During the Soviet period, this common Slavic identity frequently blurred the lines between Russians and other Slavs. Nonetheless, "Slavic culture" became synonymous with Russian culture. This cultural hegemony distinguished Russians from other Slavs.

Out of all the Successor States it is the loss of the Slavic states of Ukraine and Belarus that has proved most problematic to Russia. Because Ukraine and Belarus were economically and politically central to the Russian empire and the Soviet Union, their independence is difficult for most Russians to accept. Polling and anecdotal evidence indicate that the concept of an independent Belarus and Ukraine is not taken too seriously. In this author's experience, ordinary Russians greeted Ukrainian independence with skepticism and derision. Russians are quick to point out Ukrainian dependence on Russia and the lack of any real border between the two "countries." A Russian friend of mine held up a batch of Ukrainian [Karbovanets] coupons and declared them worthless enough to use as wallpaper; he added that though he was a "poor" Russian, in Ukraine he is practically rich by Ukrainian standards. People and goods move freely over the border. But this derision of an independent Ukraine is not indicative of any *ethnic* hostility to Ukrainians themselves. In fact the attitude toward the independent *state* of Ukraine stems precisely from the *lack* of any meaningful national distinction made by Russians between themselves and Ukrainians. One Muscovite woman I spoke with pointed out that the word "Ukraine" simply means "border," and that Ukrainians are "people who live on the border" (na ykraine). As for the question of a Belarusian State, this same woman responded "what is a Belarusian?" Belarus,

I was informed, is a region named for a particular type of Birch tree for which it is distinguished ("belo" means "white" in Russian).

Unlike the Successor States of the Baltic and Central Asia, Belarus and Ukraine (with the exception of the far western part of Ukraine) have demonstrated ambivalence about the desirability of independence and have been slow to liberalize their economies. The impetus for independence came from the Ukrainian nationalists who come primarily from Galicia, the far western portion of Ukraine which had no historic relationship to the Russian empire but had been in the past annexed to Poland and later became part of the Austro-Hungarian empire. As a result, the population is divided between staunch Ukrainian nationalists who favor independence from Russia and Ukrainians and Russians who are in favor of closer ties to Russia.

In Belarus, the population is even less differentiated from Russia. Belarusian national identity is tenuous and, though a national myth existed among many expatriate Belarusians who emigrated after WWI, it made its appearance in Belarus primarily in the nationalist movement that emerged in the late 1980s.[6] This movement lacked a clear idea of a distinct Belarusian national identity.[7] It received impetus from the discovery of mass graves in Kurapaty Wood outside Minsk. They were victims of Stalin's purges and the incident was later covered up by Soviet authorities and was revealed only through Gorbachev's policy of Glasnost in the latter half of the 1980s. This resurrected memory was a trigger for the Belarusian nationalist awakening and led to the establishment of the Martyrology of Belarus, out of which the Belarusian Popular Front (BPF) was formed. And despite the existence of a distinct Belarusian folk culture and language, the level of national consciousness among ordinary Belarusians has been low. And the nationalism exhibited by members of the BPF movement had its origins in the Soviet era.[8] Belarusian independence was the result of elite machinations, not popular sentiment nor a spontaneous national movement from below. It was the intelligentsia that brought to public awareness the mass graves; similarly it was the intelligentsia that articulated the significance of the incident to the Belarusian masses. However while the masses were outraged by the graves, this outrage did not necessarily translate into feelings of nationalism among ordinary Belarusians. The first post-Soviet Belarusian government, dominated by the BPF, recognized the low level of national consciousness among the population and acknowledged the amount of work needed to bring about a national revival among the people.[9] Likewise the subsequent defeat of the Front and the election of President Alyaksandr Lukashenka reflected public apathy toward nationalist designs. After Lukashenka extended his tenure in office in a 1996 referendum of dubious constitutional legality, the Public Association (BNF), formerly the BPF, became a part of the political opposition.

Both Belarus and Ukraine have encountered severe economic difficulties and have moved toward greater cooperation with Russia. Such developments pit two competing trends against one another: the "ideal," or the realization of a state based on the nation, and the "real," or limits on the costs people are willing to bear for independent statehood. They bring into question two assumptions: First that nationalism alone is enough to convince citizens that sovereignty and independence are worth any price, particularly if there is no shared notion of national identity, and second, the companion supposition that independent statehood is the logical, political goal of national mobilization.

In the case of Belarus, closer relations with Russia culminated in the conclusion of the Russian-Belarusian Monetary Union April 12, 1994. The treaty abolished trade barriers, established the Russian ruble as the Belarusian currency, and established a common military defense provided by Russia. This course of action is supported not only by Belarusian President Alyaksandr Lukashenka but also by the Belarusian parliament; it is one of the few things on which the two parties agreed. In fact Lukashenka has sought to dissolve parliament while parliament has attempted to have the president removed in constitutional struggle.[10] In Ukraine, the election of Leonid Kuchma, a Eurasianist (i.e., pro-Russian) who defeated nationalist Leonid Kravchuk, reflected the ambivalence of Ukrainians toward Russia. The economic catastrophe following Ukraine's attempt to dissolve economic ties to Russia upon independence apparently convinced many voters that Kravchuk's policy of independence from Russia at any cost was not a feasible or desirable option.

The organization of the chapter is as follows. First the unique aspects of the Slavic states of Belarus and Ukraine will be outlined. These aspects include their close historic relationship to Russia; common Slavic characteristics which account for the ambivalent attitude toward the Russian Federation and to Russians in general; and the particular manifestations of nationalism in Belarus and Ukraine before and after the dissolution of the Soviet Union. Second, events in the post-Soviet period will be highlighted in respect to the difficulties faced by Ukraine and Belarus and their respective relationships with Russia. These difficulties are found among all the Successor States and are complicated by the enduring influence of Russia. Third, the chapter will explore requirements needed for decreasing their dependence on Russia and the likelihood that these requirements will be met.

HISTORICAL BACKGROUND

Ukraine, Belarus and Russia: Common Slavic Origins

As is often the case among nations with close cultural, historical, and linguistic ties, the nationalists among their members (be they representatives of the government or intelligentsia) go to great lengths to emphasize their differences and de-emphasize their similarities, even when it can be argued that the latter outweigh the former. The efforts of Ukrainian and Belarusian nationalists to distance their respective histories from that of Russia are cases in point. Broadly speaking, the political cultures of the peoples of Belarus, Ukraine, and Russia have been shaped by similar forces: foreign invasion, long periods of subservience to foreign powers, warfare, serfdom, and political repression. Ukraine, Belarus, and Russia share a common history, common linguistic origins (all being part of the "East-Slavic" branch of Slavic languages), and in some instances, a common religious heritage (the Orthodox religion of Kievan Rus', from which Ukraine, Russia, and portions of Belarus emerged).[11]

Political History

The historic polity of Kievan Rus' adopted Christianity in 988; this political entity is the source of the common origins for the Belarusian, Ukrainian and Russian nations. The Mongol invasion, 1237–1240, established Mongol rule over Kievan Rus', but Lithuania, aligned with Poland, took back the territories of what is today Belarus and Ukraine; Russia remained under Mongol domination.[12] The state of Muscovy emerged and eventually successfully challenged Mongol rule in 1480.

The Mongol Horde ushered in several centuries of separation among Belarus and Ukraine, and Russia. Belarus and Ukraine, under Polish domination, developed along a path different from that of Russia under Mongol domination. The common East Slavic language and culture began to break up roughly into three spheres.

Belarus, untouched by the Mongol invasions, was a part of Poland and was not incorporated into the Russian empire until the reign of Catherine II (the Great). In fact Belarus suffered partition along with Poland and Lithuania between the Russian Empire and Prussia from 1772–1795. The Belarusian gentry was thoroughly Polandized during this time while ordinary "Belarusians" identified, or were identified, more with their religion than any sense of ethnicity.[13] The partition created no significant changes in the administration of Belarus; the Polish gentry remained in place but answered to St. Petersburg rather than Warsaw. The "Belarusian Government General" Count Zachar Cernysev, a Polish nobleman, was responsible for administering the territory now under Russian rule. Religion, not ethnicity or even language served to distinguish people. Hence in various censuses that were taken when Belarus was under Polish and later Russian rule, those who were Catholic or Uniate were counted as Polish; Orthodox believers were counted as Russian. The term "Belarusian" was used only to designate a specific territory in historical records and was not used to designate ethnicity. In 1840 the terms "Belaia Rus" and "Lietuva" were officially banned and instead the territory of Belarus was renamed the "Northwest province."[14]

Under Polish domination Ukraine retained its distinctness regarding the Ukrainian language and the Orthodox faith. The historical legacy of Ukraine differs according to region. Present-day Ukraine was historically divided into West and East Ukraine following the decline of Kievan Rus'; the histories of each are vastly different, with clear implications for the subsequent development of Ukrainian nationalism. In Western Ukraine, Galicia, which includes

Lviv and Volhynaia Oblasts, and Bukovina, fell under Polish then later Hapsburg rule. Ukrainian nationalism has its origins in Lviv and Volhynaia as a result of its contact with Austria-Hungary.[15] Transcarpathia, or Transcarpathian Oblast, was likewise a part of the Austro-Hungarian empire and the people developed a proto-national identity as Ruthenes. Transcarpathia or "Ruthenia," was a part of the new Czechoslovakian state that briefly emerged in the inter-war period. Both Galicia and Transcarpathia were not incorporated into the Soviet Union, and hence a union with Russia, until after 1940.

The central and eastern regions of Ukraine, incorporated into the Russian empire much earlier, were home to large numbers of Russians as well as Ukrainians. These areas were subjected to heavy Russian influences in language and culture. Ukrainians living in these areas do not feel themselves to be substantially different from their Russian conationals. With regards to the issue of language, a rural/urban divide could be said to be at work. Ukrainian is spoken primarily in the countryside while Russian predominates in the cities.[16] In Kyiv and Kharkiv (Kharkov) as well as the eastern industrial cities of Donetsk, Dnipropetrovsk (Dnepropetrovsk), Zaporizhzhya (Zaporozhe), and Luhansk (Lugansk), Russians comprise over one-third of the population.[17]

Portions of Ukraine and Belarus were periodically detached from Russia and absorbed by other powers. However the impact of these partitions probably had little impact on the everyday lives of the inhabitants. The masses, predominantly peasant and illiterate, were always subservient to some power, and that their awareness of the national origins of the elites governing them was low to nonexistent.

What remains to be argued then is not that the national distinctness of these three nations was significant in the historical periods before the establishment of the Soviet Union, or even the Russian Empire, but what *effects* these differences might have had on the subsequent development of national self-awareness during the waning years of the Soviet Union. National consciousness begins with elite figures such as leaders, clergy, poets and writers, historians, and others who have recorded events and were instrumental in shaping the development of written languages and otherwise keeping alive the memories of cultural practices, music, and even native custom. "Folk" culture, though practiced by the masses, is significantly reinforced by the written word. What historical writings preserved those distinct attributes? How might they later be resurrected by those who wished to develop a coherent sense of their own cultural distinctiveness?

Language: Common Origins, Different Paths of Development

How are Russian, Ukrainian, and Belarusian related languages? The Belarusian, Ukrainian, and Russian languages are descendants from Proto-Slavic as are all Slavic languages.[18] Written documents from the period

of Kievan Rus', a confederation of various provinces that include present day
Belarus, Ukraine, and European Russia, were written in Old Church Slavonic,
the chancery or high language for the East Slavic branch of Slavonic languages.[19] The dissolution of Kievan Rus' with the Mongol invasions beginning in 1240 marked the separation of Old Russian into three distinct East Slavonic languages: Belarusian, Ukrainian, and Russian.[20] The first written "East
Slavic" or Old Church Slavonic documents are not dated before the eleventh
century A.D.[21] And as is frequently the case, the chancery or elite language used
in documents was very different from what the masses spoke.

Various linguistic theories date the origins of Belarusian from the fourth
and fifth century A.D. to as late as the fifteenth and sixteenth centuries. Elements of the Belarusian vernacular began to appear in the texts of the
Belarusian provenance during the fourteenth century; as a literary language,
Belarusian appeared during the fifteenth and sixteenth centuries after it was
the official language of the Belarusian region within the Grand Duchy of Lithuania. Though close to Russian, Belarusian incorporated many words either
from Polish or from other western European languages introduced to
Belarusian through the medium of Polish.[22]

Early documents appearing in the Belarusian vernacular include statutes in
legal documents when Belarus was a part of the Grand Duchy of Lithuania,
Rus. Since Lithuanian did not become a written language until its conversion
to Christianity in the late fourteenth century, old Belarusian became the official language of the Duchy. The Litouskaia Metryka, which comprised over
600 volumes of legal documents, was written in Belarusian.[23] Other
Belarusian documents include the constitutional charters of the "Belarusian
Democratic Republic" and the Belarusian Soviet Socialist Republic.[24] Reference to the "Belarusian Democratic Republic" appeared in *Zviazda,* and referred most likely to the Belarusian National Republic (BNR) or *Belaruskaja
Narodnaja Respublika*, that was founded in March of 1918 under the authority of the Austro-German Occupation Army. Though this government lasted
only ten months, under Berlin's direction its administration managed to install
many institutions of independent statehood: consulates in Moscow, Kiev,
Odessa, Rostov, Stavropol, and Vilna; diplomatic missions to Warsaw, Berlin,
Copenhagen, Bern, and Paris; and grammar books, newspapers, and periodi-
cals in the Belarusian vernacular.[25] Most importantly Belarusian nationalists
found a precedent for an independent Belarus state in the BNR.

The literary development of Belarusian followed a long period where the
language of education and publication was either Polish or Russian. Educated
Belarusians did not have trouble reading in these languages and works translated from Latin were written with a combination of Latin and Cyrillic alpha-
bets. At times influences of Lithuanian and Ukrainian are evident.[26] When
Belarus was annexed to the Russian Empire in 1795 as a result of the partition
of the Polish-Lithuanian Commonwealth (1772–1795), tsarist authorities officially designated Belarusian as a dialect of Great Russian. They banned

Belarusian as a language of instruction in schools and prohibited the publication of works in Belarusian.[27] The first written poems exclusively in the Belarusian vernacular were an imitation of a Ukrainian parody of *Aeneid* that was followed by a poem called *Taras na Parnase*; both were anonymous and appeared during the 1800s. Other writings were unpublished poems by a Belarusian peasant named Pauliuk Bachrym whose poems were passed down then eventually written down through the efforts of scholars interested in recording and preserving the folklore of the area.[28] However there was no standard grammar text of Belarusian before 1904 when Branislau Taraskevic published his *Belarusian Grammar for Schools* that became the standard for subsequent orthographic and grammatical developments.[29]

Written evidence of a distinctive Ukrainian vernacular dates back to the twelfth century. With the fall of Kievan Rus', what is today Ukraine and Russia proper were divided and consequently a distinction between the Ukrainian and Russian vernaculars developed.[30] Ukraine came under Polish domination while the Mongol Khans ruled Russia.

The Ukrainian vernacular has a much more extensive written history that stems not only from political history, but from a literary history as well. Ukrainian place names are first documented in 1415 when Lithuania took over the Rus' principalities, which covered the territories of Belarus and Ukraine.[31] Though the dominant literary language in Ukraine was Russian (Nikolai Gogol wrote in Russian though he was a Ukrainian), Ukrainian works have been published since 1789. The year 1789 marks the publication of Kotljarevs'kyj's *Enejida* (*The Iliad*), the first time the Ukrainian spoken language was used as a literary language.[32] From that time onward, Ukrainian literary tradition expanded, especially in Western Ukraine, despite the widespread bias in Central and East Ukraine against the use of Ukrainian in literary works in favor of Russian.

Nationalism, Political Turmoil, and Two World Wars

Nationalist movements and national consciousness have their origins in the years after the Russian revolution and civil war until the conclusion of WWII. Both Belarus and Ukraine were divided between Poland and the Soviet Union. In the case of Belarus, harsh treatment by Polish authorities resulted in a more favorable view of the new Soviet State. In Ukraine, forced collectivization, famine and political repression shaped nationalist consciousness. Nevertheless Bolshevism and Communist ideology had its adherents among Ukrainian intellectuals. Though some in Ukraine attributed sovietization to the Russians, it has also been argued that Russians and Russian national identity suffered equally from sovietization. Fortunately for the Soviets, the brutalities of the German occupation eclipsed the worst of Soviet excesses. Only since the dissolution of the Soviet Union has the issue of Stalin's crimes against Ukrainians been revisited.

In Belarus, the incipient national consciousness among educated Belarusians began during the years of WWI. It later came under the influence of Russian revolutionaries following the fall of Belarusian National Republic after the conclusion of the Treaty of Brest-Litovsk in 1918 and the withdrawal of defeated German forces on whose support the newly formed BNR had been dependent. National groups of intellectuals and other politically active citizens formed a national group called the Belarusian War Relief that later became the Belarusian national committee. This group's initial aim was to present its interests to the occupying German forces. These interests included relief aid to war victims and the maintenance of Belarusian territorial integrity, which was interpreted as the continued unity of Belarus along the borders of the former Grand Duchy of Lithuania. The Germans rejoined with an offer of independent statehood, which was accepted. The Belarusian Nationalists organized themselves into the Belarusian Popular Hramada.

What followed however was a disillusionment with the German occupying authorities who preferred a Baltic state that included portions of Lithuania, Latvia, and Belarus. Under such a union, Belarusians would have become a minority. Instead the nationalists turned their attention eastward and appealed to the Petrograd Provisional Government who did not give them much support. After the Bolsheviks took power, they promised the "oppressed peoples" the status of sovereign republics in the new Soviet Union but also agreed in principle to the option of self-determination on the part of these nations. The Soviets signed the Treaty of Brest-Livtosk in February and retreated from Minsk. The Belarusian National Republic was proclaimed in March of 1918 and lasted only 10 months.

Factional infighting left the Belarusian nationalist movement ineffectual. It also suffered from a lack of popular support. The various nationalist groups as well as the newly organized Bolshevik party of Belarus of Minsk had little contact with ordinary people and did not appeal to them for support. When the first free elections to rural local governments were held, no representatives from the nationalist groups won any support from the people. In countrywide elections, only one member of the Belarusian Socialist Hramada was elected and that victory was attributed to the member's affiliation to the *Russian* Socialist Party. [33] Ultimately it was the Russians who were to appeal to the masses of Belarusians and it was the Russians who formed the Belarusian Soviet Socialist Republic in January of 1919. The new Republic was based in Minsk.

When the Germans left, Poland and Russia fought over Belarusian territory. Poland endeavored to reestablish the old Polish-Lithuanian Commonwealth along its pre-partition borders. They faced resistance from Ukrainian nationalists and later, Lithuanian and Belarusian national movements.[34] The Soviets controlled the eastern portion including the city of Minsk. Meanwhile another Belarusian National Republic in the west was formed with its capital in Vilna under the authority of General Pilsudski. For the nationalists, the union with

Poland brought some positive gains in the way of cultural autonomy, yet the heavy-handed treatment Belarus received from both the military and civilian governments would sour relations between Belarusian nationalists and Poland. The Polish-Soviet War came to an end with the signing of the Treaty of Riga. Signed in March of 1921, the treaty recognized the division of Belarusian territory between Poland and the Soviet Union. Roughly one-third of Eastern Belarus, including Minsk, went to the Soviet Union while the remaining two-thirds were ceded to Poland. The division was a reflection of the gains each was able to achieve and maintain.[35] Belarus was thus dismembered.

The same treaty was also responsible for the dismemberment of Ukraine. Ukraine had become a sovereign republic from 1917–1920 during the Civil War. Ukrainian nationalists fought both Poles and Russian Communists for independence. The fighting occurred almost exclusively in Western Ukraine. After the conclusion of the Polish-Soviet War, Western Ukraine including Lviv and Ruthenia went to Poland while the rest went to the Soviet Union.

For the remaining years before the German invasion of Poland in 1939, Belarus remained divided between West and East. West Belarus with its center in Vilna (Vilna did not became a part of Lithuania until after the conclusion of WWII), was subject to Polish cultural and linguistic influences while in East Belarus with its center in Minsk, Russian influences predominated. The two developed differently during those years. Those living in West Belarus can be said to have had more political and personal freedoms yet the economic situation was perilous. To many, the Soviet alternative held some attraction. Meanwhile, following the NEP period in Soviet history that ended in 1929, East Belarus was transformed by the Soviet process of collectivization, state-planning of the economy, and the arrest and deportation of undesirable elements including "kulaks," those engaged in trade, nationalists, and other politically active people.[36] Hence while more restrictive politically and socially, East Belarusians at least had economic security of sorts because universal employment was central to aims of the Communists. The standard of living was adequate as compared to the poor conditions typical of Belarus in the past. Belarus did not lose out economically with its merger with the USSR.

Hence from a nationalist point-of-view, Belarus was caught in a tug-of-war between two hostile powers, both of which had been ruthless in their respective policies. If Belarus cannot be said to have preferred the domination of one to the other, it was true that by the time of the German invasion of Poland, many Belarusians believed the Soviet alternative to be the lesser of two evils. When Hitler invaded in 1941, one-quarter of the population lost their lives as a result. In addition Belarus suffered inordinately from Hitler's implementation of the final solution as Belarus had been home to a large Jewish population.[37] When German tanks rolled into Poland, the Soviets quickly retook West Belarus and thus the two sides were reunited. The native Belarusian vernacular was restored and encouraged in schools but the fact remains that Russian became the language of government, higher education, and political advancement.[38] Sovietization in Western Belarus followed the same pattern that it had everywhere else, but the process did not get underway in earnest until the conclusion of WWII. The reasons for the delay are obvious; Belarus on the Western flank was hostile toward Poland and Germany, and any heavy-handed Soviet policies might have changed that balance of power in favor of the Germans. It was therefore in the interest of the Soviets to not alienate the population of Belarus.

Western Ukraine's hostility toward both Poland and the Soviet Union is not in dispute. But what of the rest of Ukraine? During the revolutionary years, Ukrainian intellectuals in Kyiv and Kharkiv were divided between those favoring Ukrainian statehood and those who supported the Bolshevik movement.[39] An independent Ukraine was established in 1917 but became a victim of the Polish-Soviet War and was dismembered. The Treaty of Riga that ended the war gave the Soviets east and central Ukraine while west Ukraine went to Poland.

The Soviets also retook West Ukraine including Lviv and Brest. In these areas, Ukrainian nationalists continued armed resistance against Polish authorities while Central and East Ukraine underwent rapid industrialization, forced collectivization, deportation, and for millions of rural inhabitants who remained, starvation. After the civil war, all of Ukraine minus Lviv and Bukovina were under Soviet rule. Following the German invasion and occupation of Ukraine, both East and West, Ukrainian nationalists and even ordinary Ukrainians collaborated with the Germans in the hope that life under German occupation would be an improvement to Soviet rule. It was not, and after the Soviets took back Ukraine, collaborationists, especially members of nationalist groups, were arrested and either deported or executed.[40]

There were several Ukrainian nationalist groups fighting against first the Poles and the Germans, and later, the Soviets. Guerrilla fighting continued in Western Ukraine and was not completely quelled until the 1950s. Nationalist groups, referred to as partisans, were distinguished by their leaders such as Bandera, Kovpak, Borovets, or Mel'nyk. Attempts were made by Soviet authorities to co-opt or control Ukrainian nationalist groups fighting against the Germans though there is little evidence to support the success of these efforts. Instead propaganda was employed for this purpose.[41] Nationalist groups such as the one led by Stepan Bandera were condemned and censured by Soviet authorities. Predictably Ukrainian nationalists currently reevaluating their history consider the activities of the partisan groups as heroic.

The history of Belarus, Ukraine, and Russia bequeathed a legacy of troubled relations. The history of the region is one of almost continual warfare, which disrupted and divided Slavic territories. The net result of this has been the denationalization of these regions and the lingering bitterness among the population.

Sovietization and Russification in Belarus and Ukraine

Belarus and Ukraine did not become wholly and fully integrated into the Soviet system until after WWII. With the incorporation of all Ukraine and Belarus into the Soviet political system as National Republics came mass education and language policies including the institution of Russian as the primary language of government, media and education.[42] Linguistic russification accompanied the opening of schools and was aided by the low esteem of the titular languages held by the rural population who flooded into the cities. Hence Russian became the language of preference by Belarusians and a significant number of Ukrainians.[43] Both were transformed politically and economically into the Soviet mold. Socially the masses were introduced into Moscow-directed Communist propaganda as the newspapers and other forms of media were placed under control of the central government.

And while all the Soviet Republics went through this process, Ukraine and Belarus became more successfully integrated into the Soviet system for a variety of reasons. The first concerns the presence of national cadres both before and after the revolution. Many Belarusian and Ukrainian nationals actively participated in the Russian Revolution and were members of the Communist Party. Second, Russians themselves did not, and still do not, consider Ukrainians and Belarusians to be ethnically and culturally, significantly different from themselves.[44] Third, the experiences of WWII destroyed much of Belarus and Ukraine, and post-war rebuilding coincided with modernization. In Belarus, resistance fighters and Red Army liberators became national heroes and this process facilitated a strong mass Soviet identity.[45]

Collectivization was implemented with particularly brutal effects in Belarus and Ukraine. Many in the Ukraine (as well as other areas of the periphery such as Kazakhstan) chose a third option to collectivization: resistance. The result was a struggle between the Communist Party and its functionaries, and the peasants. Forced requisitions of grain and the wholesale slaughter of livestock created famine in Ukraine, as well as in parts of Kazakhstan and the northern Caucasus. Belarus (East and West) lost an estimated 2 million people as a result of purges, forced collectivization, famine and deportation. The mass graves of Kurapaty forest outside Minsk were used as such from 1937–1941. Industry had to be built from scratch, as Russia had almost no industrial base. Gosplan, the Party organ in charge of setting production goals and quotas, controlled five-year plans.

Socially people faced the intrusion of the state into their personal lives. Informants were employed to spy on their neighbors and even their families. Freedom of movement was restricted with the introduction of the internal passport system (propiska). Through the introduction of personal documents the authorities were able to keep track of people. Permission by authorities to establish residence in a town or city became a requirement. The media were brought under the control of the Communist Party. Social, ethnic, and even religious organizations and traditions were co-opted and used for propaganda purposes. For instance Belarusian and Ukrainian folk traditions in music, dress, and national celebrations were promoted in order to convey the successful resolution of the age-old national question through the Soviet system where many different nationalities live together voluntarily and peacefully.

Unlike other non-Russian republics, the Soviet leadership regarded Belarus and Ukraine as an indispensable part of the Soviet Union in much the same way they were regarded as intrinsic to the Russian Empire. While the two Republics were subjected to sovietization and russification, their common cultural heritage meant that these two nationalities were not regarded as "foreign" by the Russian dominated Communist leadership. In a Russian dominated Union, this has meant that the upward mobility of Ukrainians and Belarusians was not hindered in the way that it was for other nationalities such as those from the Caucasus and Central Asia.

In contrast to the political situation in the Baltic and Central Asian regions during the revolution, communist revolutionary movements including the Bolsheviks were active in Belarus and Ukraine. National cadres were not difficult to find in Ukraine and Belarus. Hence the Soviet system could be said to have been less "foreign" to Belarus and Ukraine *relative to the way it was regarded in the Baltic region and Central Asia*. From the time of the revolution until the dissolution of the Soviet Union, Belarusians and Ukrainians had participated actively in the Soviet system. They were over-represented in the party structures in relation to their percentage of the overall population. In the 1930s there was much upward social mobility due to vacancies caused by the Stalinist purges. Membership in the Communist Party was sought less for reasons of ideological conviction than for career reasons. However before the 1930s, Ukrainians and Belarusians (as well as Jews and Latvians for that matter) were over-represented in the Communist Party. Ukrainians, comprising 21.2 percent of the population in the 1920s, counted for 42.4 percent of party membership in 1920. The figures for Belarusians were 3.2 percent and 29.8 percent respectively. After the first purge in 1926, Ukrainians still comprised 21 percent of party membership and Belarusians, 3 percent.[46]

In addition the Russians themselves did not regard Ukrainians and Belarusians as fundamentally distinct from themselves. This attitude undoubtedly had the effect of precluding discrimination against Belarusians and Ukrainians on the basis of ethnicity. Unlike other Soviet nationalities, in the RSFSR they were not discriminated against in the selection process for the Communist Party and party offices, in the procurement of permits to live in Moscow or Leningrad (St. Petersburg), or in admission to universities, to name a few examples. David Lempert's ethnographic study on Russian attitudes towards non-Russian Soviet citizens revealed that race played a large part in determining Russian attitudes towards various nationalities. According to interviews with Russians, Lempert constructed four rough categories: whites, primitives, black, and Orientals. In the context of Soviet nationalities, the "Whites" include Russians, Belarusians, Ukrainians, and the Baltic peoples. "Primitives" refer to those of African descent, but since the Soviet Union was not home to any nationalities of African descent, Russians do not become familiar with them except through foreign contacts. "Blacks" are peoples from the Caucasus and Central Asia such as Georgians, Armenians, Chechens, and Uzbeks, and so on. Chinese, Mongolians, Koreans, and Japanese fall into the "Oriental" group. Though a range of negative stereotypes were used by Russians in descriptions of non-whites, it is significant that in they included Ukrainians and Belarusians as whites and therefore as "one of us" rather than one of "them."[47]

Furthermore, Belarusians, Ukrainians, and Russians are frequently lumped together under the common category of "Slavic" people rather than separated into Belarusian, Ukrainian, and Russian. In assessing center/periphery relations in the Soviet Empire, the mass migration of "Slavic" peoples into the non-Russian periphery, especially Central Asia and the Caucasus, is regarded by indigenous peoples as evidence of the center's presence in their territory. The non-Slavic peoples of the periphery fail to distinguish among Slavs.[48]

Another measure of cultural closeness is the relatively higher numbers of Russian bilinguals in Belarus and Ukraine. Bilinguals are Russians living in Belarus and Ukraine who know the titular language of their home republic. In Belarus and Ukraine, 31 percent of Russians living in these republics have a working knowledge or better of the local language. These are the highest rates in the former Soviet Union and can be contrasted with those for Central Asia where the percentages range from 1–9 percent and those for Estonia and Latvia that range from 13–20 percent.[49] Though factors such as perceived need and length of residence are pertinent, the closeness of the three Slavic languages and the extensive interaction between Russians and Belarusians/Ukrainians undoubtedly figure prominently.[50]

Which brings us to the final point. The level of intermarriage between Russians and non-Russians indicates levels of voluntary interaction. Rasma Karklins has noted that non-Russian nationalities tend to marry only within their own ethnic group. This tendency is strong and is measured by the "Index of endogamy" that measures the level of ethnic randomness of marital unions. The higher the number, the less "random" the marital choice, demonstrating that an ethnic group consciously and deliberately chose a mate using an ethnic criterion. Hence the numerical values of endogamy are highest among the Muslim peoples: they range from 77.3 percent for Tajiks to 95.4 percent for the Kyrgyz. This is in sharp contrast to the values for Ukrainians and Belarusians: 34.3 percent and 39 percent respectively.[51] Religion plays a strong role in preventing inter-marriage between Muslims and Russians living in Muslim republics. Likewise rates of inter-marriage are stronger in urban environments than in country settings. Nevertheless when both factors are taken into account they only serve to emphasize the cultural relatedness among the Slavs, especially as compared to relations between Russians and non-Slavs.

The Soviet Breakup: National Movements in Ukraine and Belarus

The prominence of the national movements which sprang up as the result of Gorbachev's policy of Glasnost was the result of the Soviet political structure of the Federation that served to reinforce national identity rather than eradicate it. Special status given to the nationalities of the republics provided a ready-made blueprint for political autonomy and ultimately independence.[52] Any assessment of nationalism in Ukraine and Belarus should begin with a brief overview of the nationalist movements that preceded the breakup of the Soviet Union.

Except in the western areas of Ukraine, nationalist movements were more politically rather than ethnically motivated. Evidence in support of this can be found after independence, when both stressed (and continue to stress) that their respective states were not *ethnically* based. Mandates have been made inclusive enough to include other ethnic groups, especially ethnic Russians living in Belarus and Ukraine. Point 1 of Article 2 of the Ukrainian Law on Citizenship stipulates that all persons living in Ukraine at the time this law was passed (excluding foreigners who are citizens of other countries) became Ukrainian citizens unless they purposely chose to become citizens of a state other than Ukraine.[53] This is in stark contrast to the policies of other Successor States where the government expressly declares nationality to be the basis for the state. The Baltic States have gone so far as to deny other nationalities, in particular Russians, citizenship through the introduction of strict citizenship laws. Even in Kazakhstan, with Russians comprising almost half of the population, there is an effort to replace Russians with Kazakhs at every level of government and industry.

The nationalist movements in Belarus and Ukraine were not so much anti-Russian (as always the exception is Lviv) as they were anti-Communist and anti-Moscow. The impetus for Belarusian and Ukrainian nationalist demands has been the mismanagement of the economy and the cover-up of atrocities committed against their populations by the Soviet regime, particularly under Stalin. And although nationalists on both sides have variously interpreted these incidents as threats against their respective nations, the process of exposing the Soviet regime in Belarus and Ukraine was likewise mirrored in the political debates in Russia itself.

RELATIONS WITH RUSSIA AFTER INDEPENDENCE

Pursuing a path of total economic independence and maintaining an autonomous and even defiant foreign policy vis-à-vis the Russian Federation has been an untenable option for both governments for two related reasons. Both have experienced a drastic economic decline in production, wages, employment, trade and living standards, and both the lack of popular support for nationalist agendas that include anti-Russian rhetoric without economic relief.

The governments of the Slavic states along with other Successor States face the dual challenges of economic restructuring and reducing economic dependence on the Russian Federation. Poor economic performance since independence combined with continued dependence on Russia in matters of trade severely limits the options of the leadership of both states. Both are forced to turn to Russia as the primary economic partner and the only state willing and capable of restoring economic and political links. The adoption of such options is a reflection of the limits of popular endurance of hardships for the sake of national pride. It is also indicative of the lack of alternatives for both states. The continuation/restoration of former Soviet trade patterns between enterprises and closer cooperation in matters of state borders, military security and foreign policy.

The Collapse of Trade

The economic situation for Belarus, Ukraine and Russia has been disastrous following the dissolution of the Soviet Union. The formation of the CIS did little to halt decreases in production and trade (See Table 5.3). Taking 1989 as an index year, the last year of "normal levels" of Soviet production, a precipitous decline of Gross Domestic Product (GDP) in all three of the Slavic Successor States can be observed. GDP was nearly cut in half by 1994 in Ukraine and Russia while it declined to 63.4 percent in Belarus (see Table 5.1).

And while the three states represented the bulk of Soviet production and industrial development, it is nonetheless true that Russia is in a much more advantageous position vis-à-vis Belarus and Ukraine. Percentages given for production declines and declines in GDP mask the sheer size of Russia's economy vis-à-vis Ukraine and Belarus (see Table 5.2). Also, its economy is much more diverse in production, markets, and inputs.[54] Consequently Russia is not as dependent on Belarus and Ukraine, even as a source for markets; Belarus

Table 5.1
GDP Indices, 1989=100

Country	1989	1990	1991	1992	1993	1994
Russia	100.0	97.0	84.6	68.3	60.1	51.1
Ukraine	100.0	96.4	85.2	73.5	63.1	51.1
Belarus	100.0	98.0	96.8	87.5	79.2	63.4

Source: Lee Kendall Metcalf, "The (Re)Emergence of Regional Economic Integration in the Former Soviet Union," *Political Research Quarterly* (1998).

Table 5.2
Comparative Economic Indicators, 1999

	Russia	**Ukraine**	**Belarus**
GDP (US$ bn)	185.6	30.7	11.5
Exports (US$ bn)	74.5	12.5	6.0
Imports (US$ bn)	39.4	12.9	6.6

Source: The Economist Intelligence Unit Limited: EIU Country Profile 2000, Belarus (London: The Economist Intelligence Unit, 2000), p. 17.

and Ukraine however are very dependent on Russia for both their exports and industrial inputs, particularly in the energy sector. Fuel and energy account for roughly 38 percent of Ukraine's total imports.[55] Belarus likewise imports most of its fuel from Russia; it pays only half of what Ukraine must pay to Russia.[56] It is a political dividend for the close cooperation between Minsk and Moscow. Russia has less to gain economically from greater levels of economic integration with Ukraine and Belarus than do the latter. The benefits on the Russian side are political rather than economic.[57]

Trade matters have been complicated by the monetary policies of Russia. Following the dissolution of the Soviet Union, the three Slavic states met and formed the Commonwealth of Independent States (CIS). Originally the countries of the CIS agreed to retain the ruble as a common currency, control the supply of money, control budget deficits and establish a common tax code. The CIS eventually expanded to include all the Successor States except the Baltic States. In practice Russia insisted on controlling the money supply through Russian banks. From 1992–1993, political pressures from such diverse politicians as Yegor Gaidar and Vladimir Zhirinovsky to cut price subsidies to CIS states prevailed.[58] The view that the costs of retaining close economic cooperation with the CIS outweighed the benefits for Russia was widespread.

Russia employed a strict monetary policy by exercising direct control over the currency supply by the Central Bank of Russia's refusal to honor old rubles or those printed by banks other than the Central Bank of Russia. Russia freed prices, removing price controls from manufactured products and raw materials internally as well as for exports. In return for the use of the Russian ruble as currency, Russia demanded that the Successor States deposit their gold reserves in Russia. Finally Russia demanded payment in hard currency of raw materials including gas and oil.

Table 5.3
Trade

	Russia			Ukraine			Belarus		
	1991	1992	1993	1991	1992	1993	1991	1992	1993
Foreign exports US$ bn	50.9	40.0	40.0	7.3	6.0	4.9	1.66	1.06	0.7
Foreign imports US$ bn	44.5	35.0	20.0	10.0	5.5	1.7	1.96	0.7	0.7

Source: Helen Boss and Peter Havli, "Slavic (Dis)union: Consequences for Russia, Belarus and Ukraine," *Economics of Transition*, vol. 2, no. 2 (1994), p. 236.

All of this drove members of the CIS out of the ruble zone and forced them to introduce their own separate currencies. Trade among the Successor States was in large part reduced to barter arrangements since none could pay in hard currency.[59] Those who feared that Russia would dominate the CIS in the way that it did the Soviet Union need not have feared; the CIS as an organization has been ineffectual and its mandates left largely unimplemented. Russia itself reneged on many CIS agreements by freeing prices without consulting CIS member states in January of 1992. Ukraine shortly after introduced the Karbovanets (coupon) as legal tender which was eventually replaced by the Ukrainian hryvnya in September of 1996 (see Table 5.1). Even Belarus, who accepted the strict terms of Russia in order to stay within the ruble zone, was forced to introduce a parallel currency in 1992.[60] Hyperinflation in Belarus and Ukraine resulted.

Political Relations

Political relations between Belarus/Ukraine and the Russian Federation have been turbulent in the political realm but overall the disagreements resemble family bickering rather than serious quarrels indicative of animosity between rival states. In the case of Belarus, close relations with Russia, including cooperation on military matters and greater agreement in foreign policy, clearly preclude hostile bilateral relations. In the case of Ukraine, political disagreement has been more contentious to be sure, and yet overall both have managed to come to agreement on several key issues though a number of disputes still need to be worked out. But clear concessions on both sides illustrate the fact that overall relations are more harmonious than they are contentious.

Belarus

Under Lukashenka Belarus has towed the Russian line in foreign policy. Given the economic dependence of both on Russia, Belarus had less reason to oppose Moscow on key political issues such as NATO expansion and

Chechnya than Ukraine. And the trend toward closer cooperation with Russia is likely to continue. The Belarusian national revival was at its height in 1990 and perhaps shortly after the dissolution of the Soviet Union. And at its height the chairman of the Belarusian Supreme Soviet Stanislau Shushkevich, who signed the CIS accords at Belavezha and became the first Belarusian president, was a centrist not a nationalist. In 1994, he was replaced with a conservative Alyaksandar Lukashenka who was unabashedly pro-Moscow. The policy of offering Moscow political concessions in exchange for economic subsidies on energy supplies and the like gained momentum after his election to the presidency.

Belarus effectively placed the nuclear weapons left in Belarus under the Russian military command when security agreements with Moscow were reached about maintaining a common air defense and the defense of Belarusian borders. Belarus is very heavily militarized for its size. According to the London-based International Institute for Strategic Studies, its military consisted of 98,400 active troops with an additional 289,500 reservists, while its nuclear arsenal included some 18 Intercontinental Ballistic Missiles (ICBMs).[61]

In addition there is no operative border, that is, international border, between Russia and Belarus. Belarus and Russia have signed agreements to establish a common customs union, which called for the removal of demarcation posts and border guards on the border between Russia and Belarus. Accordingly Yeltsin publicly proclaimed that there is no border between Belarus and Russia.[62] In addition, Russia has agreed to pay 50 percent of the costs for border security on Belarus' western border with Poland through an agreement that was signed September 21, 1995. Costs of border maintenance include the maintenance of the border facilities themselves, technical supplies to border troops, and the upkeep and salaries of the border troops themselves. Belarusian President Lukashenka declared that the Russian government recognizes that Belarus' western border is in fact the western border of Russia.[63]

Ukraine

Though also highly dependent on Russia for imports and trade, Ukraine has other conflicts with Russia that precluded easy acquiescence to Russia on political matters. Among the major confrontations between the two were the issues of nuclear weapons, the Crimea, and the Black Sea Fleet. Nevertheless, headway and concessions have been made on these issues. Ukraine relinquished its nuclear weapons, managed to avoid armed conflict in the Crimea and has divided the Black Sea Fleet with Russia though there is still the outstanding issue of where Russia should base its Black Sea Fleet.

The dissolution of the Soviet Union resulted in the division of the Soviet nuclear arsenal among Ukraine, Belarus, Kazakhstan, and the Russian Federation. As Russia was recognized by the United States and the world community of states in general as the successor state to the Soviet Union, pressure was put on Russia to retain control over the Soviet nuclear arsenal. Russia in turn pressed Ukraine, Belarus and Kazakhstan to turn over nuclear weapons to the Russian Federation or to collaborate with Russia to have them decommissioned. Originally Ukraine under President Kravchuk sought to retain its nuclear weapons despite the fact that they needed financial assistance in their maintenance. Evidently a nuclear Ukraine was thought to hold more interest to the West than a non-nuclear one. Under pressure from the United States as well as Russia, a trilateral agreement was signed and Ukraine agreed to move its nuclear weapons to Russia where they would be dismantled. In return for Ukraine's acquiescence, economic concessions from Russia along with debt rescheduling for energy imports and economic aid from the United States were thrown into the bargain.

There are also outstanding territorial questions between Ukraine and Russia, the most notable of them being the Crimea. Ukraine is divided into several regions with different aspirations and problems. Some analysts even speculate that this fact would undermine Ukraine's survival as a state. But Kiev has thus far been able to manage regional demand while using political schisms within these regions to extend central control over Ukraine and effectively establish a unitary state.[64] The sole exception to this has been the Crimea.

Historically Crimea has been a part of Russia while economically it belongs with the Donbass and the rest of Eastern Ukraine as an industrial region. Khrushchev transferred Crimea to the Ukraine in 1954 to commemorate the 300th anniversary of the "reunification" of Ukrainian and Russian nations. The Russian population of Crimea is approximately 61.6 percent; the Crimea was granted the status of Autonomous Republic within the Ukrainian State.

Economically the Crimea along with the heavily russified areas of Eastern Ukraine (Kharkiv, Luhansk, Donetsk, Zaporizhzhya, and Dnipropetrovsk) account for the bulk of Ukrainian industry and mining, areas of the economy that contributed by far the largest share of Ukraine's GDP, export earnings and tax revenues.[65] The latest figures for Ukraine indicate that in 1996, industry contributed 32.5 percent to the GDP while the principal exports were ferrous and non-ferrous metals at 32.3 percent, compliments of the mining industry.[66] Conversely the eastern and southern regions are most dependent on Kiev for state subsidies and capital investments without which they could not survive. This fact in combination with the lack of political activism among the population and disunity among the politicians of these regions has played into President's Kuchma's hands. Kuchma, who was elected on a platform that championed greater regional autonomy, has in fact since his election in 1994 worked hard to extend and tightened Kiev's administrative control over these regions.[67] Constitutionally Kuchma has placed the government of Crimea under the direct control of the government in Kiev; the legislative assemblies and their speakers are to be directly accountable to the president.[68]

Essentially the battle between Crimea and the center in Kiev is similar to the conflict between the eastern areas of Ukraine and Kiev, except that no other region has Crimea's autonomous status. Crimea has the power to establish its own parliament and elect its own slate of politicians. The conflict between Kiev and the heavily industrialized areas of the east and south is in part caused by the reluctance of the regions to hand over tax revenues to the central government who would then, through redistributive polices, spend it on other regions of Ukraine. Hence the Russian population of Crimea, who do not regard the Crimea as a legitimate part of Ukraine, have elected a parliament that has pressed for greater autonomy from Kiev.[69]

Separatist sentiments have also been widely expressed by parliamentarians. In 1995 Crimean President Yuri Meshkov, addressing the Crimean Supreme Soviet, publicly supported the "restoration of a fraternal Slavic union and successive and gradual reunification of Crimea and Russia."[70] Likewise the former Foreign Minister Kozyrev's much publicized statement regarding the use of force by Russia in protecting Russian minorities in the near abroad was greeted enthusiastically by the Crimean leadership. In April of 1995, after Kuchma moved to subordinate the Crimean government to the central government in Kiev, the Crimean parliament formally asked for protection from Moscow. Parliament requested of President Yeltsin and the State Duma the adoption of "measures, according to their international commitments, protecting the rights of compatriots living on the territory of the Crimea and representing a national minority in Ukraine."[71]

The potential success of the separatist movement in Crimea is dependent on Russia's response to their pleas for integration into Russia. Russia for its part has expressed reluctance in Crimea's reintegration into the Russian Federation. Officially, Russia has long taken the stance that the issue of the Crimea is the internal affair of Ukraine, a claim reiterated by Russian Duma Speaker Ivan Rybkin after Kuchma's crackdown on the Crimean government.[72] There would be financial costs in reintegrating the Crimea. But the Crimean issue is closely linked to the issue of the Black Sea Fleet that was based in the Crimean city of Sevastopol.

Normalization of Relations with Russia

Though Belarus and Ukraine have had their disagreements with Russia, bilateral relations between each have taken on a less contentious tone. While Belarus' policy of forging closer relations with Russia has been clear and unequivocal, Ukraine too has recognized the need for some sort of reconciliation with Moscow.

President Kuchma for his part has expressed the desire for closer cooperation with Russia. Headway has been made on many fronts. The division of the Black Sea Fleet has been completed. The issue of where the Russian portion of the Fleet will be stationed has been partially resolved with the signing of the

Treaty of Friendship. A Treaty of Friendship had been in the works since 1995 and was finally concluded in May of 1997.[73] The provisions of the Treaty recognize the inviolability of Ukrainian and Russian borders and allow Russia to lease the port of Sevastopol for Russia's Black Sea Fleet. Though there were fears on the Ukrainian side that Moscow was deliberately delaying its signing in the hopes that separatism would gain strength in the Crimea, the Treaty was eventually signed by the Russian president in May of 1997 and ratified by the Russian parliament in January of 1998.[74]

Cooperation has been made on the economic front as well. Trade between Russia and Ukraine is projected to increase after a drastic reduction during 1997 as a result of the trade war between Ukraine and Russia.[75] The value added tax (VAT) levied on exports by both Ukraine and Russian led to what has been labeled an "economic war" between the two countries. Essentially trade between the two ground to a halt for the better part of 1997. Both sides eventually agreed to abolish the value-added tax in November of 1997, ending the six-month trade war.[76]

Relations between the two continue to be uneven. With renewed pledges to strengthen economic ties, both signed a 10-year program of economic cooperation in February of 1998. Russia's motivation for closer ties is closely linked with the business interests of Russia's oligarchs who own huge enterprises that control most of Russia's valuable resources including mineral and energy resources. Ukraine's big industries, including the extractive industries, have yet to be privatized. Should Ukraine decide, or be forced by circumstances, to privatize its industries, it is likely that the buyers will be Russian businesses. This would undermine Ukraine's sovereignty. The question remains, would it erode Ukraine's independence to the point of defacto reincorporation of Ukraine into the Russian Federation? Or would relations between the two more resemble those of other states who are dependent on their larger neighbors?

PROSPECTS FOR INDEPENDENCE

Conditions in the Center Unfavorable to the Reestablishment of the Empire

The non-interventionist mood of the Russian government and a corresponding apathy among ordinary Russian citizens regarding the recreation of the former Union favor political independence as a state and an eventual lessening of economic and military dependence from Russia. The attitude of those in the Russian government toward Ukraine and Belarus has suggested reluctance and in some instances outright rejection of the notion of reuniting with Belarus and Ukraine. Even the ultra-nationalist and bombastic Zhirinovsky believes the costs associated with reintegration to be too high for Russia who has its own economic woes. The Russian government has consistently delayed the full implementation of the Union Treaty with Belarus. In fact there are many in the Russian government and opposition who actively oppose the Union with Belarus on economic grounds. And among the general population there is the widespread feeling that Russia is better off without the republics.[77]

Conditions in the Periphery Unfavorable to Independence from Russia

As stated in chapter 2, there are several factors that can make the periphery more vulnerable to imperial conquest: a politically divided population, low levels of nationalism, and economic instability. The first applies to Ukraine with its regional divisions while the second applies to both Belarus and Ukraine with their low levels of national consciousness. Strife between the titular citizenry and the Russian minorities has been minimal and localized. Lastly, the poor state of both economies has produced the attendant social ills and general instability, which is manifest in all the Successor States to some degree.

Belarus

Belarus is not a divided country in that there are not significant pockets of ethnic minorities or other politically motivated malcontents. This might be a source of strength against a return to Russian hegemony except that the population is united by the feeling that the dissolution of the Soviet Union was a mistake and that the way to improved living conditions is through renewed close contacts, if not reunification, with Russia. President Lukashenka, the successor to Stanislau Shushkevich, the man who signed the CIS accords abolishing the old Union, publicly declared that the breakup of the Soviet Union was a political mistake. He further argued that capitalism is alien to "Slavs" and that any attempt to impose "ruthless capitalism" will fail because it is incompatible to the mentality of Slavs.[78] In his use of the term Slav he is equating Belarusians with Russians (and Ukrainians). It is also worth noting that Lukashenka, whatever conflicts he has had with his own parliament and the Russian government (the detention of ORT [Russian Public Television] journalists), still commands more votes than his political opposition. He was elected in 1994 with 80 percent of the total votes cast. At the end of 1997 Lukashenka received the highest approval rating (44 percent) while the leader of the main opposition party, the People's Front of Belarus (PFB) received the highest no-confidence rating (22 percent).[79] His grip on power is furthered by the lack of unity among the opposition.

Belarusian national consciousness is likewise low. Though Belarusian and Russian are mutually intelligible languages, Russian is the principal language spoken among people, Belarusians and Russians alike. Even government business is conducted in Russian. As late as September of 1996, the Belarusian Supreme Soviet attempted to conduct its session in the Belarusian language, an effort that was noted in the media because of its novelty. The session held no other interest for the media despite the fact that a new constitution was being debated. Minsk BTK Television Network commented on the use of Belarusian on this occasion, the implication being that the use of Belarusian departs from the normal conduct in parliament in spite of the fact that the Supreme Soviet Chairman Syamyon Sharetski "promised" to conduct government in Belarusian.[80]

The final factor working against Belarusian independence is the poor economic situation in the country as well as the political polices pursued by the Belarusian president. Far from cultivating alternative sources of raw materials, energy supplies and markets, Belarus has endeavored to increase its connection to Russia rather than the opposite. This is not only a matter of practicality but also a conscious political choice by a popularly elected Lukashenka who openly laments the breakup of the Soviet Union and expresses his hostility to market reforms.

The economic situation, in particular GDP, as well as the living standard of the population declined drastically since 1991. Belarus has long been recognized by the IMF and World Bank as being the most reluctant to introduce market reforms. In fact Lukashenka's economic policy reverts back to Soviet style central planning. His plans were summarized in November of 1997. They include the restoration of the privileged status of the defense industry in government-provided capital investments. State enterprises were authorized to grant employee and management pay bonuses for meeting and exceeding quotas. The majority shares of "private" enterprises including joint-stock companies are to be owned by the state. The plan also includes increases of state funding for research and development, and electricity subsidies for light (consumer industry). And to ensure that energy needs are met, overall energy consumption is to be frozen from 1998 to 2000.[81] The Belarusian economy has retained its Soviet character intact from the time of the breakup. Its Soviet trade patterns are likewise the same. Trade with Russia has increased from 1996 to 1997. Exports to Russia have increased by 53 percent and imports from Russia by 31.5 percent. Russia accounted for 41.6 percent of Belarusian exports and 50.5 percent of Belarusian imports.[82]

Accordingly the Belarusian economy is doing well on paper. The economy grew by 10 percent in 1997 and unemployment fell to 2.3 percent of the workforce. However according to the Economist Intelligence Unit, these increases were the result of a government-supported policy of pumping money into industry through increased subsidies and expanding public works such as housing construction to reduce unemployment. The growth in the economy was not demand-driven and therefore growth is unlikely to be sustainable. Better indicators of real economic performance as it relates to living standards are the high levels of inflation and increases in prices (in real terms). By 1999, the economy showed a 3 percent growth, but production price inflation was at 242.2 percent while consumer price inflation stood at 251.3 percent.[83]

Ukraine

Ukraine unlike Belarus is divided regionally. With regards to the Russian Federation and the Russian minority living in Ukraine, only the Western region, with its center in Lviv, has consistently been nationalistic and antagonistic toward Russia. The central, eastern and southern regions by contrast exhibit lower levels of Ukrainian national consciousness; but even more significantly, are not hostile toward ethnic Russians or Russia in general. In fact surveys taken to gauge inter-ethnic relations between Ukrainians and Russians all indicate that there is little ill will between the two. Many respondents were unable to tell how many of their friends and acquaintances fell into each ethnic group![84] As always the exception to this has been in Lviv, where Ukrainians there harbor unfavorable stereotypes of Russians to a greater extent relative to the rest of Ukraine, while Russians in Lviv (unlike Russians elsewhere in Ukraine) report feeling like outsiders in a foreign land.[85] And as previously noted, the eastern and southern regions actually favor closer ties to Russia if not outright annexation.

As for nationalist fervor, it has noticeably declined since independence. Local elections held in 1990 and again in 1994 show that the Democratic Bloc, which included the nationalists, gained many seats and even won the majority of seats in many areas of western Ukraine. But in the rest of Ukraine, Soviet-era local elites have held on and have even gained strength as voters, after 1994, became disillusioned with the nationalists mishandling of the economy and their dogmatic nationalist beliefs. The nationalists, who included former dissidents and intellectuals, were not politicians and failed to meet the expectations of their constituents.

The power of the nationalists was at its peak in 1990 but that changed, particularly after 1994. Bad economic conditions persisted throughout the 1990s, which did not add to the popularity of the nationalists. Ukraine's economy continues to contract, though at a much slower pace than in the past. Real GDP has declined by more than half since 1992.[86] Kravchuk was replaced by Kuchma (who hails from Dnipropetrovsk), a fact which by all accounts signaled a shift in the Ukrainian government away from nationalist rhetoric. A recent pole in Ukraine that asks people how they will vote in the next elections revealed that 22 percent would vote for the communists or socialists, 20 percent for the democrats and liberals, but only 5 percent would vote for the nationalists.[87] Kuchma was reelected in 1998 and though the election was a contentious one, the nationalists did not figure prominently among those who opposed Kuchma.

Economically Ukraine has not moved away from Russia as a trading partner. In fact trade with Russia is up after both agreed to eliminate the VAT on imports. Even in 1997 during the trade war, Russia remained Ukraine's primary trading partner, accounting for 47 percent of total imports and 26 percent of total exports. Barter trade amounted to 10.5 percent of exports and 10 percent of imports. The following year those figures rose to 60.7 percent and 33 percent respectively.[88] Russia still supplies Ukraine with most of its oil and gas though Ukraine has recently signed a deal with Turkmenistan for the latter to supply Ukraine with natural gas. But Russian cooperation is a necessity for this agreement since Turkmenistan relies on Gazprom (Russia's gas monopoly) for use of its pipelines. Russian goodwill is also necessary for the rescheduling of Ukraine's energy debt to Gazprom, which was done in December of 1997 while a new gas supply agreement was signed for 1998.

And economic cooperation (or integration?) between Ukraine and Russia will only intensify in the future. Unlike Lukashenka, Kuchma decided to privatize some of Ukraine's big state industries, and predictably the interested parties are Russian businesses. In January of 2000, the Ukrainian government made a formal announcement to privatize some of the biggest industries. Mykolayiv (Nikolaev) aluminum plant was sold to Sibirskii Aluminum on March 29. Tyumen Oil and Lukoil are actively pursuing the acquisition of Ukraine's oil refineries.[89]

Some Western analysts expressed concern that Ukraine's sovereignty will be compromised by the sell-off of Ukraine's prime industries to Russian business. Such concerns ignore the reality of the "New World Order" where international corporations play a huge role in the development or deterioration of the national economies of the countries in which they function. If this is true of Ukraine, the same could be said of many developing countries. Foreign investment in Ukraine is low in part due to the ambiguous and unenforceable commercial laws. The arbitrary business climate is no hindrance to Russian investment since the business climate in Russia is similarly unpredictable. But more importantly Russians and Ukrainians are accustomed to dealing with each other, and after all, it is they who shaped the very post-Soviet economic environment that Western businesses find so unnerving. The feuding between President Kuchma and parliament exacerbates the situation.[90]

CONCLUSION

Although conditions in Belarus and Ukraine would seem to favor the restoration of the empire, conditions in Russia itself preclude that scenario. A more likely scenario is the progression of unbalanced bilateral relations similar to those between a powerful, large state, and its tiny neighbor(s).

It is unlikely that any other large power will challenge Russia's influence in these states as the international community, in particular the United States and the European Union, whatever it may declare publicly, has shown by its inaction that it is not all that interested in Ukraine. The United States and the European Union are interested primarily in two things: nuclear weapons and avoiding any accidents at Ukraine's several nuclear power plants. The former issue has been successfully resolved while long-term solutions to the latter problem have yet to be worked out though an international conference held in

New York pledged to pay Ukraine $337 million to repair the crumbling sarcophagus that was hastily built to contain the Chernobyl nuclear power plant.

And though disagreements remain between the governments of Belarus and Ukraine on the one hand, and the Russian government on the other, Belarus and Ukraine have both show a willingness to work closer with Russia despite the critics from the nationalist oppositions in both countries. It is also important to note that disagreements between governments are not indicative of inter-ethnic strife between ethnic Russians, Belarusians, and Ukrainians.

NOTES

1. Konstantin Zatulin and Andranik Migranyan, "SNG posle Kishineva: nachalo kontsa istorii," *Nezavisimaya gazeta (sodruvzhestvo ng)*, December (1997) pp. 1–2.

2. Viktor Litovkin, "Ofitserskoe krepostnoe pravo otmeneno," *Izvestiia*, April 8 (1998) pp. 1–2.

3. Anatol Lieven, "Russia's Military Nadir," *The National Interest*, Summer (1996) pp. 27–32.

4. Gerhard Simon, *Nationalism and Policy Toward Nationalities in the Soviet Union* (Westview: Boulder, 1991) pp. 114–124.

5. Adam B. Ulam, *Stalin: The Man and His Era* (Boston: Beacon Press, 1989), pp. 345–350.

6. Nicholas P. Vakar, *Belorussia: The Making of a Nation* (Cambridge: Harvard University Press, 1956) pp. 41–42.

7. Karen Dawisha and Bruce Parrott, *Russia and the New States of Eurasia: The Politics of Upheaval* (Cambridge: Cambridge University Press, 1994) pp. 74–76.

8. Kathleen J. Mikhalisko, "Belarus: Retreat to Authoritarianism," in *Democratic Changes and Authoritarian Reactions in Russia, Ukraine, Belarus, and Moldova*, edited by Karen Dawisha and Bruce Parrott (Cambridge: Cambridge University Press, 1997) p. 236.

9. Dawisha and Parrott, *Russia and the New States of Eurasia*, pp. 74–76.

10. Ustina Markus, "A War of Referenda In Belarus," *Transition*, 13 December (1996) pp. 13–14.

11. Kenneth Katzner, *The Languages of the World* (New York: Funk & Wagnalls, 1975) pp. 14–15.

12. Ihor Stebelsky, "The Toponymy of Ukraine," *Post-Soviet Geography and Economics*, vol. 38, no. 5 (1997) pp. 278–279.

13. Vakar, *Belorussia*, pp. 65–66.

14. Mihalisko, "Belarus," p. 228.

15. Paul Kolstoe, *Russians in the Former Soviet Republics* (Bloomington: Indiana University Press, 1995) p. 172.

16. Georgiy I. Mirsky, *On the Ruins of Empire: Ethnicity and Nationalism in the Former Soviet Union* (Westport: Greenwood Press, 1997) pp. 124–125.

17. Evgenii Golovakha, Natalia Panina, and Nikolai Churilov, "Russians in the Ukraine," in *The New Russian Diaspora*, ed. by Vladimir Shlapentokh, Munir Sendich, and Emil Payin (New York: M. E. Sharpe, 1994) p. 59.

18. Bernard Comrie and Greville G. Corbett, "Introduction," in *The Slavonic Languages*, edited by Bernard Comrie and Greville G. Corbett (New York: Routledge, 1993) p. 1.

19. Alan Timberlake, "Russian," in *The Slavonic Languages*, p. 827.

20. Peter Mayo, "Belorussian," in *The Slavonic Languages*, p. 887.

21. Vakar, *Belorussia*, pp. 29–30.

22. Mayo, "Belorussian," p. 888.

23. Mihalisko, "Belarus," p. 226.

24. Jan Zaprudnik, "Belarusian Identity and Foreign Policy," in *National Identity and Ethnicity in Russia and the New States of Eurasia*, edited by Roman Szporluk (New York: M. E. Sharpe, 1994) p. 141.

25. Vakar, *Belorussia*, pp. 103–106.

26. Ibid., pp. 76–79.

27. Mayo, "Belorussian," p. 888.

28. Vakar, *Belorussia*, p. 79.

29. Ibid., p. 78; Mayo, "Belorussia," p. 888.

30. Mirsky, *On the Ruins of Empire*, p. 118.

31. Stebelsky, "The Toponymy of Ukraine," p. 279.

32. Dmytro Cyzevs'kyj, *A History of Ukrainian Literature* (Littleton, Colorado: Ukrainian Academic Press, 1975) pp. 366.

33. Vakar, *Belorussia*, pp. 92–97, 108.

34. Ivan L. Rudnytsky, "Observations on the Problem of 'Historical' and 'Non-Historical' Nations," *Harvard Ukrainian Studies*, vol. 5, no. 3 (1981) p. 366.

35. Ibid., pp. 116–117.

36. Vakar, *Belorussia*, pp. 117, 155, 165–166.

37. Mihalisko, "Belarus," p. 233.

38. Vakar, *Belorussia*, p. 157; Simon, *Nationalism and Policy Toward the Nationalities in the Soviet Union*, pp. 326–328.

39. Armstrong, *Ukrainian Nationalism*, p. 12.

40. Ibid., pp. 293–300, 302, 304–305.

41. Ibid., pp. 131–138.

42. Simon, *Nationalism and Policy Toward the Nationalities in the Soviet Union*, pp. 326–328.

43. Mihalisko, "Belarus," pp. 235–236; Ilya Prizel, "Ukraine Between Proto-Democracy and "Soft" Authoritarianism," in *Democratic Changes and Authoritarian Reactions in Russia, Ukraine, Belarus, and Moldova*, edited by Karen Dawisha and Bruce Parrott (Cambridge: Cambridge University Press, 1997) p. 336.

44. David H. Lempert, *Daily Life in a Crumbling Empire: The Absorption of Russia into the World Economy* (Boulder: East European Monographs, 1996) p. 295.

45. Mihalisko, "Belarus," pp. 232–233.

46. Lempert, *Daily Life in a Crumbling Empire*, p. 290.

47. Ibid., p. 295.

48. Rasma Karklins, *Ethnic Relations in the USSR: The Perspective from Below* (Boston: Allen & Unwin, 1986) pp. 51–52.

49. Ibid., pp. 59, 231.

50. Ibid., p. 59.

51. Ibid., pp. 156–157.

52. Philip G. Roeder, "Soviet Federalism and Ethnic Mobilization," in *The Soviet Nationality Reader: The Disintegration in Context*, edited by Rachel Denber (Boulder: Westview Press, 1992) pp. 148–149.

53. *FBIS-SOV*, 11 April (1995) p. 46.

54. Lee Kendall Metcalf, "The (Re)Emergence of Regional Economic Integration In the Former Soviet Union," *Political Research Quarterly*, (1997), p. 3.

55. *The Economist Intelligence Unit Limited: EIU Country Profile 1999–2000, Ukraine* (London: The Economist Intelligence Unit, 1999) p. 30.

56. *The Economist Intelligence Unit Limited: EIU Country Profile 2000, Belarus* (London: The Economist Intelligence Unit, 2000) p. 15.

57. Ibid., p. 7.

58. Helen Boss and Peter Havlik, "Slavic (dis)Union: Consequences For Russia, Belarus and Ukraine," *Economics of Transition*, vol. 2, no. 2 (1994) p. 243.

59. Paul D'Anieri, "Dilemmas of Interdependence: Autonomy, Prosperity, and Sovereignty in Ukraine's Russia Policy," *Problems of Post-Communism*, January/February (1997) p. 20.

60. Ustina Markus, "Belarus, Ukraine Take Opposite Views," *Transition*, 15 November (1996) p. 21.

61. Michael Evans, "Moscow Plans Pact With Belorussia if NATO Expands," *The Times*, 15 May (1996) p. 1.

62. *FBIS-SOV*, 31 May (1995) p. 75.

63. *FBIS-SOV*, 12 September (1996) p. 30.

64. Sarah Birch and Ihor Zinko, "The Dilemma of Regionalism," *Transition*, 1 November (1996) pp. 23–24.

65. Ibid., p. 22.

66. *The Economist Intelligence Unit Country Report: Ukraine, 1st Quarter* (London: The Economist Intelligence Unit, 1998) p. 5.

67. Birch and Zinko, "The Dilemma of Regionalism," p. 23.

68. *FBIS-SOV*, 12 April (1995), p. 54.

69. Ian Bremmer, "The Politics of Ethnicity: Russians in the New Ukraine," *Europe-Asia Studies*, vol. 46, no. 2 (1994), p. 265.

70. *FBIS-SOV*, 7 April (1995) p. 61.

71. *FBIS-SOV*, 21 April (1995) p. 45.

72. *FBIS-SOV*, 11 April (1995), p. 51; *FBIS-SOV*, 26 April (1995) p. 15.

73. *The Current Digest of the Post-Soviet Press*, vol. XLIX, no. 35 (1997) p. 20; *The Economist Intelligence Unit Country Report: Ukraine, 1st quarter* (London: The Economist Intelligence Unit, 1998) p. 11.

74. *FBIS-SOV*, 3 May (1995) p. 48.

75. *FBIS-SOV*, 9 September (1996) p. 51.

76. *The Economist Intelligence Unit Country Report: Ukraine, 1st quarter* (London: The Economist Intelligence Unit, 1998) pp. 11, 23, 30.

77. This view was the one most commonly observed in Russia among ordinary Russians by the author in 1994. It is my opinion that this attitude will increase rather than decrease over time.

78. *FBIS-SOV*, 27 November (1995) p. 52.

79. *The Economist Intelligence Unit Country Report: Belarus/Moldova, 1st quarter* (London: The Economist Intelligence Unit, 1998) p. 12.

80. *FBIS-SOV*, 5 September (1996) p. 38.

81. *The Economist Intelligence Unit Limited: EIU Country Profile: Belarus* (London: The Economist Intelligence Unit, 2000) pp. 16–18.

82. *The Economist Intelligence Unit Country Report: Belarus/Moldova, 1st quarter*, (London: The Economist Intelligence Unit, 1998) pp. 6, 17.

83. *The Economist Intelligence Unit Limited: EIU Country Profile: Belarus* (London: The Economist Intelligence Unit, 2000) p. 16.

84. Ian Bremmer, "The Politics of Ethnicity: Russians in the New Ukraine," *Europe-Asia Studies*, vol. 46, no. 2 (1994) pp. 273–275.

85. Ibid., p. 265.

86. *The Economist Intelligence Unit Country Report: Ukraine, 1st quarter* (London: The Economist Intelligence Unit, 1998) p. 17.

87. *The Economist Intelligence Unit Country Report: Ukraine, 1st quarter* (London: The Economist Intelligence Unit, 1998) p. 8.

88. Viktor Luhovyk, "Seductive Sellouts," *Transitions* 9 May (2000).

89. Ibid.

90. Ibid., p. 25.

Chapter 6

The Central Asian Successor States

INTRODUCTION

In common with Belarus and Ukraine, conditions in the Central Asia do not favor independence from Russia. However the reasons are very different from those in the Slavic and Baltic States. Central Asia faces many development problems similar to those of Third World states. The leaders of the Central Asian states did not come from any opposition group nor did they break from the Communist Party to become nationalist leaders. They are Soviet-era bureaucrats trained and socialized in that tradition; they are neither champions of "democracy" nor proponents of free market capitalism free of government direction and intervention.[1] They are faced with the policy dilemma of promoting economic development through foreign investment and increasing trade while at the same time trying to protect uncompetitive domestic enterprises so as to not worsen inflation and unemployment. They are attempting to achieve all of this against the backdrop of declining social services, infrastructure, and the growing destitution of a population that was already among the poorest within the Soviet Union.[2]

Like the Slavic and Baltic Successor States, the Central Asia periphery is vulnerable to Russian influence, though for different reasons. Central Asia needs to retain its trade links with Russia and it needs Russian aid for national defense and energy. Unlike the Baltic and Ukrainian leaders, the leaders of Central Asia have few nationalistic hang-ups (i.e., agonizing over the "loss of sovereignty" and so forth) about forging close links with Russia although that does not mean Central Asian leaders will act according to Russian wishes regardless of the situation. They simply see cooperation with Russia as the most viable alternative available to them. The Soviet links are still there, such as the close personal contacts between Central Asian and Russian leaders that are holdovers from the Soviet era.[3]

What makes Central Asia susceptible to Russian influence in the post-Soviet era? The lack of political and economic alternatives due to geographic isolation accounts for much of Central Asia's dependence on Russia. Despite the expansion of foreign relations with states outside the post-Soviet space, Russia remains the primary economic and political partner of the Central Asian states and continues to exert considerable leverage over them.

The Central Asian Republics became independent by default after Russia, Ukraine and Belarus signed the CIS accords in December of 1991, and Russia is no more anxious to reintegrate the Central Asia states than it is the states of Belarus and Ukraine. Independence was never the goal in Central Asia. The lack of nationalist, independence movements during the Gorbachev era is indicative of this. After the dissolution of the Soviet Union, the Slavic states formed a post-Soviet arrangement that became the CIS. Angry for having been excluded from this, the Central Asian states demanded to be included in any post-Soviet arrangement. Having had independence forced upon them, the states of Central Asia face many economic and social problems that, given the demographic and ethnographic reality, have the greatest potential for generating unrest and open conflict. The civil war in Tajikistan is a case in point. Independence has actually made the task of managing these problems more difficult for the leaders of these countries must deal with the consequences of social and public unrest. They can no longer depend on logistical support from Moscow. This chapter will examine the distinctive nature of the Central Asian periphery, comprised of Kazakhstan, Kyrgyzstan, Uzbekistan, Turkmenistan, and Tajikistan, within the Soviet Union and the pattern of dependence on the Russian Federation in the post-Soviet period.

THE DISTINCTIVENESS OF CENTRAL ASIA

There are several features that distinguish Central Asia as a region from the Slavic and Baltic Successor States. First, the conquest and recolonization of Central Asia by Soviet Russia resemble more the manner of overseas colonies of France and Britain where the culture of the colonizers differ vastly from those of subject nations.[4] The culture and society of Central Asia differed substantially from those of Russia.[5] The peoples of Central Asia are predominately Muslim with a traditional societal structure based on kinship ties. In many areas including Kazakhstan and Kyrgyzstan the people were nomadic and were forcibly settled only in the Soviet era. With the exception of Tajik, Central Asian languages belong to the Turkic branch of languages. Linguistically they are the most different from Russian, a fact that accounts in part for the low level of bilingualism among Russians living in these states.[6]

Second, the treatment of this region under the Soviets gave it peculiar characteristics, in particular its role in providing the Soviet Union with raw materials such as cotton, non-ferrous metals, minerals, natural gas and petroleum. The process of modernization affected Central Asia much less than it did in other areas of the former Soviet Union. The level of urbanization in the Central Asia during Soviet times was among the lowest of the Soviet Republics, a fact that holds true today. As late as 1987, the percentage of urban dwellers was only 41 percent on average for Central Asia while the average for the USSR was 66 percent, a figure that includes the Central Asian average with that of the other Republics (see Table 6.1). When the ethnicity of urban inhabitants is taken into account, the percentage of ethnic Kazakhs in Kazakhstan living in urban areas amounted to only 32 percent and in Tajikistan, Tajiks comprised only 28 percent (other Central Asian Republics falling between these two figures).[7] Even today the majority of Central Asians live in rural areas. Kazakhstan is the only country where a majority of the total population lives in urban areas. Out of a population of 16,913,000 as of 1993, 9,655,000 are urbanites while fully 7,257,000 live in rural areas.[8] As for the other Central Asian states, the rural population in total numbers exceeds that of the urban by a low ratio of 2:1 to as much as 3:1 (see Table 6.6).[9]

Central Asia has also experienced the highest total population growth since the 1970s. This is the result of higher birth rates, high fertility rates (the average number of children for each women of childbearing age), and a high percentage of women of childbearing age (45.6 percent of the total female population of Central Asia).[10] Birth rates in Central Asia were the highest in the Soviet Union and remain so today. They range from 28.1 to 42 births per thousand; the average for the USSR was 20 per thousand (see Table 6.3). Fertility rates in Central Asia range from 4.2 to 5.7 children per woman of child-

Table 6.1
Urbanization, Percentage of Total Population

Region	1913	1926	1939	1950	1959	1970	1979	1987
Uzbek SSR	24	22	23	31	34	37	41	42
Kyrgyz SSR	12	12	19	28	34	37	39	40
Tajik SSR	9	10	17	26	33	37	35	33
Turkmen SSR	11	14	33	36	46	48	48	48
Central Asia	19	18	23	30	35	38	41	41
average for USSR	18	18	32	39	48	56	62	66

Source: Goskomstat SSR (Moskva: Naseleniye SSSR, 1987), pp. 8–15.

Table 6.2
Settlement Patterns for Asians and Russians

Nationality	Reside in titular Republic			Reside in contiguous Republic			Reside elsewhere in the USSR		
	(1970)	(1979)	(1989)	(1970)	(1979)	(1989)	(1970)	(1979)	(1989)
Uzbeks	84.1	84.8	84.6	15.0	14.4	99.0	0.9	0.8	---
Kazakhs	78.5	80.7	80.3	12.2	11.0	91.9	9.3	8.3	---
Tajiks	76.3	77.2	75.1	22.4	21.3	98.7	1.3	1.5	---
Turkmen	92.9	93.2	92.9	4.6	5.2	98.3	2.5	1.6	---
Kyrgyz	88.5	88.5	88.0	10.0	10.0	98.1	1.5	1.5	---
Russians	82.5	82.6		---	---	---	16.5	17.4	---

Source: Rasma Karklins, *Ethnic Relations in the USSR: Perspective from Below* (Boston: Allen & Unwin, 1986), p. 232; Robert J. Kaiser, "Nations and Homelands in Soviet Central Asia," in *Geographic Perspectives on Soviet Central Asia*, edited by Robert A. Lewis (London: Routledge, 1992), p. 290.

Table 6.3
Birth Rates: Central Asia and the USSR (per thousand)

Republic	1940	1960	1970	1986
Uzbek SSR	33.80	33.60	37.80	39.80
Kyrgyz SSR	33.00	30.50	32.60	36.90
Tajik SSR	30.60	34.80	42.00	33.50
Turkmen SSR	36.90	35.20	36.90	42.40
Kazakh SSR*	---	26.20	28.10	---
USSR	31.20	17.40	20.00	24.90

*Southern Kazakhstan.
Source: Ozod Baba-Mirzayevich Ata-Mirzayev and Abdukhakim Abdukhamidovich Kayumov, "The Demography of Soviet Central Asia and Its Future Development," *Geographic Perspectives on Soviet Central Asia*, edited by Robert A. Lewis (London: Routledge, 1992), p. 215; Richard H. Rowland, "Demographic Trends in Soviet Central Asia and Southern Kazakhstan," in *Geographic Perspectives on Soviet Central Asia*, p. 224.

bearing age. Comparable rates for the RSFSR and the USSR are 2.2 and 2.5 respectively (see Table 6.4). The infant mortality rate in Central Asia is the highest among the Successor States as it was during Soviet times (see Table 6.5). In 1994, infant mortality rates ranged from a "low" of 27.4 (per 1,000 births) for Kazakhstan to a high of 47 for Tajikistan. These numbers are high compared to the Russian rate of 18.7 (which itself is high compared to rates for European countries).[11]

Economic development in Central Asia during the Soviet period centered on extractive and mining industries, and irrigated agriculture, the products of

Table 6.4
Total Fertility Rates in Central Asia, Russia, and USSR, 1958-87; Average Number

	1965-6	1969-70	1975-6	1978-9	1982-3	1986-7
Uzbek SSR	5.5	5.7	5.7	5.1	4.6	4.6
Kyrgyz SSR	4.6	4.9	4.9	4.5	4.1	4.2
Tajik SSR	5.4	5.9	6.3	6.0	5.5	5.7
Turkmen SSR	6.0	6.0	5.7	5.3	4.7	4.8
RSFSR	2.1	2.0	2.0	1.9	2.0	2.2
USSR	2.4	2.4	2.4	2.3	2.3	2.5

Source: Richard H. Rowland, "Demographic Trends in Soviet Central Asia and Southern Kazakhstan," in *Geographic Perspectives on Soviet Central Asia*, p. 226.

Table 6.5
Infant Mortality: The Number of Deaths before One Year of Age per 1,000 Births

State	1970	1980	1985	1989	1990	1992	1994
Russia	23.0	22.1	20.7	17.8	17.4	18.0	18.7
Kazakhstan	25.9	32.7	30.1	25.9	26.4	26.1	27.4
Kyrgyzstan	45.4	43.3	41.9	32.2	30.0	31.5	29.4
Tajikistan	45.9	58.1	46.8	43.2	40.7	45.9	47.0
Uzbekistan	31.0	47.0	45.3	37.7	34.6	37.4	28.3
Turkmenistan	46.1	53.6	52.4	54.7	45.2	43.6	46.4

Source: James H. Bater, *Russia and the Post-Soviet Scene* (London: Arnold, a member of the Hodder Headline Group, 1996), pp. 305, 309.

Table 6.6
Population Statistics, 1993 (in thousands); Total Gross Domestic Product (in
$bn) and Per Capita GDP

country	population	urban	rural	GDP($bn)	per capita
Kazakhstan	16,913	9,655	7,257	43.4	$2,632
Uzbekistan	21,608	8,489	13,119	47.6	$2,009
Kyrgyzstan	4,469	1,662	2,807	7.4	$1,250
Turkmenistan	3,846*	1,718	2,128	5.8	$1,250
Tajikistan	5,555*	1,689	3,866	3.6	$ 599

Source: Statistical Handbook 1994: States of the Former USSR (Washington: The World Bank,
1994), pp. 257–58, 303–4, 537–38, 583–84, 675–76; *The Economist Intelligence Unit
Country Report: Uzbekistan, 1st Quarter* (London: The Economist Intelligence Unit, 1998),
pp. 34–35.

which were distributed to the rest of the Union.[12] The economies of Central
Asia most resembled those of developing countries with raw materials and cash
crops (e.g., cotton) comprising the bulk of exports. Furthermore Central Asia
depended upon imports of basic foodstuffs including grain and other manufactured goods including clothing made from the very cotton grown in Central Asia. The traditional social structure centered around the Islamic
community is still the principal moral force uniting diverse peoples including
non-religious, non-practicing Muslims. Islam is more than a religion. It serves a
political and social function that provides a basis for morality and community. One
need not be a devoted or even practicing Muslim to be a part of the community.[13]

Third, Central Asia is politically distinguished by the lack of viable nationalist movements during the era of Perestroika and Glasnost. That is not to say
that Glasnost was not felt in Central Asia or that nationalism was not a social
force; indeed there were communal riots in places such as Osh, Kyrgyzstan and
Alm-Alta (renamed Almaty after independence), Kazakhstan. Nevertheless
nationalist movements resembling those in other Republics that advocated autonomy and later independence did not emerge as a viable political opposition
to the Soviet political leaders in power in Central Asia. All of the elected leaders
are former Soviet apparachiki and are therefore politically "trained" and socialized in the Soviet system.

These former peripheral administrators retained their power base and
stayed in power following the breakup. The Soviet First Secretaries or bosses of
these Republics managed to retain their political power after independence in
Turkmenistan and Kyrgyzstan (Saparmurad Niyazov of Turkmenistan and
Askar Akaev of Kyrgyzstan). In Kazakhstan and Uzbekistan their respective
First Secretaries were purged due to the anti-corruption campaign carried out

during Gorbachev's administration. Because of this, lower ranking party offi-cials rose to become the elected leaders of Uzbekistan (Islam Karimov) and Kazakhstan (Nursultan Nazarbayev). And, in spite of the many political changes in Tajikistan, former communists figure prominently. Former Tajik Communist First Secretary Rahmanov Nabiev replaced Kakhar Makhkamov barely three months before the formal dissolution of the Soviet Union in De-cember of 1991. Nabiev was ousted by Islamic activists who felt they had no say in the coalition governing Tajikistan and were themselves ousted and re-placed by the pro-Communist secular regime of Emomali Rahmonov. His rule in Tajikistan was contested by what can be regarded as an anti-Soviet opposi-tion and open civil war was the result.[14]

The idea presented earlier that Central Asia was essentially a third world col-ony implies a colonial dependency that carried over into the post-Soviet era. In the case of Central Asia, this dependency is marked because of the low level of development and high levels of political and economic instability. Hence the post-imperial relations are characterized by the same dependency dynamic that marked relations between center and periphery in the former empire.

HISTORICAL BACKGROUND

The manner in which the center conquered and administered the Central Asian periphery has a direct bearing on the post-Soviet pattern of relations be-tween the former center and periphery. Though the economies of all of the re-gions were directed toward the center and away from foreign powers and each other, Central Asia suffers more from this because of its economic underdevel-opment in the Soviet period. The Slavic and Baltic States are comparatively more politically stable with less ethnic tension and fewer potential border dis-putes. They also benefit from being in a more stable region of the world, a fact that has undoubtedly had a salutary effect on political and economic coopera-tion among these states. And though the Baltic and Slavic States depend on Russia and other Successor States to buy their goods, they are economically more self-sufficient relative to Central Asia.

The remainder of this section will outline the following: the form that the Soviet conquest took and the high level of popular resistance to it in Central Asia; political polices including the creation of the Central Asian Republics; the establishment of artificial borders and the Soviet attempt to suppress Is-lam; and Soviet economic policies including collectivization, the settlement of nomads, and the establishment of an economy based on the extraction of raw materials and the production of specialty agricultural commodities.

Central Asia: The Soviet Takeover and Armed Resistance

The Russian Revolution marked the conquest of Turkestan by Soviet Rus-sia. The consolidation of Soviet power in Central Asia was essentially the recolonization of the area by Russians. The reason for such a statement lies in the complete incompatibility of the Russian Revolution—its aims, goals, and ideology—with the political aspirations of the principal political entities of Turkestan.[15] The spread of Soviet power in Central Asia contrasts with that in Belarus, Ukraine, and the Baltic states in the absolute foreign nature of the imperial center vis-à-vis Central Asia. And although generalizations can be made about the Soviet transformation in what became the Republics, Central Asia was unique in that the distinctive culture and character of the region endured.

In the Soviet representation of history, political events were dichotomized. Characters in Soviet historical dramas were typically placed into one of two groups. There were various types of anti-Soviet "reactionaries" (the bad guys), and pro-Soviet "progressives" or "revolutionaries" (the good guys). Accordingly, the success of the October Revolution in Turkestan was the result of an alliance between Russians and Muslims against reactionary forces.[16] This simplistic approach overlooks the fact that political life in Central Asia was very fractious with different factions pitted against one another.

The reality was more complex. As in the Baltic and Slavic regions, the consolidation of Soviet power in Central Asia occurred in stages. First the Bolsheviks aligned themselves with the various local communist movements. During the civil war, before the Bolsheviks consolidated their rule in Russia, the Bolsheviks under Lenin's direction made it policy to publicly support independence for the peoples of Central Asia. The role of national communists in Central Asia was crucial in introducing communist ideas to the population of Central Asia. After Soviet rule took hold, they used their political contacts to promote political movements sympathetic to the Bolshevik Revolution. Support from the Russian revolutionaries as well as promises of independence provided the political bond between the national communists indigenous to Central Asia and the Russian Bolsheviks.

Marxist ideas came to Central Asia and were adopted by many Central Asian intellectuals and revolutionaries. Muslim leaders sought to reconcile Marxist ideas with the very different cultures of the Tartar, Caucasian, and Central Asian Muslims.[17] Led by Sultan Galiev, a Tartar from the Volga region, Muslim leaders sought to modify Marxist ideas to conditions in non-Russian areas. The reasons for doing so had to do with the emphasis on the working class in Communist doctrine, and suspicions of Russian dominance of Communist revolutionary organizations. Galiev's ideas became the basis for what became known as "national communism."

The first of these revisions was based on Lenin's work, *Imperialism: The Highest Stage of Capitalism*. Galiev distinguished between bourgeois and proletarian *nations*.[18] The world division of labor created a world system divided into what he termed "oppressor" and "oppressed" nations. European countries that exported capitalism to the non-European "underdeveloped" areas of the world caused this situation. He further stipulated that oppressed nations could progress from feudalism directly to socialism, thus bypassing the capitalist phase of history. Galiev thus altered Marx's definition of proletariat by extending the term to include Muslims of *all* classes! "All Muslim colonized peoples are proletarian peoples and as almost all classes in Muslim society have been oppressed by the colonialists, all classes have the right to be called 'proletarians.' "[19] In this way, national communism reinforced national differences rather than rising above them. Galiev then rejected Marx's stand on nationalism; Marx believed that the similarities among members of the same class superseded the differences between nations as a whole.

The second major revision of Galiev's pertained to his assertion that the ascendance of socialism did not mean the end of the national question. Marxist-Leninist doctrine stipulated that the national question would be solved because the source of exploitation (i.e., capitalism) would have been removed. Galiev by contrast did not assume that Russian domination would cease with the revolution and based this belief in Russia's historical behavior towards Muslim minorities. Socialism cannot be expected to change the natural aggressiveness of the Russians! National communists needed to guard against the imperialist aims of the Russians and maintain their self-reliance.[20]

Galiev's notion of national communism had a significant influence on Central Asian revolutionaries and intellectuals. The attraction of Marxism to Central Asians did not center on Marxist notions of class conflict and his critique of capitalism. Rather its attraction had to do with the more general idea of oppression and oppressed nations. In the milieu of Central Asia, the "oppressed" meant the native peasants and bourgeoisie while the "oppressors" were members of the Russian imperialist government and possibly even the Russian Bolshevik revolutionaries. Hence Marxist ideas were incorporated with indigenous customs such as Islam and were to form the basis for national liberation. More ominously from the standpoint of Russian Bolsheviks were the pronouncements of the Socialist Party of Turkestan (ERK) whose leaders urged Muslim peoples to unify on a national rather than class basis. They proclaimed as their goal, an independent, unified Turkestan.[21]

Essentially the aim of the Soviets was to integrate Central Asia into the Soviet Union while giving the appearance that this act was a purely voluntary one. Armed resistance in Central Asia continued up until about 1933.[22] Soviet rule was not fully consolidated in Central Asia before then. But the Soviet government did have control over the administrative centers, that is, the Republican capitals, which had been established by 1923. This allowed the Soviet government to begin the work of integrating Central Asia into the Soviet Union.[23] The armed movement, the Basmachi partisan movement, originated in the Fergana Valley and was dedicated to fighting Soviet power. As the Soviets consolidated their power via the Red Army in areas of Central Asia, the armed movement spread, as did its popularity. The Red Army eventually prevailed, in part due to the political divisiveness within the Basmachi movement itself.[24]

Stalin eventually purged the national communists as he consolidated Soviet power in Central Asia. In 1928, Stalin had Galiev arrested and deported to the

Solovki camps where his fate is unknown. What is known is that his arrest signaled the inward turning of the Russian Revolution following the failure of the revolution in Europe. Consolidating the Russian Revolution at home took precedence to supporting communist revolutions abroad, particularly in Asia. Galiev and other national communists had pushed to aid communist movements in the Soviet southern borderlands, in countries such as Turkey, Afghanistan, and Iran. After Stalin took power, aid to communist movements in Asia ceased in favor of establishing bilateral relations with the national governments of neighboring countries.[25]

The Creation of the Central Asian Republics

Historically Central Asia had been divided into several states or other political units according to shifting political fortunes of conquerors indigenous (Central Asia) and foreign (Russian, Chinese, and Mongol).[26] On the eve of the Russian Revolution, there were three coherent political entities on the territory of what is today considered Central Asia: Khiva, Bukhara, and Kokand. These territories along with those areas outside the borders of these units (portions of present-day Turkmenistan and Kyrgyzstan), were lumped together to form what is generally referred to as Turkestan.[27] What is today northern Kazakhstan was under Soviet control and constituted the Kyrgyzstan ASSR.[28]

These conditions made possible the Russian conquest of Central Asia that began in the mid-nineteenth century and the reconquest by the Soviets during and immediately after the Civil War (1917–1920). The Soviets exacerbated these divisive tendencies by how they drew the Republican borders. Following independence, the now "international" borders complicated inter-ethnic relations within these states which in turn complicated relations among the Central Asian states themselves and weakened their individual bargaining power with respect to Russia.

The Central Asia Republics were officially established in 1924 after the Civil War.[29] Central Asian borders among the Republics and Autonomous Oblasts shifted and were reorganized several times before they took on their present form. The last of these reorganizations came after the Kyrgyzstan and Kazakhstan attained Republican status in December of 1936.[30]

The modern borders of the Central Asian states are totally artificial in that they represent neither the boundaries of historical polities, nor the national, ethnic, or linguistic boundaries. The boundaries of the Soviet Central Asian Republics were the artificial creation of the Soviet government and divided Central Asia in such a way as to deliberately divide nations. The Soviet Republican boundaries of today's Successor States generally conform to national boundaries: Estonia comprised of the territories inhabited mostly by Estonians, Lithuania by Lithuanians, and so on. By contrast the peoples of Central Asia were united by a common religion (Sunni Islam) and mutually intelligible

Turkic languages (except Tajik, which is a form of Persian and closely related to Dari, and Farsi, spoken in neighboring Afghanistan and Iran respectively).[31]

Areas clearly dominated by one ethnic or linguistic group were ceded to the titular Republic of another. For instance, the territories of the feudal states of Khiva and Bukhara were divided among the five Republics rather than retained as individual units. The historic cities of Samarqand and Bukhara were traditional Tajik cities where the majority of inhabitants spoke the Tajik variety of Persian. They were cultural and political centers of the Indo-European Tajiks, not the Turkic Uzbeks, to whose titular Republic they were grafted by Soviet authorities. Consequently there are large numbers of Tajiks living in Uzbekistan.[32] Rather than designating one of these cities as the capital of the Tajik Republic, both were ceded to Uzbekistan while the relative backwater city Dushanbe was made the capital. Likewise, the city of Osh in present-day Kyrgyzstan is located in a portion of the Fergana Valley and is an Uzbek city. There are large numbers of Kyrgyz living in Tajikistan and vice versa. The ancient Turkmen capital of Khwarazm, now Khiva, is located in Uzbekistan.[33]

As suggested previously, the cultural unity of the region historically tended to outweigh divisiveness. Or more to the point, borders were drawn to create political and ethnic divisions in a region that was more or less united by a common religion and a common language group. This had the effect of weakening the Central Asia periphery by sowing the seeds for internal ethnic conflict. But in the name of federalism, cultural autonomy, and the linguistic development of national languages, the nascent Soviet government under Lenin divided Central Asia into five separate Republics. The potential for a united Central Asia based on a pan-Turkic and pan-Islamic national identity was regarded as a potential threat to Soviet communism. With the political division of Central Asia, the threat of a united Turkestan was avoided.

At the time of the Russian Revolution, there were only three identifiable political units in Central Asia, one of them, Kokand, controlled by pre-revolutionary Russia. Ultimately the five Central Asian Republics were formed according to identifiable common Turkic dialects and prominent ethnic groupings in the course of establishing Soviet federalism. Lenin sought to pacify the "oppressed peoples" of the Russian Empire (many of whom originally opted for independence from the Soviet Union) by adopting a federal structure for the new Soviet state.[34]

The Soviets devoted much time and energy into developing national languages, that is the languages of the new Republics. They went so far as to resurrect languages such as Belarusian, though most Belarusians spoke Russian as their first language. This policy also created written languages out of what were previously only spoken languages. In the case of Central Asia, great effort was expended to elevating the status of the national languages of the Central Asian Republics so as to emphasize their differences in the name of "cultural egalitarianism."[35]

The Soviet attempt to politically divide Central Asia also included attempts to curb Islam. Communism was essentially an atheist ideology and religion was direct competition for the loyalties of people. So for reasons of ideological purity and political advantage, religion was discouraged and at times actively persecuted. Religious places of worship, including Russian Orthodox churches, were closed to worshippers, put to uses other than religious ones (many small churches in Novgorod for example were used for storing grain), or razed. This included mosques. Ultimately this policy was a failure, and the reason for its failure lies in the resilience of Islam, as religious authorities understand it and believers practice it.

Unlike other religions, the practice of Islam is not inhibited by the absence of formal places of worship. Nor is the practice of Islam limited strictly to religious worship. Besides serving a religious function, Islam also serves an important social function; it defines a community or "Ummah." All are members of this community regardless of the level of individual piety. Centrals Asians routinely identify themselves as "Muslims," yet, in the next breath, declare themselves to be non-believers or undecided in their religious piety.[36] Islam is an integral part of *national* identity. It provides social and moral guidelines that serve to unify people around the community. It cements the roles and obligations of members and provides social cohesion in a region that might otherwise be "lawless" in the Western sense of the term (that is the absence of positive law, as exemplified by the impartial application of legal codes, court trials, and punishments). In the post-Soviet period, the resurgence of interest in Islam was in large part the conscious restoration of a national identity and tradition that is opposed to communism and indigenous to Central Asia.

Because Russian cultural and political incursions of Central Asia remained shallower than that of other peripheral regions, Islam, with its system of social order and law, remained a useful way to control the population. Therefore it was tolerated to a certain extent, and the Soviet authorities sought to co-opt and control Islam. Soviet Islam was placed under the authority of four "spiritual leaderships" or *Muftiates* that are named for the cities in which they were located: Ufa, Tashkent, Buynaksk, and Baku. It is the Tashkent Muftiate that had under its jurisdiction the Sunni Muslims of Central Asia.[37] Of the Muftiates, the Tashkent one was the most powerful: under its jurisdiction were the only two Muslim universities; it was authorized to print the Koran and the Muslim calendar; and it served as the Soviet emissary to the Muslim world outside Soviet borders.[38]

The legacy of this policy is felt in Central Asia today. Essentially it allows for a loose interpretation of Islam that recognizes the separation of religion from political life. Such a distinction between secular governments and religion is atypical of Islam, and in this way Central Asia is distinct from the Islamic world of the Middle East. The flexibility that allowed Islam to survive in the Soviet period helped to create a broad-based support for secular government which helps to explain the political survival of so many Soviet era bureaucrats and leaders.

The Economic Development of Central Asia during the Soviet Era

Though Soviet economic planning meant that the Republics tended to specialize in some area of production, the industrial and agricultural bases of the former Republics, with the possible exception of Moldova, were more diversified than those of the Central Asian Republics. The Baltic States were home to much of Soviet industry, both light and heavy. However they also produced food in sufficient quantities as well as dairy and meat products that could either be consumed locally and/or sold abroad at higher prices than grain. The same is true of Ukraine and Belarus. Even in the industrial sphere, products can be used locally because people and businesses need manufactured goods. And since manufactured products command higher prices than raw materials, the Baltic and Slavic Successor States are better off than Central Asia despite economic losses due to inefficient production methods.

Central Asia was never industrialized to the same extent as the Baltic and Slavic States. In the Soviet economic division of labor, Central Asia was assigned the role of providing agricultural goods and raw materials and minerals to the rest of the USSR. Agricultural products included some specialty items such as melons, but by far the dominant agricultural product grown in Central Asia was cotton. The primary products of Central Asia were, and continue to be, coal, iron, oil, natural gas, and non-ferrous metals.

The economy of Central Asia, which was a separate economic zone during Soviet times,[39] was characteristic of developing countries in two ways. First, primary products were shipped out of Central Asia and processed elsewhere in the USSR. And second, Central Asia was not self sufficient in food and became dependent on Russia for food imports.[40] During Soviet times cotton production became the dominant feature of Central Asian agriculture. Furthermore this imposition of what is termed the "cotton monoculture" was forced on an unwilling population and a resisting national elite. Even today cotton production remains the primary agricultural commodity of Central Asia although there has been some diversification in agricultural production.

Russian imperial authorities first introduced cotton production in Central Asia during the American Civil War in an attempt to lessen dependence on foreign cotton imports.[41] However the amount of cotton grown relative to other crops, as well as the total amount of acreage devoted to agriculture, expanded greatly during Soviet times. The consequences of this dependence on a single commodity are grave. Cotton is destructive to grow and unpredictable in terms of sales profits. Its near exclusive cultivation ensures a continued dependence on food imports and undermines state sovereignty.

The region of Central Asia is arid and dominated by deserts, but its climate is continental. Agriculture is made possible with the irrigation of its two main river systems, the Syr Dar'ya and the Amu Dar'ya. Both rivers have their origins in the eastern highlands: the Syr Dar'ya in Kyrgyzstan and the Amu Dar'ya in Tajikistan. Both flow westward and empty into the Aral Sea.

During Soviet times the amount of water diverted for irrigation increased dramatically because of the center's high production quotas for cotton. The amount of land devoted to grain and other food crops, already lowered during the last half of the nineteenth century by Tsarist Russia, decreased greatly in the Soviet era. Investment in Central Asian agriculture went into projects for expanding cotton production, including the building of hydroelectric dams, the construction of canals for water diversion, and the production of fertilizers and pesticides. The construction of the Kara Kum Canal was one such project. It was an expensive project to expand the acreage for cultivation across the Kara Kum desert in Turkmenistan. The Kara Kum Canal links the Amu Dar'ya with the Murgab river and cuts across the Kara Kum desert.

The transformation of Central Asian agriculture into a cotton monoculture was the result of Soviet economic policies and ran contrary to the interests of the people and against the objections of Soviet Central Asian cadres.[42] Objections were the result of the turbulent times from WWI through WWII when grain deliveries from Russia were unreliable and deficient. During WWI, grain deliveries decreased as food was diverted to the Western front and the war effort. After the Russian Revolution, communications to and from Central Asia ceased altogether. Grain imports from Russia ceased and shipments of raw cotton and cotton seed oil from Central Asia were left undelivered due to interruptions in rail service. Later during the 1930s, Stalin's collectivization drive resulted in drastic reductions in grain harvests and again the amount of grain delivered to Central Asia was cut back.[43]

Unreliable grain deliveries naturally led peasants to eschew cotton for grain production. Those efforts were harshly dealt with during collectivization. Soviet authorities forcibly requisitioned grain. Central Asian cadres who voiced opposition to the expansion of cotton production during times of food shortages and famine were purged. Cotton production expanded from 1.46 million acres to 3.71 million acres between 1925 and 1930. When grain deliveries decreased during this period, Faizulla Khodzhaev, chairman of the Uzbek Council of People's Commissars, told central planners that the fulfillment of cotton quota depended upon increases in grain deliveries from Russia. He publicly opposed placing cotton at the center of economic development and tried unsuccessfully to persuade central planners to construct factories and other industries in Uzbekistan. He later became a victim of Stalin's purges and was tried and executed.[44]

Popular resistance to the imposition of cotton was evident in a resurgence of the Basmachi movement. The forced settlement of nomads and the persecution of clergymen, along with Soviet grain requisitions and the imposition of cotton, fueled anti-Bolshevik sentiment among people and provided the resistance with recruits. In Tajikistan and Turkmenistan rebels managed to capture and control parts of each Republic until Soviet armed forces launched a military offensive against them.[45] Armed resistance continued until 1933.[46]

The Soviet forced settlement of nomadic people and their attempts to force them to become peasants were disastrous both in terms of declines in agricultural productivity and in human suffering. Without sufficient planning and money, people were forced into regions and towns without adequate housing or fertile soil on which to grow crops. Attempts to force them to grow cotton largely failed; unfamiliar as they were with farming they could not feed themselves or their livestock. The settlement of nomads in Kazakhstan resulted in famine and emigration to China. According to Soviet sources, the number of Kazakh households declined from 1.2 million in 1929 to 565,000 in 1936. In Tajikistan, 45,000 families were relocated from the mountain areas to the lowlands where they were forced to grow cotton. Only about one-third of them stayed in the areas to which they were relocated while fully two-thirds either fled to Afghanistan or joined the Basmachi movement.[47]

The other area of economic development in Central Asia pursued by Soviet authorities was the expansion of resource extraction. Central Asia is generally a resource poor region, especially compared to Siberia. Before the Russian Revolution, there was virtually no industry of any kind in Central Asia. Mining and oil production were under-developed in Central Asia, and Russian authorities had not even conducted geological surveys of the region.[48] Hence the infrastructure of Central Asia was developed almost wholly under the Soviets.

The infrastructure was built with the idea of supporting largely extractive industries. Economic planning was the key motivation for developmental projects in the region. Roads and railways were built to ship resources to and from Central Asia. Steel production was necessary for the maintenance of local railroads and steel plants were constructed in Uzbekistan and southern Kazakhstan.[49] Hydroelectric dams were constructed in order to provide local industries and towns with electricity. The hydroelectric potential of the highlands of Kyrgyzstan and Tajikistan was utilized for the construction of power plants that provided local cities and industries with electricity. The Kyrgyzstan dam along the Narin river provides electricity to the Republican capital of Frunze (Bishkek) and to portions of the Fergana Valley.[50] In fact Kyrgyzstan now exports hydroelectric power to eastern areas of Uzbekistan. Uzbekistan also produces electricity, though its need is greater than its output.

The most significant resource of Central Asia was petroleum and natural gas. It was important during Soviet times because it helped to alleviate the need for petroleum imports from other areas of the USSR. Where possible, Soviet planners sought to support local industries with local sources of energy. Oil production increased considerably in Turkmenistan and Uzbekistan under the Soviets, though regional needs outstrip local output.[51] Today the importance of oil and energy production is even greater, involving as it does the new states of Central Asia, Russia, and a host of foreign companies, all with an interest in exploiting Central Asia's energy reserves. New sites for petroleum have been discovered under the Caspian Sea floor while natural gas deposits in Turkmenistan are currently a lucrative source of revenue for Ashkhabad.

Many of the primary products grown or mined from Central Asia could have contributed to the development of local industries if it were not for Soviet central planners who diverted these resources to industries elsewhere in the USSR. Gas and petroleum products might have been refined in Central Asia instead of Russia.[52] Raw materials and non-ferrous metals might have been processed locally; the same goes for cotton. Khodzhaev for example unsuccessfully demanded the construction of a cotton-processing facility in Uzbekistan.[53] All of the above would have greatly increased the value and hence the price of Central Asian goods. They would have also diversified the economy by increasing the number of jobs in a region with comparatively higher levels of unemployment and underemployment. But central planning served to integrate the USSR by making the Republics dependent on Russia, either as a direct source of food and resources, or as a transportation link between the Republics. The economic cornerstone during Soviet times, Russia continues to play a pivotal role in the economies of the former Republics. And in the case of Central Asia, this dependence extended to food.

Independence by Default

The dissolution of the Soviet Union and the center's voluntary and abrupt abandonment of its periphery was a shock to the Republics of Central Asia which found themselves cast adrift from the Union. Efforts to reestablish a new Union ultimately failed but were vigorously supported by the leaders, now presidents, of the newly independent states. Unlike the leaders in the other Successor States, the leaders of the Central Asian Republics were not nationalist leaders and did not seek or originally support independence. The nationalist movements that emerged during the Gorbachev years in the other Republics actively sought public support and in fact were the very manifestation of popular will. Nationality was the issue around which popular anti-Communist and/or anti-Russian sentiment naturally coalesced. The national movements that emerged in Central Asia by contrast were more elitist and lacked a broad support base. That is not to say that Central Asia did not have its share of ethnic conflicts during this period. In fact some of the bloodiest ethnic riots occurred there. But the nationalist movements seemed to lack the ability to mobilize for political purposes and were not generally aimed at the Russians.

Mikhail Gorbachev's momentous reforms preceded (some would say caused) the break up of the Soviet Union. The formal dissolution came with Yeltsin who promised Republican leaders autonomy and independence in order to win their political allegiance in his rivalry with Gorbachev. Gorbachev's policy of Glasnost, or openness, unleashed a storm of criticism against corrupt local leaders, the police, bad housing, health care and education, and finally against the Communist Party and the central government. Eventually the criticism enveloped Gorbachev himself.

The most notable effect of Glasnost was the rise in ethnic tension and nationalism in the Republics. During the latter half of Gorbachev's tenure, the Republics declared autonomy, then later independence from the Soviet Union. This development was an unwelcome shock to Gorbachev as the intention of Glasnost was to bring pressure to bear on corrupt officials, factory managers, and other bureaucrats so as to garner support for economic reforms, or Perestroika. The idea of state-sponsored reform was to make the Soviet Union stronger, especially economically, not to dismember it. It was thought that greater openness would strengthen the Union by providing an open forum to discuss pressing problems. What occurred instead was his ouster in favor of Yeltsin.

Ethnic tension in Central Asia gathered force with the anti-corruption campaigns conducted by the center, and Glasnost, which made public economic decline and environmental degradation in Central Asia. The decline in the standard of living particularly affected the titular nationalities. Higher levels of unemployment among them vis-à-vis the "foreigners" living in "their" Republic heightened feelings of resentment. Glasnost gave these feelings a voice. Clashes between titular nationalities and assorted "foreigners" or immigrants occurred with increasing ferocity during the latter half of the 1980s.

Gorbachev was determined to strengthen the Soviet system by cracking down on corruption within the party. His mistake is that he began his campaign in the periphery against the very people, the peripheral administrators, who supported the Union. The territorial integrity of the Soviet Union depended on the cadre system whereby administrators were left to manage their Republics in return for continued loyalty to the central government in Moscow to which they owed their positions. Gorbachev's anti-corruption campaign fundamentally undercut this relationship.

Gorbachev targeted the Central Asian Republics primarily because they were the biggest drain on the Soviet budget. As a region, they were the most dependent on subsidies from the center. Accordingly the burden of restructuring would fall hard on Central Asia. His policies of restructuring indicated a desire to cut subsidies to the Central Asian Republics.

The first such campaign was directed against the head of the Communist Party of Uzbekistan, Sharif Rashidov, in January of 1986. What began as a campaign to root out corruption, ended in the condemnation of an entire people, their social and political culture.[54] What made Rashidov's downfall so spectacular was its very public nature. In the era of Glasnost, the Soviet press was relentless in its scathing coverage of first the political leaders, then those "corrupt" Uzbek traditions.

The smear campaign was so complete that it led to the unmistakable conclusion that the rehabilitation of Uzbekistan would be impossible without outside intervention. At first the scandal concentrated on uncovering the extent of Rashidov's falsification of Uzbek cotton harvests, but it quickly spread to dozens of minor officials and involved other institutions such as the state-run University of Tashkent. Officials administering the university were accused of granting admission and diplomas based on nationality (favoring Uzbeks), political connections, and nepotism. The Uzbek affair dragged on into 1988 with new and shocking revelations about the corruption and depravity of the Uzbek government and militia (police) and their ties to the Uzbek Mafia. It was uncovered for example that the Uzbek Mafia ran protection rackets, monopolized the trafficking of legal and illegal goods and services, and even served as hired killers. All of this occurred with the complicity of the Uzbek government. These denunciations were aired publicly in Party Congress forums and in the media.[55]

The tone of the media coverage suggested that Uzbek corruption was somehow unique in its magnitude, a contention that provoked popular indignation in Uzbekistan. The perception that Uzbekistan was singled out and unfairly attacked was undoubtedly heightened by the policy of Glasnost that ensured these denunciations would be very public and harsh. Before Glasnost, Rashidov and his accomplices might have been quietly removed and broader judgments about Uzbek traditions and corrupt practices would have been avoided. As it stood, attacks from the center motivated Uzbeks to support their leaders regardless of the charges against them. The Uzbek scandal also raised the question of whether or not the center, that is the Russians, should step in to govern Uzbekistan. The corruption scandal justified Russian authority over the Muslim periphery.[56]

This idea of russifying the higher echelons of power in the periphery had immediate consequences in Kazakhstan. The First Secretary of the Communist Party in Kazakhstan, Dinmukhomed Kunaev, was deposed in a similar anti-corruption campaign conducted by the center. A Russian, Gennady Kolbin, replaced Kunaev, an ethnic Kazakh. The reaction of the Kazakhs was immediate; Kolbin's appointment sparked rioting in Alma-Ata in December of 1986, where demonstrators shouted nationalist slogans and demanded the return of the Republic to the Kazakhs. The appointment of an ethnic Russian to a post usually reserved for cadres from the titular nationality was interpreted as a repressive move.[57] Although the riot was quickly put down, it was a signal of events to come.

The anti-corruption campaigns in Central Asia and the subsequent popular outrage they provoked among the peoples against whom these campaigns were waged were a prelude to the ethnic disturbances and rioting that plagued the Central Asian Republics during the waning years of the Soviet Union. Many of these riots resulted in extensive property damage, injuries, and even deaths. The riots had one common denominator. They were spontaneous outbursts directed at "foreigners," that is minorities. Chiefly these minorities were displaced peoples who had been resettled in Central Asia.

That Central Asia became a dumping ground for political dissidents and collaborationists was a serious bone of contention because their numbers were significant enough to tilt the ethnic balance away from the titular nationality. And these minorities did not assimilate but maintained their separate national identity. Foreigners also came to Central Asia to work, and not just Russians. In several cases, the minority group in question had the added distinction of being in an enviable economic situation vis-à-vis the locals. The rallying cry of demonstrators consistently proclaimed that their Republic belonged to them (the titular nationality) and that all foreigners should leave.[58]

On May 6, 1989, a day after the May Day celebrations in Ashkhabad in the Turkmen Republic, a riot erupted. It included mostly young people who rampaged through the city and demolished kiosks and other businesses. Reports of the incident were sketchy, but the daily *Turkmenskaya iskra* blamed the incident on hooligans and other criminal elements who took advantage of what were mostly privileged youths, and incited them to riot. The daily stated that these youths, as members of the more prosperous segment of the population, resented Perestroika because it meant the forfeiture of their privileges.[59] The daily went on to describe how the youths shouted ethnic slogans aimed at inciting ethnic conflict and vandalized foreign-run businesses. It mentioned that the ethnic slurs were directed against Armenians but failed to report the national origins of those who ran the businesses that were vandalized.[60]

On May 23, 1989, an argument in a produce market in the small city of Kusavia near Tashkent in the Uzbek Republic turned into a full blown riot that quickly spread to neighboring towns in the Fergana valley. Uzbek gangs targeted those of Caucasian nationality, set houses on fire, assailed public buildings, and attempted to raid police headquarters to seize weapons.[61] The Meskhetian Turks were targeted in the Fergana Valley; several of them were killed and their homes burned.

The Meskhetian Turks are a Caucasian people who were deported by Stalin to the Uzbek Republic. Reportedly they refused to join the Uzbeks in a pan-Islamic front that was to drive out the Russians.[62] As the riots spread throughout the Fergana Valley, Uzbek groups demanded the removal of the Meskhetian Turks from Uzbekistan. The Uzbek riots were the most spectacular in the number casualties. In all more than one hundred died, thousands were injured, hundreds of homes and buildings were destroyed, and more than 34,000 Meskhes were forced to leave the Uzbek Republic.[63] The "situation" in the Fergana Valley was not stabilized before the 19th of June.[64]

June 16, 1989 in the town of Novy Uzen in the Kazakh Republic, a fight in a dance hall broke out between Caucasian nationals and Kazakhs which escalated into rioting, with rioters vandalizing buildings and attacking people with crude weapons. They targeted the building of the city's Internal Affairs Department. Demonstrations in front of the city's government buildings followed the next day, with demonstrators complaining about high prices and general social conditions. They demanded that all people of Caucasian nationality be deported from the city and that the tour-of-duty method of procuring workers for the oil and gas industries be stopped. The Caucasians in Novy Uzen were guest workers who had superior standards of living as compared to the titular nationality.[65] Unrest in Novy Uzen continued for the better part of two weeks. According to the Kazakh daily, *Kazakhstanskaya pravda*, five people died of their injuries and 20 people were hospitalized.[66]

In January of 1990, Frunze, the capital of the Kyrgyz Republic, was the site of an anti-immigrant demonstration. It seems that there were rumors that refugees from the civil war in Azerbaijan were to be resettled in the Kyrgyz Republic. On the basis of these rumors, the Kyrgyz came out to demonstrate against the movement of people into their Republic. They camped out on vacant land in Frunze. No people were subsequently settled in the Kyrgyz Republic though it was determined that the refugees in question were Russian and that authorities were considering where to settle them. Later that year, in June, ethnic clashes broke out in the Kyrgyz City of Osh between Kyrgyz and Uzbek residents.[67]

In the Tajik Republic, demonstrations against non-Tajik minorities targeted Russians indirectly, and Uzbeks and smaller minorities of the Pamir directly. Tajiks were angered over the treatment of Tajiks in Uzbekistan and demanded the return of the cities of Bukhara and Samarqand.[68]

Although incidents of ethnic discord became prevalent in Central Asia, the ethnic component of these disturbances was largely overshadowed by low standard of living and poor social conditions. The immigrants who settled in the Central Asian Republics were a reminder of the technological backwardness of the titular nations and their low status within the Soviet Union.[69]

Gorbachev's policies of Glasnost and Perestroika unleashed tension and conflict in Central Asia. The targets for Central Asian frustrations were non-titular minorities. These conflicts, though ethnic in form, were the result of economic decline and worsening social conditions, especially unemployment. It is curious that Russian minorities were targeted less than non-Russian minorities. Most often clashes occurred between two Muslim nationalities. Social unrest in Central Asia was a reflection of local tensions and not of defiance against Moscow, much less a push for independence. Cutting ties to the Russia was never in the political equation of Central Asia.

RELATIONS WITH RUSSIA

The following sums up relations between Russia and the Central Asian states immediately following the dissolution of the Union. The Central Asian states sought to retain close links to Russia while the actions of the latter demonstrated a clear unwillingness to bear the cost of supporting the former Central Asian Republics. Central Asian leaders were the most vigorous supporters of maintaining the Union, and later signing the amended Union Treaty drawn up by Gorbachev that other Republics had refused to sign. Efforts to form a new union to replace the old remained stillborn largely due to Moscow's indifference. Of all the regions of the former periphery, Russia is least committed to Central Asia. As it became clear that an unstable Central Asia represented a security threat to the Russian Federation, and that the power vacuum left by Russia's retreat might be filled by undesirable (from the Russian point of view) elements, Russia made efforts to retain its presence in Central Asia.

Several analysts have noted that the Central Asian states had independence pushed on them. The Central Asian states supported the new Union Treaty unveiled by Gorbachev in March of 1991. That plan fell through with the ascendancy of Yeltsin and the introduction of a tripartite union agreement among the Slavic states of Russia, Ukraine, and Belarus. The Central Asian states, led by Nazarbayev of Kazakhstan, expressed dissatisfaction that they should be left out.[70] After Russia declared its independence in early December of 1991, the Central Asian states immediately set about looking for another union to replace the Soviet Union. The CIS was born.

As noted previously, the purpose of the CIS was to minimize the difficulties of the post-Soviet era by maintaining a common economic space. This meant the use of a single currency and the prohibition of tariffs and other impediments to trade. The CIS was also to provide members with a common security umbrella. The CIS busily passed provisions and decrees that remained unenforced and was eventually declared defunct by many as it became clear that multilateral diplomacy was giving way to bilateral relations between Russia and each of the Successor States.

Russia itself spearheaded the demise of the CIS. By its actions, Russia sealed the fate of the CIS. In direct violation of its provisions, Russia terminated the ruble zone by restricting its monetary policy and imposing outrageous currency and banking restrictions on the Successor States that most of the Successor States, including even Belarus, were forced to introduce their own currencies. The erection of trade barriers among the Successor States soon followed. The terms of trade such as the currency to be used (hard currency or "soft") or whether to conduct old-fashioned, Soviet-styled barter trade, became a matter of bilateral relations among the Successor States and in fact differed from state to state according to the commodities in question. For example, the terms of Russian energy deliveries to the former periphery are negotiated separately between Russia and individual Successor States.

The same was true with military and security arrangements. With Kazakhstan, Russia was concerned with the dismantling of nuclear weapons that were placed there. With Turkmenistan, Kyrgyzstan, and Tajikistan, mutual security arrangements centered on the defense of the southern borders with Iran, China, and Afghanistan respectively. For instance, the Russian presence in Tajikistan was so extensive that Afghan border guards negotiated directly with Russian military commanders.[71]

PROSPECTS FOR INDEPENDENCE

Though there are factors that could facilitate Central Asian development away from dependence on Russia, on balance there are many more significant factors working against it. The main factor that may mitigate dependency on Russia is the negligent attitude of Russia itself. The perception of the southern periphery as burdensome is hardly conducive to economic and political inter-vention, much less outright acquisition that would be even more costly. Still geopolitical realities will force Russia to recognize the need for continued in-teraction with Central Asia for security reasons.

At present the geopolitical realities of the post-Soviet space have remained constant. The Central Asian cadres, now leaders of sovereign states, are con-cerned with the development of their respective countries, and of avoiding economic collapse. They also must be concerned with their own political sur-vival. Central Asian leaders will look for investment aid wherever they can find it. This leaves the potential for outside states to fill the power vacuum left by the Soviets. For various reasons, however, Central Asian leaders have found it easier to make use of their Soviet-era political connections with the center, as much out of habit as necessity.

Factors Favoring Independence from Russia: Political Attitudes in Russia

Neither the Russian government nor the Russian public is mentally or phys-ically prepared to undertake a military operation to restore the empire. This is due to the lack of national will on the part of the Russian government for a massive military venture on a scale large enough to overcome the popular re-sistance that is bound to be exhibited. In the case of Central Asia, the geo-graphical remoteness of Central Asia and the "foreignness" of its people no doubt contribute to the Russian public's apathy toward Central Asia and an-tipathy toward military adventurism.

The high level of support shown among ordinary Russians and the Russian government for reintegration of Belarus and Ukraine (which, although high, is not universal), drops off considerably when the question of Central Asia is added to the equation. The general perception is that Central Asia is not "Rus-sian" land (with the possible exception of northern Kazakhstan). In addition Central Asia, being the poorest region of the former Soviet Union, was consid-ered to be an economic drain on Russia. The perception I encountered was that Russia was better off without Central Asia.[72] Central Asians are regarded as "foreign" by Russians despite having coexisted within the same political system.

This fact is supported by, and probably the result of, a combination of fac-tors that have isolated Central Asians from Russians and other Slavs. Geo-graphically Central Asia is far removed from European Russia. In comparison to nationals of the other Republics, Central Asians were the least likely to live outside of their native homeland. Of those that did reside outside the borders of their titular Republics, most lived in adjacent areas within Central Asia (see Table 6.2).[73] These exceptions are the result of the artificial nature of the borders drawn among the Republics by the Soviet authorities that divided a once united region. Borders were deliberately drawn so as to limit the potential for cooperation among the Central Asian Republics.

Interaction between Russians and Central Asians was minimal except in the Central Asian Republican capitals where there were substantial numbers of Russians. And as illustrated by the data collected by Rasma Karklins, levels of intermarriage between Russians and Central Asians were very low. Out of all the Soviet peoples, the highest values for the Index of endogamy (in excess of 90 percent except for Tajiks) went to Central Asians.[74]

Factors Working against Independence from Russia

Conditions in the Central Asian periphery on balance do not favor full independence from Russia. The conditions that make peripheral territories vulnerable to conquest, or in the case of Russia and Central Asia, extensive influence and interference from the former center, are all applicable to Central Asia. These conditions include the following: (1) enduring imperial linkages between the Russian and the Central Asian governments; (2) the absence of effective, workable relations among the Central Asia states; and (3) disunity within the states themselves and the potential for popular resistance to government that makes them more vulnerable to Russian influence (i.e., they will take what they can get from Russia if it bolsters their position vis-à-vis the political opposition and a potentially restive population).

The Endurance of Old Imperial Links

The old imperial links are still the most dominant ones. The phrase "imperial links" refers specifically to the vertical administrative links maintained between Russia and the administrative apparatus (now the governments) of each of the Central Asian states. The vertical pattern of political and economic linkages between the center and each of the respective peripheral territories was identified as one of the definitive characteristics of empires. The Central Asian leaders rely on this vertical structure. All of the Successor States, and the Central Asian states are no exception, have tended to favor bilateral relations with Russia rather than multilateral relations where the Successor States in effect compete with one another. And since Central Asia leaders have no nationalist objections to a Russian presence (in fact they welcome it), this situation is unlikely to change in the foreseeable future.

Russia is in fact the only power recognized as the legitimate mediator among the Central Asia states. A summit held by four CIS member states in 1997—Russia, Belarus, Kazakhstan, and Kyrgyzstan—with the intent to establish a common market modeled on the EU made little headway because of Belarusian-Kazakh competition as to which state will be closer to Russia. Kazakh President Nazarbayev upstaged Belarusian President Lukashenka when he submitted a draft document for the proposed common market at the meeting. Lukashenka's resentment of the Kazakh president translated into possible Belarusian resistance to integration along the lines presented by Nazarbayev unless the Kazakh president were to be supported by Russia in which case Belarusian acquiescence is assured.[75]

Another example of Russia's mediation is its role in the Tajik conflict. It was Russia that sent troops to Tajikistan to shore up the "Soviet-style" Tajik government of Emomali Rahmanov. And though Iran tried to mediate the conflict (on the side of the Islamic opposition), as did Uzbekistan (on the side of Rahmanov and against the Islamic opposition), it was Russia that played a pivotal role in the peace process. The Tajiks publicly acknowledged this themselves. In a statement to journalists the Tajik leadership emphasized Russia's role in the region. "Tajikistan's leadership has welcomed . . . all constructive initiatives . . . from the United Nations and other influential international organizations . . . and above all from Russia which is the most vigorous mediator in the process of ensuring regional security and stabilizing the sociopolitical situation in Tajikistan and a guarantor of peace and stability in the region."[76]

The bulk of peacekeeping troops sent to Tajikistan came from Russia though there were a few units from Kazakhstan, Uzbekistan, and Kyrgyzstan. All the units are under Russian command.[77] The primary purpose of sending Russian troops was to regain control of the Tajik border with Afghanistan, a border that was porous and problematic to patrol.[78] Russian border troops have frequently been the target of armed attacks by militant Muslims and several have been killed.[79] The very fact that Russia sent troops to defend the border of a state with a secular government in power pitted Russia against the Tajik opposition. The most powerful faction of the opposition is the Islamic faction, as it is the Tajik Islamists and their counterparts in Afghanistan, Pakistan and Uzbekistan who stand the most to gain from an open border. Nevertheless, with Russian support (though many in Russia believed this to be a huge mistake) Rahmanov signed an agreement to share power with the opposition.[80] And in its attempt to foster a dialogue with the Tajik opposition, Russia appealed not to neighboring countries, but to the United Nations and supported a strengthening of the UN mission in Tajikistan. Likewise, the UN envoy met with high-ranking members of the Russian Defense Ministry and the Federal Border Service, not with Iran, Pakistan, or Uzbekistan.[81]

The lack of international support for these countries forced them to rely on Moscow for assistance, both military and economic. This is especially true of Tajikistan and Kyrgyzstan. Resource-poor Kyrgyzstan is hardly an investment magnet. The only resource of any value is gold, but Kyrgyzstan's gold reserves require much investment before their extraction produces any profit. And since 1990 Kyrgyzstan's economic decline has been the most drastic of the former Republics. Unemployment exceeds 25 percent in many areas; the Kyrgyz government consistently runs budget deficits while uncollected taxes account for an estimated one-quarter of total state revenue.[82] Russia remains Kyrgyzstan's main trading partner while Uzbekistan runs a close second. Russia however remains the most attractive partner since Uzbekistan has taken flagrant advantage of Kyrgyzstan's plight (this will be discussed more fully in the following section).[83] Tajikistan, torn by conflict and with few natural resources, is not even in the running for foreign investment. Russia remains the main source of aid and the principal trading partner.[84] Other countries shy away from trade due to the weakness of the som and Tajik ruble and the fact that neither country can pay world prices for commodities (except China, which does a roaring informal border trade with Kyrgyzstan, largely through barter).[85] Russian interest in both areas lies primarily in the concern for Russian minorities and patrolling the borders with China and Afghanistan. Trade with these countries is not in Russia's economic self-interest; Russia's decision to trade with both countries is a political rather than economic one.

Strained Relations among Central Asian States

Relations among the Central Asian states themselves remain underdeveloped and are characterized by a great deal of mistrust. If a vertical pattern of political and economic linkages between the center and each of the respective peripheral territories was identified as one of the definitive characteristics of empires, a related characteristic also definitive of empires is the absence of horizontal linkages among the peripheral territories. This leaves each of the Central Asia states to deal with Russia on its own. Furthermore, as compared to neighboring Central Asian states, each tends to regard Russia as the lesser of two evils.

The different foreign policy agendas pursued by the Central Asian states reflect the differences among them in terms of relative economic strength and geography. In short, the small Central Asian states distrust the large ones. By far the largest state in the region, by population and the size of its economy, is Uzbekistan (see Table 6.6). Kazakhstan runs a close second, but Kazakhstan seeks a balanced foreign policy since it alone among the Central Asian states shares a long border with Russia. In relations to its smaller neighbors, Uzbekistan's population is four times the size of the third most populous country in the region, Tajikistan.[86] Uzbekistan is strategically located, occupying the fertile Fergana valley. Uzbek President Karimov has pursued an openly hegemonic foreign policy; Uzbekistan has militarily intervened in Tajikistan against the Tajik Islamic opposition and bullied Kyrgyzstan. Karimov's foreign policy in the region in large part reflects his domestic political policies.

Karimov has been determined to stamp out Islamic opposition. The Uzbek government distinguishes between government sanctioned Islam and Islam not sanctioned by the government. The latter is considered to be criminal.

Uzbekistan has retained the Soviet institution of Mufti. Islamic clerics and mosques must be registered and approved by the government in order to become legal. Karimov has used the police to arrest unregistered Islamic clerics and their followers. Arrests of clerics and their followers have occurred since independence and Karimov has publicly blamed Kyrgyzstan and Tajikistan for training Uzbek youths as Islamic militants.

More recently, the Uzbek Foreign Minister Abdulaziz Kamilov publicly accused Pakistan of training guerrillas with the express purpose of overthrowing the Uzbek government in the beginning of 1998. The camps where guerrillas are being trained have been positively identified inside Pakistan. According to the Uzbek Ministry of Foreign Affairs, it was the Pakistani trained guerrillas who were responsible for the attacks that killed at least four policemen in the Namagan Province in late 1997.[87] Namagan is located in the middle of the Fergana Valley and is the center for religious activity.[88] Several of the camps were identified through the testimonies of those guerrillas who were arrested. The Uzbek Ministry of Internal Affairs stated that these guerrillas are receiving Islamic indoctrination of an extremist Islamic philosophy based on Wahhabism, a variant of Islam practiced in Saudi Arabia.[89] Despite some misgivings toward Islamabad, Kamilov publicly stated that his government did not believe that Pakistani officials were involved.[90]

Karimov's preoccupation with Islamic fundamentalism prompted him to intervene in Tajikistan on the side of the pro-Communist Tajik government that won 57 percent of the vote in the first presidential election in 1991. When the Communist government in Tajikistan refused to share power or institute democratic reforms that might have provided a legal, legitimate role for the opposition, the two largest opposition groups, the Democratic Party and the Islamic Renaissance, formed a political alliance in what became the United Tajik Opposition, or UTO. Fighting broke out after anti-government political demonstrations took place from March to May of 1992 in Dushanbe when people from several clan groups were bused in to participate. As a result of the demonstrations, a coalition government was formed.[91]

But Tajik government forces and their Russian and Uzbek patrons retaliated. Pro-Communist forces with help from Russian and Uzbek troops attacked various Tajik factions or clans that were known to support the opposition (the Kulobis, the Pamiris, and the regions of Qurghonteppa and Vakhash Valley which are home to the Gharmis).[92] Essentially these armed attacks were large-scale massacres involving the razing of entire villages and the migration of hundreds of thousands of refugees to Afghanistan. Uzbek troops were directly involved in these massacres.[93] Under such circumstances, these clans eventually began to fight back and the political plank of the Islamic forces became much more radical.

The Uzbek government began to support peace efforts to end the war after it became apparent that a continuation of the war would only prolong the Russian presence in Tajikistan. A strong Russian presence in Tajikistan is regarded as a direct challenge to Uzbek supremacy and Karimov was anxious to establish Uzbekistan's leadership position in the region.[94] But the Uzbek role in the Tajik civil war has made the Tajik government wary of Uzbek intentions and so ensures that the Tajik government will keep a line open to Moscow.

When the Tajik government eventually agreed to share power with the Islamic opposition, Dushanbe began to distance itself from Uzbekistan. Having been torn by civil war and having had a succession of defunct governments, Tajikistan, currently headed by President Emomali Rahmonov, formally legalized the Islamic Renaissance Party and the secular Democratic Party of the UTO. As a result of the 1997 peace agreements, the government agreed to allot 30 percent of government posts to opposition members.

But the political feud in Tajikistan is not yet in the past. Since the agreement was reached, its implementation has been a source of contention. The leader of the UTO, Abdullo Said Nuri, walked out of talks with Rahmonov over disagreements on the transfer of posts to the opposition.[95] The UTO accused Rahmonov of ill will and Rahmonov accused the UTO militants of ties to the Afghani government, not registering with the Tajik government, and not surrendering weapons.[96] The UTO also has close ties with Uzbek guerrillas in the Fergana Valley.[97] Power sharing nonetheless was implemented with Russian backing, though the Uzbek government and some Russian analysts warned that sharing power with the Islamists was a fatal error; it is a statement that reflects the concerns of both Russia and Uzbekistan over Islam as a political force.[98]

Tajikistan mistrusts Uzbekistan and has preferred to turn to Russia for trade and mediation in its internal conflicts in order to lessen its dependence on Uzbekistan, who is its second largest trading partner. Tajikistan seeks a stable, balanced relationship with Afghanistan and Iran.[99]

Kyrgyzstan for its part distrusts Uzbekistan. Uzbek territorial claims on the city of Osh are no secret and Karimov openly criticizes Bishkek for its treatment of the Uzbek minority. Akaev has reason to fear Uzbekistani intervention should ethnic tensions reminiscent of the 1990 Osh riots erupt again.[100] There is a real danger that Uzbeks in Osh will one day demand to be united with Uzbekistan.[101]

Uzbekistan's military involvement in Tajikistan demonstrates the willingness of Tashkent to flaunt its growing influence in Central Asia. Shortly after the Kyrgyz som was introduced as currency in 1993, Tashkent cut off gas supplies to Kyrgyzstan until the latter used $13 million of its IMF loan to stabilize the Uzbek economy by buying up Kyrgyz rubles that had ended up in Uzbekistan! After Uzbekistan again cut gas supplies to Kyrgyzstan in 1993, Akaev had to devote much energy to flattering Karimov at a Kyrgyz-sponsored ceremony given by the quasi-governmental society Rukhniyat (or Spiritual Renewal) in January of 1994. The ceremony was in honor of Karimov who was awarded the society's "Man of the Year for 1994." Apparently when Nursultan Nazarbayev was awarded this honor the month before for 1993, Karimov was angered.[102] The only country trusted by Kyrgyzstan is Kazakhstan. Kyrgyzstan is closely integrated with Kazakhstan being Kyrgyzstan's second most important trading partner after Russia.[103]

Turkmenistan has sought to avoid conflicts with its neighbors and promote diplomacy abroad by declaring neutrality. To this end Niyazov has made appeals to the world community to grant Turkmenistan the status of a neutral state.[104] Claims to neutrality aside, Turkmenistan's relations with its neighbors, particularly Uzbekistan, are difficult. Fortunately for Ashkhabad, Tashkent's attention has been directed primarily towards Kyrgyzstan and Tajikistan. Still there are some outstanding issues between Turkmenistan and Uzbekistan such as Turkmenistan's claims to the city of Khiva, and conflicts over the waters of the Amu Dar'ya. The Amu Dar'ya comprises much of the Uzbek-Turkmen border. Both states are heavily dependent on its waters for irrigation. The Kara Kum canal, which diverts a considerable amount of water for irrigation for Turkmenistan alone, is a potential source of tension between the two states that are heavily dependent on the river.[105]

Disunity within the Central Asian States

There is disunity and the potential for conflict *within* each of the Central Asian states as well as among them. Their internal political turmoil makes them vulnerable to pressures from the former imperial center. It also accounts for the lack of enthusiasm for independence on the part of the Central Asian leaders. Each of the five Central Asian states suffers from two broad conditions that have the potential for generating instability and perhaps war. They are poor, even by the Soviet standards, and they have large numbers of minorities resulting from the Soviet-drawn borders and Soviet policies of resettling "enemy" peoples in Central Asia. In practice, both conditions are intertwined. As evident in the riots of the latter half of the 1980s, socioeconomic conditions played a key role in exacerbating inter-ethnic tensions. The perception that some groups, particularly those not from the titular nationality, have superior access to superior housing and jobs fuels popular rage. The disturbances in Novy Uzen for example centered on the employment practices of the oil and gas companies. This would not have been such an explosive issue if Novy Uzen did not suffer from high unemployment rates among ethnic Kazakhs. As many as 1,500–2,000 young Kazakhs were estimated to be out of work.[106] Similar frustrations led to the rampages in Uzbekistan; Uzbek demonstrators complained that the good jobs were taken by the Azeris and that they were condemned to work in the cotton industry for low pay.[107] Though these riots threatened the unity of the Soviet Union, future disturbances will threaten the unity and stability of the Central Asian states.

In Kazakhstan, the main internal threats to stability lie in the fact that almost half of its population is Russian and resides primarily in the north. The Russian minority has so far concentrated its energies on complaining about the treatment of Russians at the hands of Kazakhs. It has been alleged that Russian farmers have been robbed and harassed and that the Kazakh government has failed to prosecute the culprits because they (the culprits) are Kazakh and have family connections to the government. They also resent the imposition of the Kazakh language and feel that they are being shut out of political life. Indeed since independence, civil administrative positions have increasingly gone to ethnic Kazakhs. In the March 1994 parliamentary elections, Kazakhs won 105 of the 177 seats. The resignation of Prime Minister Sergei Tereshchenko later that year eliminated the last Russian, indeed Slav, from the top echelon of the Kazakh government.[108]

Ethnic tensions between Russians and Kazakhs have been fueled by the deteriorating economy. The northern town of Zhanatas for example has suffered from massive layoffs, and a large segment of the population is unemployed. Those still working have not been paid for over two years. Most homes are without electricity, gas, or plumbing; residents have been installing old-fashioned wood-burning stoves. Hunger strikes have been held in front of Fosforit, the principal employer in the city. The Kazakh government had barred Russian television film crews from reporting on the situation in Zhanatas. Clashes between Russian film crews and the Kazakh Special Forces resulted in the confiscation of filmed footage.[109] All of this has been reported in the Russian press.

Nazarbayev's motion to move the capital of Kazakhstan from Almaty (so renamed after independence) to Akmola reflects his concern that the Russian minorities, who inhabit the northern area of Kazakhstan that borders on the Russian Federation, might in the future demand succession from Kazakhstan and integration with Russia. The motivation behind the move is twofold: the move to Akmola would shift the weight of government to the north and dilute the power and influence of southern Kazakh factions entrenched in the south.[110] This suggests that Nazarbayev's power is not fully secure, even among Kazakhs in the south.

Akmola is a small town located in northern Kazakhstan in the heart of the Russian area; in order to serve as a capital, basic infrastructure is needed including roads, electricity, and plumbing for sewage and drinking water. In short an entire town will have to be built virtually from scratch. Nazarbayev has solicited financial aid from foreign investors, and has placed the cost of building new embassies on the visiting states. The move from Almaty to Akmola has met with considerable resistance from Nazarbayev's own government, not to mention foreign diplomats, and foreign investors. Nazarbayev had conducted periodic checkups on his ministers to ensure they do not sneak back to Almaty![111] Nazarbayev then changed the name of Akmola to Astana in June of 1998 because the former means "white grave" in Kazakh. Though the Kazakh president fervently denied that Akmola meant white grave, he nonetheless changed the name. This author found in a Russian-Kazakh dictionary that the meaning given to "belyi" (white in Russian) was "ak." One of the

Kazakh words given for the meaning "mogli" (grave in Russian) was "mola."[112]

The potential for instability is still high in Tajikistan. Although open conflict has ceased and a power sharing arrangement worked out between the opposition and the Rahmanov government, hostilities could resume, particularly if the Islamists attempt to implement the more radical elements of their political platform. By contrast, Rahmanov has expressed the view that Tajikistan will be a secular, democratic state governed by the rule of law. Turadzhonzoda, the leader of the Tajik opposition, has declared that the express goal of the Movement for the Islamic Revival of Tajikistan was the Islamization of Tajikistan.[113] Thus far the power sharing arrangement seems to have moderated the actions of the Islamic opposition. Should that state of affairs change, armed conflict could resume.

In Uzbekistan, the potential for internal instability stems from the growing impoverishment of the country combined with the social consequences for the desiccation of the Aral Sea. The desiccation also affects Kazakhstan and Turkmenistan. But it is Turkmenistan and Uzbekistan that grow most of Central Asia's cotton and hence are dependent on the waters of the Amu and Syr Dar'ya that empty into the Aral Sea. Because most of the water from both rivers is diverted to irrigation, only a trickle reaches the Aral Sea.

Measured in the 1980s, the social consequences of this crisis are many. People from afflicted areas have moved to neighboring towns in large numbers. Unemployment is endemic for those who remain (in the Kazakh city of Aralsk, fully one-half of the population is unemployed). Health hazards such as hepatitis, dysentery, and tuberculosis have reached epidemic proportions.[114] Infant mortality is three to four times the Soviet average as recently as 1988 in Karakalpakstan, Uzbekistan and in the Tashauz province in Turkmenistan.[115] Pesticides and fertilizers have contaminated groundwater but the people, lacking any alternatives, continue to drink it.[116] Reports on clashes between inhabitants on either side of the Amu Dar'ya have been suppressed in the media. People living downstream are forced to use water that has been contaminated by fertilizers and pesticides. Turkmenistan is essentially dependent on Uzbekistan for water for the Tashauz province since the river at that point runs though the Uzbek territory of Khorezm.[117]

The economic and social crisis in both Turkmenistan and Uzbekistan could result in the strengthening of the Islamic forces (that is those not co-opted by the state). And although there are a fair number of minorities—Tajik, Kyrgyz, Russian, and so forth—Uzbekistan is not threatened by irredentism among its minority populations.

In Kyrgyzstan, the principal source of internal instability continues to be the exodus of the Russian minority and the lack of ethnic cadres to fill managerial positions. However the reason for the mass flight from Kyrgyzstan has less to do with ethnicity and more to do with living conditions in Kyrgyzstan that are low even by the standards of Central Asia. Simply put, there are few prospects for the Kyrgyz economy.

The only thriving area of the economy seems to lie in the production and trafficking of narcotics. Drug usage among Kyrgyz citizens represents a potential social problem. The southern portion of Kyrgyzstan has become an important source of cannabis that is estimated to cover as much as 60,000 hectares. Traditionally Kyrgyzstan grew opium poppy though as a result of its having been banned, its growth and cultivation seem to be limited to backyard, private plots.[118]

Another threat to the internal stability of Kyrgyzstan is the Uzbek minority that is concentrated in the Kyrgyz portion of the Fergana Valley and its largest city, Osh. The aggressiveness of Uzbek foreign policy and nationalist rhetoric has the potential for inciting the Uzbek population across the border into Kyrgyzstan. As it is, Uzbek news broadcasts are easily picked up in Osh. The issue of ethnic tension in Osh is an extremely sensitive one for the Kyrgyz government. As mentioned previously, Kyrgyzstan is vulnerable to Uzbek pressures. A repeat of the 1990 incident, in which thousands died, might provoke more than a verbal response from Uzbekistan.[119]

CONCLUSION

Conditions in the Central Asian periphery are not favorable for the elimination of the dependency of these governments on Russia. Central Asia's economic and social underdevelopment has hindered the creation of coherent national identities. This lack of nationalism on the part of these states is crucial to understanding Central Asia's post-Soviet dependency on Russia. The importance of nationalism in breaking away from a former imperial power is perhaps best illustrated by the Baltic case.

NOTES

1. David Rieff, "From Khan to Tsar to Comrade to Khan," *Transitions*, vol. 4, no. 1 (1997) p. 14.

2. Ibid., p. 19.

3. Martha Brill Olcott, *Central Asia's New States: Independence, Foreign Policy, and Regional Security* (Washington, D.C.: United States Institute of Peace Press, 1996) p. 46.

4. Marco Buttino, "Politics and Social Conflict during a Famine," in *a Collapsing Empire: Underdevelopment, Ethnic Conflicts and Nationalisms in the Soviet Union*, edited by Marco Buttino (Milan: Fondazione Giangiacomo Feltrinelli, 1993) p. 258.

5. Ralph S. Clem, "The Frontier of Colonialism in Russian and Soviet Central Asia," in *Geographic Perspectives on Soviet Central Asia*, edited by Robert A. Lewis (London: Routledge, 1992) pp. 24–25.

6. *The Soviet Union: A Systematic Geography*, edited by Leslie Symons (New York: Routledge, 1983), p. 101; Rasma Karklins, *Ethnic Relations in the USSR: The Perspective from Below* (Boston: Allen & Unwin, 1986) p. 233. Gennady V. Kolbin, the First Secretary of the Communist Party of Kazakhstan officially noted this low level of bilingualism, in a speech given to Kazakh journalists. Appointed to the post by Gorbachev to replace Kunaev (a native Kazakh) following rioting in Alma-Ata in 1986, Kolbin, who was a native Russian and therefore not popular in Kazakhstan, acknowledged that bilingualism in Kazakhstan was "mainly a phenomenon" of Kazakhs rather than Russians. According to Kolbin, Russians were not making an effort to learn Kazakh and further noted that Kazakh was "poorly taught and poorly respected. See "Address of the First Secretary of the Communist Party of Kazakhstan Gennady V. Kolbin to the Seventh Congress of Kazakh Journalists," in *Perestroika in the Soviet Republics: Documents on the National Question*, edited by Charles F. Furtado, Jr., and Andrea Chandler (Boulder: Westview Press, 1992) pp. 472–473.

7. Gerhard Simon, *Nationalism and Policy Toward the Nationalities in the Soviet Union* (Boulder: Westview, 1991), pp. 390–391.

8. *Statistical Handbook 1994: States of the Former USSR* (Washington, D.C.: The World Bank, 1994, p. 257–258.

9. Ibid., pp. 675–676, 303–304, 583, 537–538.

10. Ozod Baba-Mirzayevich Ata-Mirzayev and Abdukhakim Abdukhamidovich Kayumov, "The Demography of Soviet Central Asia and its Future Development," in *Geographic Perspectives on Soviet Central Asia* edited by Robert A. Lewis (London: Routledge, 1992) p. 216.

11. James H. Bater, *Russia and the Post-Soviet Scene* (London: Arnold, a member of the Hodder Headline Group, 1996) p. 309.

12. Ian Murray Matley, "Agricultural Development," in *Central Asia: A Century of Russian Rule*, edited by Edward Allworth (New York: Columbia University Press, 1967) p. 289–290; Ian Murray Matley, "Industrialization," in *Central Asia: A Century of Russian Rule*, pp. 334–339.

13. Shahram Akbarzadeh, "The Political Shape of Central Asia," *Central Asian Survey*, vol. 16, no. 4 (1997) pp. 5245; Helene Carrere d'Encausse, *Decline of an Empire: The Soviet Republics in Revolt* (New York: Newsweek Books, 1979) pp. 233–234.

14. Martha Brill Olcott, *Central Asia's New States*, pp. 28–29.

15. Helene Carrere d'Encausse, *Islam and the Russian Empire: Reform and Revolution in Central Asia* (London: I.B.TAURIS 7 Co Ltd. Publishers, 1988), p. 147; Helene Carrere d'Encausse, "The National Republics Lose Their Independence," in *Central Asia: A Century of Russian Rule*, p. 256.

16. Helene Carrere d'Encausse, *Islam and the Russian Empire: Reform and Revolution in Central Asia*, p. 148.

17. Alexandre A. Benningsen and S. Enders Wimbush, *Muslim National Communism in the Soviet Union: A Revolutionary Strategy for the Colonial World* (Chicago: University of Chicago Press, 1979) p. 41.

18. Ibid., p. 42.

19. Ibid.

20. Ibid., p. 46.

21. Ibid., p. 44.

22. Gerhard Simon, *Nationalism and Policy Toward the Nationalities in the Soviet Union*, p. 104.

23. Helene Carrere d'Encausse, "Civil War and New Governments," in *Central Asia: A Century of Russian Rule*, p. 253.

24. Ibid., pp. 250–251.

25. Alexandre A. Benningsen and S. Enders Wimbush, *Muslim National Communism in the Soviet Union*, p. 90.

26. Anthony Hyman, "Turkestan and pan-Turkism Revisited, "Central *Asian Survey*, vol. 16, no. 3 (1997), pp. 339–340.

27. Helene Carrere d'Encausse, "Civil War and New Governments," in *Central Asia: A Century of Russian Rule*, p. 224.

28. Ibid., p. 240.

29. Helene Carrere d'Encausse, *Decline of an Empire: The Soviet Republics in Revolt* (New York: Newsweek Books, 1979), p. 23.

30. Helene Carrere d'Encausse, "The Republics Lose Independence," in *Central Asia: A Century of Russian Rule*, p. 257.

31. Shahram Akbarzadeh, "The Political Shape of Central Asia," p. 517.

32. Ibid., p. 518.

33. Martha Brill Olcott, *Central Asia's New States*, p. 42.

34. Helene Carrere d'Encausse, *Decline of an Empire: The Soviet Republics in Revolt*, p. 23–24.

35. Ibid., p. 26.

36. Ibid., p. 229.

37. Ibid., p. 229–230.

38. Ibid., p. 230.

39. *The Soviet Union: A Systematic Geography*, pp. 248–249.

40. Gehard Simon, *Nationalism and Policy Toward the Nationalities in the Soviet Union*, p. 105.

41. Ian Murray Matley, "Agricultural Development," in *Central Asia*, p. 275.

42. Gehard Simon, *Nationalism and Policy Toward the Nationalities in the Soviet Union*, p. 105.

43. Ian Murray Matley, "Agricultural Development," in *Central Asia*, pp. 284–285.

44. Gehard Simon, *Nationalism and Policy Toward the Nationalities in the Soviet Union*, pp. 105–106.

45. Ibid., p. 106.

46. Ibid.

47. Ibid., pp. 106–109.

48. Ian Murray Matley, "Industrialization," in *Central Asia: A Century of Russian Rule*, p. 319.

49. Ibid., pp. 332–333.

50. Ibid., pp. 333–334.

51. Ibid., pp. 335–336.

52. *The Soviet Union: A Systematic Geography*, pp. 264–265.

53. Gehard Simon, *Nationalism and Policy Toward the Nationalities in the Soviet Union*, p. 105.

54. Helene Carrere d'Encausse, *The End of an Empire: The Triumph of the Nations* (New York: BasicBooks, 1993) p. 18.

55. Ibid., pp. 18–20.

56. Ibid., pp. 20–21.

57. Ibid., pp. 32–33.

58. Ibid., pp. 101–108.

59. *The Current Digest of the Soviet Press*, vol. XLI, no. 25 (1989) p. 23.

60. Ibid.

61. Ibid., p. 98.

62. *The Current Digest of the Soviet Press*, vol. XLI, no. 25 (1989) p. 22.

63. Helene Carrere d'Encausse, *The End of an Empire*, p. 99.

64. *The Current Digest of the Soviet Press*, vol. XLI, no. 25 (1989) p. 22.

65. *The Current Digest of the Soviet Press*, vol. XLI, no. 25 (1989) p. 19.

66. Ibid., p. 21.

67. Helene Carrere d'Encausse, *The End of an Empire*, pp. 100–101.

68. Ibid., p. 105.

69. Ibid., p. 107.

70. Shireen T. Hunter, *Central Asia Since Independence* (Westport, Connecticut: Praeger, 1996) p. 107–108.

71. *FBIS-SOV*, 9 September (1996) p. 65.

72. This conviction is vindicated by the author's own experience while in Russia during 1994 in discussions with ordinary Russians and Russian university students. This perception has also been noted in Martha Brill Olcott, *Central Asia's New States: Independence, Foreign Policy, and Regional Security* (Washington, D.C.: United States Institute of Peace Press, 1996).

73. Rasma Karklins, *Ethnic Relations in the USSR: The Perspective from Below* (Boston: Allen & Unwin, 1986) p. 232. The percentages of Kazakhs, Uzbeks, Kyrgyz, Turkmen, and Tajiks living in places other than their titular Republics or adjacent areas of Central Asia are 8.3 percent, 0.8 percent, 1.5 percent, 1.6 percent, and 1.5 percent respectively in 1979. These were among the lowest levels of settlement outside native areas from among the titular nationalities of the Soviet Union.

74. Ibid., p. 156.

75. Gaiaz Alimov, "Nursultan Nazarbaev predloshil kollegam idti navstrechu prostym liudiam," *Izvestiia*, January 24 (1998) pp. 1, 3.

76. *FBIS-SOV*, 5 April (1995) p. 67.

77. *FBIS-SOV*, 5 April (1995) p. 67.

78. *FBIS-SOV*, 11 April (1995) p. 76.

79. Ibid., pp. 76–77.

80. *The Current Digest of the Post-Soviet Press*, Vol. 50, no. 8 (1998) p. 19.

81. *FBIS-SOV*, 12 September (1996) p. 3.

82. Olcott, *Central Asia's New States*, pp. 98–99.

83. Ibid., p. 108.

84. *The Economist Intelligence Unit Country Report: Tajikistan, 1st quarter*, (London: The Economist Intelligence Unit, 1998) p. 22; *The Economist Intelligence Unit Country Report: Kyrgyz Republic, 1st quarter* (London: The Economist Intelligence Unit, 1998) pp. 6, 8.

85. Olcott, *Central Asia's New States*, p. 109.

86. Richard H. Rowland, "Demographic Trends in Soviet Central Asia and Southern Kazakhstan," in *Geographic Perspectives on Soviet Central Asia*, p. 233.

87. *The Current Digest of the Post-Soviet Press*, vol. 50, no. 7 (1998) p. 20.

88. Olcott, *Central Asia's New States,* p. 115.

89. *The Current Digest of the Post-Soviet Press,* vol. 50, no. 7 (1998) p. 20.

90. Ibid.

91. Nasrin Dadmehr, "Tajikistan—Inevitable War? Inevitable Peace?" *Central Asia Monitor,* no. 1 (1998) p. 2.

92. Ibid.

93. Ibid., pp. 2–4.

94. Ibid., p. 5.

95. Boris Vinogradov, "V Dushanbe snova nespokoino," *Izvestiia,* January 17 (1998), p. 3.

96. Ibid.

97. Aleksei Nazarov, "Islamisty protiv svetskogo gosudarstva," *Pravda-5,* February 25 (1998) p. 1.

98. Ibid.

99. *The Economist Intelligence Unit Country Report: Tajikistan, 1st quarter* (1998) pp. 20, 22.

100. Olcott, *Central Asia's New States,* p. 106.

101. *The Economist Intelligence Unit Country Report: Kyrgyz Republic, 1st quarter* (1998) p. 7.

102. Olcott, *Central Asia's New States,* p. 108.

103. *The Economist Intelligence Unit Country Report: Kyrgyz Republic, 1st quarter* (1998) p. 6.

104. *FBIS-SOV,* 11 April (1995) p. 77.

105. Dmitrii B. Oreshkin, "Ethnic Dimensions of the Aral Sea Crisis," in *In a Collapsing Empire,* pp. 286–287.

106. *The Current Digest of the Soviet Press,* vol. XLI, no. 25 (1989) p. 20.

107. Helene Carrere d'Encausse, *The End of an Empire,* p. 107.

108. Martha Brill Olcott, "Post-Soviet Kazakhstan: The Demographics of Ethnic Politics," *Problems of Post-Communism,* March/April (1995) p. 25.

109. *The Current Digest of the Post-Soviet Press,* vol. 50, no. 6 (1998) p. 19.

110. *The Current Digest of the Post-Soviet Press,* vol. 50, no. 9 (1998) p. 10.

111. *The Economist Intelligence Unit Country Report: Kazakhstan, 1st quarter,* (1998), pp. 13–14.

112. *Russko-Kazakhskii slovar'* (Moskva: Gosudarstvennoe izdatel'stvo inostrannykh i natsional'nykh slovarei, 1954) pp. 42, 349.

113. Aleksei Nazarov, "Islamisty protiv svetskogo gosudarstva," *Pravda-5,* February 25 (1998) p. 1.

114. Dmitrii B. Oreshkin, "Ethnic Dimensions of the Aral Sea Crisis," in *In a Collapsing Empire,* pp. 282–283.

115. Ibid., p. 283.

116. Ibid., p. 280.

117. Ibid., p. 289.

118. "Narcotics in Central Asia," *Central Asia Monitor,* no. 2 (1998) p. 20.

119. *The Economist Intelligence Unit Country Report: Kyrgyz Republic, 1st quarter* (1998) p. 12.

Chapter 7

The Baltic Successor States

INTRODUCTION

Conditions in the Slavic and Central Asian states have not been supportive of independence. Political instability, economic decline, ethnic divisiveness, and the lack of a unified or even coherent sense of national identity have served to weaken the states of these regions, making them more susceptible to pressure from Russia.

The Baltic region by contrast is the exception that proves the rule because conditions in this peripheral region *are* conducive to independence. And yet tense relations with Russia have similarly troubled the Baltic transition to independence. All three regions remain economically and even politically dependent on Russia though the Baltic States have gone furthest to rid themselves of these dependencies. However the "success" of the Baltic States remains conditioned upon cordial relations with Russia. But Russia's aggressive opposition to Baltic membership in NATO and its delay in signing border agreements have hindered the efforts of the Baltic States to integrate with the West. Cooperation with Russia is also beneficial in conducting trade. For instance economic cooperation between Latvia and Kazakhstan would be greatly facilitated by Russia's willingness to allow both countries to use its rail and airspace so that more costly means of transport could be avoided.[1]

Why have the Baltic States opted to distance themselves from Russia as much as possible? How do conditions differ in the Baltic States from those in the other two regions under study? The remainder of the chapter addresses these questions. First the distinctive characteristics of the Baltic region will be touched upon for perspective vis-à-vis the other two regions. The Baltic region differs from the Slavic and Central Asian regions in several significant respects.

These differences account for the prevailing conditions that have made the pursuit of independence a national imperative. National agreement on the goal and desirability of independence is a crucial ingredient to the relative (to the other regions) success of the Baltic States. This unity has made possible government resistance to economic pressures from Russia because the population is more willing to endure hardships for the sake of national pride. It is also important to note that living conditions in the Baltic States were among the highest within the former Soviet Union and therefore references to "economic hardships" should be viewed in relative terms.

Second, relations with Russia following independence will be examined with particular attention to those aspects that presented difficulties to the state-building endeavors of the Baltic States. Relations immediately following independence were strained. Issues of contention included the stationing of Russian troops in the Baltic States, intermittent deliveries of Russian oil and gas, Russia's concern about the treatment of Russian minorities, and Moscow's opposition to Baltic membership in NATO. While the issue of Russian troop withdrawal was successfully resolved by the mid-1990s, other issues have been given added urgency. Since the NATO bombing of Serbia, a nation friendly to Russia, Russian relations with the West have been strained. NATO actions proved to Russia that its interests are not taken seriously and that NATO is a potential security threat. The precedent set by NATO's defense of a region in one country from that country's government looked ominous from Moscow's vantage point given the ongoing conflict in Chechnya. All this has hardened Russia's opposition to NATO expansion into the Baltic States. Russian compliance is crucial to the acceptance in Western economic and political organizations, which has been the cornerstone of foreign policy of the Baltic governments.

Third, the prospects for independence will be outlined. In particular conditions favorable to the Baltic States will be highlighted. These include the successful resolution of key issues with Russia, economic growth due to a dynamic private sector and foreign investment, and favorable reviews from European countries regarding EU and NATO membership. Though progress has been made in relations with Russia, some issues remain outstanding and continue to hinder Baltic integration into Western institutions.

HISTORICAL BACKGROUND

The Distinctiveness of the Baltic States

There are several characteristics peculiar to the Baltic States that account for the strong show of national unity and the determination to move away from Russia's sphere of influence that each has exhibited. Geography has made the Baltic States the most "western" of the Soviet territories. As a result, the Baltic States were the most "European" of the Soviet Republics, a fact that has given the Baltic States an alternative identity to that of a Soviet one.

The strong sense of national identity exhibited by the Baltic States stems from a combination of factors: their proximity to Europe and the Baltic languages which distinguish them from Russian and other Slavic languages. Latvian and Lithuanian belong to the Baltic branch of the Indo-European family of languages. Estonian however belongs to the Finno-Ugric group of languages, which are classified with the Turkic family of languages.[2] The distinctiveness of these languages made them difficult for Russian authorities to absorb or distort in a manner similar to what occurred to Belarusian and Ukrainian. Unlike the Slavic states, the Baltic States do not suffer from an ambiguity in national consciousness nor conflicting loyalties as to which state members owe their alliance. And unlike the situation in the Central Asian States, high levels of economic and social development (as measured by classic developmental indicators including urbanization, mortality, education, income, and consumption) contributed to the development of nationalism and the political mobilization that led to the early declarations of independence from the Soviet Union.

The above particulars of the Baltic States are the result of two broad themes of Baltic history that distinguish them from the other regions of the former Soviet Union. First, the Baltic States are closely linked to Europe, both by reason of geography and culture. Their subjugation by Russia had been comparatively recent and superficial (at least until the Soviet period). But the centuries spent under German and Polish domination more fundamentally shaped the social development of the Baltic States. Second, the Baltic States have a living memory of independence. Their independence lasted for almost a generation.

Historically, the Baltic States have been closely linked to Europe. Throughout their history, the territories of the Baltic States have been dominated by foreign powers, especially Sweden, Poland, and Germany. Estonia and Latvia came under German influence while Lithuania had traditionally been dominated by Poland. However the contacts with western European powers went deeper than conquest to include profound and lasting cultural influences. Conquest of the Baltic lands began with German crusaders who in the twelfth century brought Christianity to the Baltic peoples, the latter whom were among the last remaining pagan peoples in Europe. Catholicism came to Lithuania via Poland. In 1346, the Danes sold the rights to the territory of Estonia (called Estland) to the Teutonic Order which ruled Estland, Courland and Livonia (present-day Latvia) until the Protestant reformation.[3] The Germans managed to transpose their economic and political institutions in the Baltic lands. The Germans formed an exclusive trade and fraternal organization, the Hanseantic League, and its member city-states included several Baltic cities including Riga, Tallinn, and Tartu.

In the sixteenth century, the reformation served to secularize Baltic lands that German landlords possessed. The native Baltic peoples comprised the peasant classes. The secularization of the lands was the first stage in the process of modernization in the Baltic States. Over time the adoption of the Lutheran religion transformed the political, economic, and social institutions of Estland, Courland, and Livonia. Martin Luther's push for reforming the Catholic Church resulted in revolutionary changes in the lands where it had taken hold. Liberal towns were pitted against conservative ones and Catholicism became identified with feudalism and serfdom. Protestantism by contrast was closely linked with the spread of literacy (encouraged so that the masses may read the bible for themselves) and trade.[4] Max Weber's theory on the effects of the Protestant mentality on the rise of industry and commercial trade was borne out in Estonia and Latvia. Feudalism gave way to capitalism (á la Adam Smith) and a growing indigenous (rather than German) middle class eventually became the basis for an emerging sense of national identification.

When Peter the Great conquered the Baltic lands in the Great Northern War, the treaty of Nystad in 1921 maintained the privileged position of the Baltic Germans and the Lutheran Church. The Baltic Germans continued the day-to-day administration of the Baltic provinces. Baltic German privileges meant that there would be no attempt to force either the Russian language, the Orthodox religion, or even the administrative and legal institutions of the Russian empire upon the Baltic territories. It was the German landlords that abolished serfdom in Estonia (1816), Courland (northwest Latvia, 1817), and Livonia (1819), before it was abolished in Russia itself. Its abolition furthered the growth of an indigenous middle class in the Baltic lands, which in turn fueled nascent Baltic national identity.[5]

The privileges of the Baltic Germans were not challenged until the reign of Alexander III in 1881. Russification of the Russian borderlands was given impetus by growing Russian nationalism. Alexander III made Russian the compulsory language of government and administration in 1885. Russian was also introduced into the schools, including universities. Name changes also accompanied linguistic russification. In Lithuania russification was more extreme because its ruling class was Polish gentry who had a history of harboring anti-tsarist sentiment (as evident in the rebellions of 1830 and 1863). Hence Lithuania was regarded as more seditious. Along with the imposition of the Russian language in government and schools, other policies were implemented in Lithuania. Land was confiscated from the aristocracy and was divided and distributed to the peasants. There was a concerted effort to convert the Catholic Lithuanians to Orthodoxy.[6] The nationalist response of the Baltic peoples to all of this has been a wholesale rejection of both German and Russian attempts to assimilate them.

In spite of being under foreign domination for the better part of its history, the Baltic States have known periods of independence. Independence came to the Baltic States with the collapse of the Russian Empire and the defeat of Germany following WWI. Russia, having withdrawn from the war with the signing of the Treaty of Brest-Litovsk, lost much of its western borderlands including the Baltic lands.

The period of independence in the Baltic States was significant because it signaled the beginning of modernization in these lands along the spread of nationalism. More importantly it also gave these states practical administrative experience and provided a precedent for the domestic and foreign policies that were reinstated in the 1990s.

During the interwar period, independence inspired the Baltic States to establish modern political systems and imbue them with historical legitimacy. Forging enduring institutions of statehood was a conscious goal on the part of Baltic leaders. Traditional symbols were resurrected such as flags and coats-of-arms, even though, with the exception of Lithuania who had a period of independence in the Middle Ages, those emblems had their origins in periods of foreign rule.[7] Such tactics reflected the desire of these governments to establish links between themselves and the past in order to strengthen their legitimacy. The governments that were established at the conclusion of WWI were Republics rather than Monarchies or some other traditional form of political system. These Republics had all the trappings of modern political systems including political parties and elections. During the period of independence, there is evidence of a significant degree of popular political participation.[8]

RELATIONS WITH RUSSIA

The formal dissolution of the Soviet Union left a number of issues unresolved. From the standpoint of the newly created Baltic States, these issues were obstacles to the transformation of their national territories from Soviet Republics to independent, sovereign states. As the governments of the Baltic States took on the responsibilities of independent states, points of contention between the Baltic States and Russia became evident.

The Disruption of Trade

Naturally the immediate pressing issue between Russia and the Baltic States involved the disruption of inter-Republican trade which hurt the economies the Baltic States. Deliveries of oil and gas hurt industrial production. As the most industrialized Republics of the former Soviet Union, the Baltic States depend on Russia for energy deliveries. Markets for Baltic goods were suddenly cut off. This is because the Baltic States refused to join the CIS and as a result they were the first to leave the ruble zone. The introduction of new currencies further complicated trade with CIS countries.

From the beginning, the Baltic States were determined to lessen their economic dependence on Russia and diversify their import and export markets. Upon independence the Baltic States introduced their own currencies fully aware of the disruption in trade that it would cause. In June of 1992, Estonia introduced the kroon, which was fully convertible because the Estonian Bank backed it with gold reserves and then pegged it to the German deutsche mark. For every kroon issued by the Estonia bank, there were reserves of hard currency, in this case German Deutsche marks.[9] The Bank of Estonia has followed a tight fiscal policy that has kept inflation down. Public spending did not exceed revenues and exports outstripped imports.[10] The Latvian government and the Bank of Latvia introduced the Latvian lat as the sole currency of Latvia in July of 1992.[11] Latvia, like Estonia, instituted very strict monetary policy which kept inflation down.[12] Lithuania was the last to introduce its own currency, the litas, doing so in July of 1993. Lithuania was less successful in keeping down inflation due to budget deficits. The litas was pegged to the dollar and was thus made fully convertible.[13]

The Baltic countries broke away from the ruble zone and prepared to absorb the negative impact of economic transformation. Industrial production sharply declined and industries were forced to export their commodities. Though the Baltic States lost much of the CIS market for their goods, they made it a priority to diversify their export markets. For the most part they have been successful in reorienting their trade away from Russia and the CIS. Estonia has been the most successful in becoming less dependent on Russia for trade. Lithuania and Latvia by contrast still have Russia as their largest trading partner, though the percentage of trade with Russia has deceased with Lithuania and Latvia as well.

Estonia has been the most successful in reorienting its trade away from Russia and the CIS due to a tripling in the volume of goods exported to Estonia by Finland.[14] In 1992, Russia accounted for 20.83 percent of Estonia's exports and 22.65 percent of Estonia's imports. In 1993 the percentage for exports increased to 22.61 percent while imports declined to 17.16 percent. Finland replaced Russia as Estonia's primary trade partner, though Russia remains the second largest trade partner. In 1996, 19.8 percent and 15.7 percent of Estonian exports went to Finland and Russia respectively. Corresponding figures for imports were 36.7 percent and 10.9 percent.[15]

Though Russia remains the primary trading partner for Latvia and Lithuania, the percentage of total trade with Russia has decreased while trade with Western countries has increased. The general trend in trade for both countries has been away from Russia and the CIS. In 1993, Latvia's imports and exports with Russia and the CIS countries totaled 38.23 percent and 47.59 percent respectively.[16] In 1996, those percentages dropped to 20.2 percent and 22.8 percent, though these figures only include trade with Russia. In the same year Latvia's other main trading partners included Germany, Great Britain, Sweden, and Finland.[17]

Of the Baltic States, Lithuania trades the heaviest with Russia, its principal trading partner, though the volume of trade between the two is likewise declining. Lithuania receives most of its imports from Russia: 63.94 percent (according to the Ministry of Industry) in 1992 and 74 percent in 1993. Exports to Russia totaled 31.8 percent and 43.5 percent in 1992 and 1993.[18] In 1996, imports from Russia declined to 23.8 percent and exports decreased to 29.1 percent. Lithuania too has diversified its import and export base to include Germany, Poland, Denmark, and Italy.[19]

Import figures include imports of Russian oil, much of which was utilized by Lithuania's oil refinery in Mazeikiai. The oil refinery allows Lithuania to export petroleum products. Furthermore, recent geological surveys indicate that Lithuania has a large reserve of oil. Foreign companies have expressed an interest in constructing an oil terminal in the port of Klaipeda for the eventual export of oil. Currently Lithuania extracts between 1.2 and 1.5 million tons of oil, but this is not enough to cover domestic consumption.[20] This reserve of oil could potentially alleviate Lithuania's dependence on Russian oil imports.

The Baltic States' dedication to decreasing reliance on Russia has resulted in concerted efforts on the part of the Baltic governments to strictly adhere to IMF standards in managing their economies. Strict monetary polices and more or less balanced government budgets have lessened inflation, and liberal foreign investment and privatization polices have increased trade with Western countries and modernized the industrial bases of these countries.[21] Their national cohesiveness has added to the general stability within these countries and a willingness to bear the costs of the transition thus far. Even the Russian populations in these countries have not been a source of instability. In fact most of the Russia population in all three countries supported their former Republic's move to independence and expressed solidarity with their new countries. The main source for instability is the continuing restrictions in Estonia and Latvia in the admittance of Russian speakers as citizens. Still this issue has not greatly hindered the economic transformations of the Baltic States.

The Withdrawal of Russian Troops

The stationing of Soviet troops in the Baltic States was regarded as threatening to the new governments who immediately called for their removal. Strategically located on the Soviet Western front, the Baltic States were heavily militarized. An estimated 200,000 troops were stationed in the Baltic States at the time of independence.[22] The majority of military personnel were Russian. The issue of troop removal was complicated by a number of factors including Baltic perceptions of Russian imperialism, the question of logistical support for the removal and resettlement of military personnel, and Russian efforts to link troop withdrawals with the treatment of the Russian minorities in the Baltic States.

Without exception, the Baltic governments, chosen by an electorate comprised mainly of members of the titular nationalities, regarded the presence of troops as a holdover of Soviet/Russian imperialism. Popular support for the removal of Russian troops was evident in a number of incidents dating back to independence when the issue first became prominent. The Latvian Citizens' Congress Committee printed and mailed leaflets to officers of the Skrunda

Military Camp. The leaflets informed the officers that they were living illegally on Latvian territory and that they ought to promptly leave before they "provoke the activation of forces that are prepared to resolve the question of *Latvia's decolonization by violent means*" (emphasis added).[23] The Latvian Citizens' Congress was a grassroots, nationalist organization established for the purpose of reconstituting the Republic of Latvia that existed prior to June 17, 1940, the date of the signing of the Molotov-Ribbentrop pact that effectively ceded the Baltic States, including Latvia, to the Soviet Union. The Citizens' Congress regarded this pact as illegal and considered present-day Latvia as the successor to the Republic of Latvia.[24] When the pro-Soviet "equal rights" faction of the Latvian Republic Supreme Council complained on behalf of the officers to the Latvian General Prosecutor against the Citizens' Congress Committee, pressing him to prosecute the latter for fanning inter-ethnic strife, the General Prosecutor failed to find the Committee's actions unlawful.[25] When the Latvian government attempted to order Russian troops to leave, the Russian Federation successfully overrode Riga's authority by ordering military personnel to stay put. In a formal statement, the Latvian Defense Ministry denounced this action as Russian interference in Latvia's internal affairs.[26]

In Estonia, hostility toward Russian troops turned violent. A nationalist military organization called Kaitsliit (Defense League) had a reputation for attacking Russian border troops and was credited with the orchestration of armed attacks on Russian servicemen.[27] Fights between newly formed Estonian defense forces and Russian base troops broke out periodically in the years after independence and before the last of the Russian troops were removed.[28] July 14, 1992, a gunfight between Estonian frontier guards and Russian servicemen occurred. According to the Chief of Estonia's border protection department, Russian military personnel fired the first shots. According to Russian military personnel, the frontier guards were believed to be members of Kaitsliit.[29] The incident soured Russo-Estonian talks pertaining to the status of Russian troops. While the Russian press lambasted Estonian authorities for discriminating against non-Estonian residents, that is, Russians, the Chairman of the Lithuanian parliament, nationalist Vytautas Landsbergis, expressed solidarity with Estonia against Russia's tough policy against Estonia. As a result of the July 14 incident, the Russian parliament had passed a resolution expressing concern over what it termed the violation of human rights (of the Russians) in Estonia.[30]

In public statements and legislative resolutions the Baltic governments have been unequivocal in their opposition to the presence of Russian troops and the procrastination of the Russian government in setting deadlines for their removal. From the time of independence, the Estonian government refused to sign treaties or conclude agreements that would allow for the lawful presence of Russian troops on Estonian territory.[31] The Latvian government prepared written proposals outlining the details of the removal of Russian troops from

Latvian soil.[32] The presence of Russian troops merely reinforced the perception of Russian imperial aggressiveness toward its small neighbors.[33]

The second factor that complicated troop withdrawal had to do with the costs of resettling troops and disagreements over who owned what. On several occasions the Russian government expressed reluctance to the speedy removal of troops due to the costs associated with repatriating them. Specifically Russian officials endeavored to impel the governments of the Baltic States to allow military personnel to privatize their living accommodations. The Russian government persuaded Lithuania to do just this. Russian officials argued that Russian officers would simply go to Russia, then return to Lithuania under the guise of family reunification. If officers were allowed to remain where they were stationed, they would not immigrate later and thereby add to the acute housing shortage in Vilnius or some other Lithuanian town likely to attract immigrants.[34]

The most stunning example of Baltic resistance to this argument is the case of Estonia. After more than a year of Russian procrastination, Estonia finally concluded an agreement with Russia. Estonia essentially paid the Russians to leave by absorbing some of the costs of moving and providing logistical support for the movement of equipment and personal property. The Estonian government allowed military personnel to evacuate all movable military equipment to Russia.[35] In addition, the provisions of a repatriation agreement signed by Estonia and Russia stipulated that Russians in Estonia would be able to take their property with them and dispose of property they cannot take with them in Estonia on favorable terms.[36]

Bickering over military equipment and other properties of military settlements was typical. Basically the Baltic States regarded military installations and equipment to be the property of the territory on which they were located. Latvian inspectors overseeing the Russian troop withdrawal from the military base in Dobele found much of the installation badly maintained. They reported that Russian authorities had not issued orders for transferring all equipment to Latvian authorities, which confirmed Riga's view that the military installations and equipment belonged to the Latvian State.[37] Estonia found it expedient to relinquish its demands on military equipment in order to expedite troop withdrawal.

The Russian government for its part regarded the installations and equipment to be the property of the Russian Federation. Equipment that could not be carried away was systematically demolished. Latvian authorities found the Dobele base run down and its equipment badly maintained and generally neglected.[38] The Russian navy destroyed its nuclear base at Paldiski in Estonia. Torpedo casings were systematically cut up, light bulbs were shot out, and furniture chopped to pieces. They even tried to burn the buoys in the harbor![39]

The third issue was Russia's public insistence on linking troop withdrawal with the treatment of the Russian minorities. Troop withdrawal was hence more complicated for Estonia and Latvia since both were home to a large Rus-

sian-speaking minority. In addition, Estonia and Latvia were more strategically
important than Lithuania and therefore were home to greater numbers of
troops. Restrictive citizenship laws combined with a large Russian minority
made Estonia and Latvia the primary targets of Russian obstructive stratagems
and outright obstinacy.

Former Russian Foreign Minister Andrey Kozyrev's remarks about Russia's
intention of protecting the rights of Russian minorities by the use of force if
necessary were clearly worrisome to the Baltic leaders. A year before on the eve
of Russia's military withdrawal from Estonia, Kozyrev mentioned Estonia by
name, stating that once the troops were gone, economic and political and psy-
chological pressure would be applied by Moscow in order to ensure the rights
of the Russian minorities.[40] The Baltic Assembly, an inter-parliamentary organization consisting of twenty legislators from each of the Baltic States, discussed Kozyrev's remarks and agreed that they are an expression of aggression
by Russia and constitute a security threat.[41] Estonian President Lennart Meri
termed the remarks "belligerent and bellicose," and noted with derision "the
army in Russia is regarded as a force capable of solving political problems,"
adding that "several months of slaughter in Chechnya call for a new political
logic."[42] Still the public reaction of Baltic leaders was relatively measured in
spite of the inflammatory tone of Kozyrev's remarks, a fact that was in all prob-
ability a reflection of the political climate in Moscow. The Estonian Foreign
Ministry issued a statement merely saying that Kozyrev's remarks were "not
corresponding to international norms."[43] Then Latvian Foreign Minister
Valdis Birkavs and the chairman of the Saeima (the Latvian parliament) Commission on Foreign Affairs, Aleksandrs Kirsteins, declared that Kozyrev's remarks should be regarded as "the personal statements of a politically unstable
diplomat, to please Russian chauvinist forces."[44]

Lithuania, home to a Russian population that comprises just 9.4 percent of
the population (though minorities include roughly 20 percent of the population of Lithuania), had an easier time negotiating Russian troop withdrawals.[45] Lithuania also adopted more liberal citizenship laws that reflected an internal political climate less hostile to minorities in general. Undoubtedly this
more liberal attitude was a reflection of the fact that Lithuanians are a numeric
majority within Lithuania and did not feel ethnically threatened. In contrast,
Estonians made up 61.5 percent of the population of Estonia while Latvians
comprised only 52 percent of the population of Latvia at independence.[46]

Eventually the issue of troop withdrawal was resolved by 1994, despite procrastination on the part of Russia in its negotiations with Estonia and Latvia. In
Estonia, a tentative deadline was set for 1993. Talks broke down and were re-
scheduled for February 1 and 2, 1994. A new deadline was scheduled for August 31, 1994.[47] In spite of Russia's foot dragging, troops were being
continually withdrawn from Estonia throughout 1993. Army installations
were formally turned over to the Estonian government and its defense minis-

try at the beginning of the year.[48] By the end of 1993, only 3,000 or so Russian troops remained.[49] The last of the troops left in August 1994.[50]

By the end of 1993, 15,000 Russian troops remained in Latvia. After much bargaining, a troop withdrawal treaty was drafted, and according to it, Russia withdrew the remainder of its troops by August 31.[51] According to the treaty, Latvia guaranteed pension payments to military personnel who opted to retire in Latvia.[52] Provisions in the treaty addressed the issue of the destruction of facilities and equipment, rendering such acts illegal unless with the express permission of Latvian authorities. Special consideration was given to the status of the Skrunda radar station. Russia insisted on retaining control over the Skrunda radar station, which was considered to be central to CIS air defense. According to the provisions of the treaty, the Skrunda station ceased operations by August 31, 1998 and be dismantled beginning in September of the same year.[53]

In Lithuania, agreement was easily reached on the major issues surrounding troop withdrawal including property and logistical matters. Most of the troops left according to schedule and were not pulled out piecemeal, as was the case in Estonia and Latvia. Russian troops left by August 1993, a year earlier than Estonia and Latvia.[54] The small number of military personnel who stayed behind to oversee the transfer of the bases to Lithuania left by December 1, 1993. The only remaining and continuing military issue between Russia and Lithuania pertains to the regulation of military transits through Lithuania to Kaliningrad Oblast. This issue has been closely linked with the maintenance of bilateral trade agreements[55] Lithuania is the shortest land corridor connecting the Kaliningrad Oblast to Russia.

As mentioned previously, Russia linked the issue of troop withdrawal with the treatment of the Russian minorities. Estonia and Latvia experienced difficulties in negotiations with Russia for this reason. The treatment of the Russian minorities is directly related to their legal status in the newly independent Republics which is in turned is the result of citizenship laws that determine who is and is not a citizen.

Russian Minorities and the Issue of Citizenship

The issue of citizenship has been a contentious one for the Baltic States excluding Lithuania. Essentially Estonia and Latvia passed citizenship laws granting automatic citizenship to only a small number of people. Those eligible for automatic citizenship included only those of the titular nationality. Naturalization laws were equally exclusionary due to provisions that were difficult for non-Estonians to meet and restrictions placed on the number of non-Estonians that could be naturalized each year. As a result, most Russian speakers were denied citizenship, and naturalization became almost unobtainable due to restrictive quotas, residency permits, and language exams that were next to impossible to pass due to a lack of language teaching in the titular language.

This resulted in the alienation of Russian speakers, many of whom supported independence only to find themselves disenfranchised.[56]

There are two paths to citizenship. The first is meeting the qualifications for automatic citizenship and the second is naturalization. Automatic citizenship is the unconditional acceptance of that individual's citizenship. Citizenship is thus granted without conditions such as language tests and minimum residency requirements. Those who qualify need only take a loyalty oath and renounce citizenship of any other state. Naturalization is a more complicated process and is contingent upon meeting certain requirements. Requirements for naturalization are determined by the length of an individual's residency and the ethnicity of one's parents. In its various forms, naturalization in Estonia and Latvia involves language tests and minimum residency within the state.

The differences between being a citizen and a "non-citizen," a term used to describe those who lived in each Republic prior to independence who were not eligible for automatic citizenship, is crucial. Without citizenship, people are unable to vote (thereby assuring their non-representation in government), run for office, and hold certain jobs. Non-citizens were barred from voting in national elections, and in the case of Latvia, could not vote in local elections either.[57] The exclusion of these voters greatly affected the political outcomes of elections. In Estonia, non-citizens could not run for office or become members of political parties. The fact that they can vote in local elections but not run for office themselves has resulted in some interesting outcomes. In Narva, a city 95 percent Russian, an Estonian runs the city.[58] In Estonian national elections for the State Assembly (Estonia's legislature) held in September of 1992, the first elections to be held in independent Estonia, nearly half of the population were ineligible to vote due to the restrictive laws on citizenship.[59]

Access to housing is restricted, as non-citizens are not legally able to own property. Nor can they privatize their apartments. The issue of job restrictions is crucial in a country with a large public sector. In Latvia, non-citizens may not serve as judges or barristers; be employed in the diplomatic or consulate services; hold civil service jobs; and may not serve in police departments. They are prohibited from owning land, purchasing housing from the state (the only source of housing), and buying privatized cooperative flats. Their movements within Latvia are restricted, as they are not allowed to choose their place of residence under the law. If they should travel abroad, they are not guaranteed the right to reenter the country.[60]

Last, in all three Baltic States, only citizens may claim minority rights. Although these rights are impressively extensive, they are useless if citizenship laws systematically exclude those not from the titular nationality; and minorities by definition are not members of the titular nation. All three of the Baltic States passed laws on the protection of minorities in 1990 and 1991. All three laws stipulate the right of minorities to the preservation of their national culture and education in their national language (as well as the state language). The Lithuanian constitution stipulates the state funding for educational, cultural, recreational, and other public services for minorities. In Estonia, minorities may establish local government institutions, and in locales where they constitute the majority, they may use their own language in local government administration.[61] None of these constitutional provisions currently apply to the Russian speakers, except for those in Lithuania who have taken Lithuanian citizenship. Discrimination against non-citizens is exacerbated by the slow rate of naturalization of even those who are eligible for citizenship in Estonia and Latvia.

In essence, Estonia and Latvia have kept Russian speakers from acquiring citizenship in several ways, most of which were deemed discriminatory by the OSCE. First the citizenship laws of Estonia and Latvia were highly restrictive, particularly in their first drafts. In both Estonia and Latvia, automatic citizenship was granted only to those who were registered residents in both countries prior to 1940 and their descendants. Under both the Estonian and Latvian laws, ethnic Russians did not qualify for automatic citizenship, even those born in the Republic with a knowledge of the titular language.[62] This meant that Russians wanting citizenship had to be naturalized. Language requirements were difficult to meet, as there was a dearth of language teaching facilities in both states.

Lithuania by contrast adopted a more inclusive citizenship law. Originally, Lithuania extended citizenship to those who were residents in Lithuania prior to 1940 and their descendants. But added provisions broadened the number of people who can qualify for automatic citizenship. First, all permanent residents who could show that one of their parents or grandparents was born in Lithuania were eligible for automatic citizenship. Second, those who did not meet the above criterion could become citizens if they reside in Lithuania and take an oath of loyalty within two years after independence.[63] As a result, more than 90 percent of non-Lithuanians are now citizens of Lithuania.[64]

Second, naturalization quotas and restrictions on when people could apply for citizenship served to keep Russians stateless. Quotas restricted the number of people who could be granted citizenship each year. Time limits were placed on naturalization creating a small window of opportunity in which Russians could apply and be approved citizenship. Conversely, Russians could not apply for naturalization until they first applied for residency permits. Then they faced minimum residency requirements before they could apply.

Restrictive citizenship laws have had several consequences for Estonia and Latvia. First, the number of stateless Russians remains high while the number of those approved for citizenship remains low. In Latvia fewer than a thousand people were granted citizenship in 1996 out of a total of 33,000 applicants *who met the naturalization requirements!* Latvian law limited the number of naturalizations of non-Latvians to fewer than 2,000 a year.[65] In Estonia 80,259 non-Estonians received citizenship as of August 1, 1996 out of a total of 602,791 non-Estonians (of which Russians make up about 475,000).[66]

Second, a substantial number of Russian minorities in these states have opted to take *Russian* citizenship. Russian citizenship laws granted citizenship to all former citizens of the USSR who had not claimed citizenship of another state. Most importantly, former USSR citizens could become citizens of Russia even if they reside in the Successor States.[67] That means that in Estonia and Latvia there are a substantial number of citizens of Russia. In Estonia the number of Russians optioning for Russian citizenship outnumbered those who have obtained Estonian citizenship: more than 110,000.[68] The implications for this situation are serious. No longer may the Baltic States or any Western state criticize Russia for protecting *its own nationals* from discrimination. Hence a Russian fifth column may be in the making.

Third, the restrictive laws have hindered Baltic integration with Europe. Estonia and Lithuania were admitted into the Council of Europe in 1993. Latvia was rejected due to citizenship laws that were more restrictive than those of Estonia. By 1993 Estonia had eased restrictions on citizenship somewhat.[69] The issue of citizenship has been and remains an ongoing process. Essentially Estonia and Latvia have slowly, in a piecemeal fashion, amended restrictions on citizenship and naturalization requirements, in particular residency requirements. Pressure from Russia and Europe was the primary motivation.

The real impediment to resolving the crisis has not been the content of the laws themselves, but the slow process of naturalization due to low quotas on the number of people allowed to apply for citizenship and on the number of those actually admitted once they have met the requirements. Instances of qualified Russian speakers being denied residency permits and citizenship are common in both states. The implementation of these laws is dependent on the discretion of Estonian and Latvian authorities who can deny citizenship without having to account for the reasons. One woman interviewed who was Russian, but fluent in Estonian, was denied citizenship. A fifty-four year old physicist took one language test, passed, and then was told he would have to take another after the Estonian parliament amended the requirements for naturalization.[70]

As late as May of 1998, Russia condemned Estonia for its failure to grant citizenship to greater numbers of Russian speakers. A Russian Interior Ministry spokesman is quoted as saying that Estonia had not eliminated massive statelessness.[71] Such incidents of arbitrary behavior on the part of Estonian officials reinforce the perception among Russian officials that the Russian speakers are discriminated against.

And not until this year did the Saeima propose amendments to Latvia's citizenship laws that would lift naturalization quotas.[72] The amendment was approved by a vote in the Saeima on June 22, 1998. The amendment grants citizenship to stateless children born in Latvia since August 21, 1991 (the date of Latvia's independence) and eases the naturalization process for elderly non-citizens.[73] Though this amendment will further Latvia's cause with the OSCE High Commissioner on National Minorities (one Max van der Stoel at the time of this writing), it does not address the problem of statelessness among adult Russians.

Russia wishes to see citizenship offered to Russians without qualifications. Estonia and Latvia for their part simply do not want to see so many Russians admitted as citizens. Citizenship would give them a political voice that might compromise the goals of Estonians: the reconstitution of Estonian culture and language. As late as September 2000, a public opinion poll showed that nearly half of respondents thought that the Russian minorities were not loyal to Estonia and that they should leave.[74] There is also an overriding moral issue; Estonians and Latvians are galled by the fact that most of the Russian speakers immigrated during the Soviet period, a period regarded as an illegal and a humiliating chapter in their respective histories. In the case of Latvia, whose naturalization laws are even stricter than Estonia's and are recognized as such by Russia, it is argued by Latvian authorities that Soviet "colonization" came close to making ethnic Latvians a minority and that restrictive citizenship laws are simply a way to correct this imbalance.[75]

However attempts to exclude Russian speakers from the political processes of these countries may ultimately backfire on them. Their treatment of the Russian speakers as "occupiers" and fifth columnists only alienates Russians who would otherwise prove loyal to the new states. And if they are continually denied citizenship, more and more Russians may opt to take Russian citizenship. This would leave Estonia and Latvia in the position of having over one-third of their residents foreign nationals of a powerful, neighboring state.

Border Disputes

Outstanding territorial disputes between the Baltic States and Russia reflect national aspirations in both the former center and periphery. The Baltic nationalities have a clear sense of national identity and shared future. The point of departure lies in the basic assumptions upon which the legitimacy and logic of the Baltic States rest. When the Baltic States became independent, they believed their governments to be the successors of the interwar independent Republics. The Baltic governments adopted the premise that the interwar Republics continued to exist in name, and that their annexation into the Soviet Union was an illegal act followed by an illegal occupation. With the end of the "occupation," the laws of the interwar states and the peace treaties signed by those states would necessarily be reenacted.[76]

By contrast Russians themselves disagree as to how the Soviet period fits into notions about the Russian nation. The Russian government regards the Russian Federation to be an entirely new state, not based on the Soviet Union.[77] Because of this, the Russian government is disinclined to accept the Baltic States' account of Soviet history. The peace treaties signed by the Soviet government at the conclusion of WWI were rendered invalid with the 1940 annexation and the establishment of inter-Republican borders in 1944.[78]

As was the case with most of the Successor States, the borders of the Baltic States were altered when the Soviets drew their internal Republican borders. After independence those Republican borders became international borders. Estonia and Latvia want Russia to recognize the validity of the peace treaties each concluded with the fledgling Soviet State at the conclusion of WWI. Those peace treaties demarcated borders. On the basis of these treaties, Estonia and Latvia have territorial claims on Russia. Border disputes have their origins in the treaties between the Soviet State and the Estonian and Latvian Republics signed at the conclusion of WWI. In the case of Estonia, it was the Treaty of Tartu concluded February 2, 1920; for Latvia, it was the Riga Peace Treaty adopted August 11, 1920. After the Soviets "liberated" the Baltic territories in 1944, northeastern portions of Estonia, now the Pskov Oblast, were incorporated into Russia. Latvia's eastern district and town of Abrene were likewise annexed to the RSFSR. Lithuania actually gained territory from the RSFSR.

But these treaties have significance beyond territorial demarcation. More importantly for the Baltic States, the treaties stipulated that the Soviet Union recognize the sovereignty of Estonia and Latvia and relinquish any claims to Baltic territory. Russia is unwilling to recognize the validity of these treaties because it would be tantamount to acknowledging the illegal nature of the 1940 annexation.

In the first half of the 1990s, negotiations between Russia and Estonia surrounding the formal demarcation of their common border have not progressed very far because of Estonian insistence on Russian recognition of the Treaty of Tartu as the point of departure for border talks. It is unlikely that Estonia would actually demand the territories back from Russia given that Russians now inhabit those areas almost exclusively.[79] In fact Estonia agreed to renounce its claims to Russian territory in exchange for Russia's recognition of the validity of the treaty. But recognition of the treaty would mean the relinquishment of Russian claims to Estonian territory and admitting culpability in an illegal act that would leave Russia open to future demands for reparations.[80] Russia has countered Estonian demands by putting forth its own claims to Narva in the northeastern part of Estonia.[81] Former Russian Deputy Foreign Minister Vitalii Churkin implied is that if Estonia refused to recognize the present borders, Russia could make counter claims to Estonian territory that had formally belonged to the Russian Empire. In response to Estonian claims, Churkin responded, "there is no need to create additional irritants, which will bring no practical results. We can take retaliatory measures, and our Estonian partners will not like it. This [the Pskov Oblast] is Russian territory, it is controlled by Russia and our present border with Estonia has the status of a state frontier."[82]

The impasse over the Treaty of Tartu was not the last word on border talks. Estonia and Russia have gone ahead with demarcation and have signed border protocols. The demarcation of the Estonian/Russian border began in 1994, with Russian government geologists and cartographers consulting historic maps. Russian officials then proceeded with installing border crossings and armed border troops. These actions were in response to the latest incident of the shooting of a Russian border guard by who ITAR-TASS referred to as "contrabandists specializing in arms trade."[83] In 1995, Estonia and Russia signed a border protocol regulating the activities of the border guards including cooperation and coordination on dealing with border violations related to the trafficking of narcotics, illegal immigration, and organized crime.[84]

Border talks between Latvia and Russia have been more cordial due to Latvia's reluctance to aggressively demand Russian recognition of the Riga Peace Treaty before the issue of troop withdrawal had been resolved. Latvia however did want Russia to recognize the Treaty of Riga for the same reasons the Estonians wanted the validity of the Treaty of Tartu recognized. The Latvian Supreme Council issued a Degree on the Non-Recognition of the Annexation of the Town of Abrene and the District of Abrene in December of 1992 that declared the recognition of the treaty as the point of departure for border talks.[85]

Unlike Estonia, Latvia had not given much priority to border issues beyond decrees on interwar agreements. Latvia was more concerned with expediting Russian troop withdrawal. Also unlike Estonia, the areas of dispute are small compared to the areas of agreement. Less than two-thirds of Latvia's border with Russia is under dispute.[86] Given that troop withdrawal had not been effectively resolved before 1994, the issue did not gain prominence until 1996. Even then, the government itself was divided about what approach to take. The Saeima took a hard line toward Russia regarding the territorial dispute by issuing a decree declaring that Latvia had been occupied territory of the Soviets and calling for the international community to aid Latvia in removing all traces of that occupation.[87] President Guntis Ulmanis and the Latvian Foreign Ministry disassociated themselves from parliament's actions.

As in the case of Estonia, Russia's refusal to recognize the Treaty of Riga did not prevent the normalization of those areas of the border that are not in dispute. Both Latvia and Russia have been working quietly in demarcating their mutual border in the midst of troop withdrawal.[88] But still no formal border treaty has been signed due to Russia's refusal to recognize the Riga Peace Treaty and Latvia's refusal to drop references to it.[89]

In contrast to Estonia and Latvia, Lithuania did not lose territory with its annexation to the Soviet Union, and it does not share a common border with Russia proper. It does however share a common border with the Kaliningrad Oblast. In fact Lithuania gained territory when the Soviet Union took over areas of formerly eastern Poland and incorporated them into the Lithuanian SSR including the city of Vilnius (which is claimed by Poland). But the Lithuanian leadership does not question Russia's jurisdiction over Kaliningrad Oblast or the position of the border. Demarcation of the Lithuanian/Kaliningrad border was well underway by 1994.[90]

The Russian government is in disagreement over the signing of a formal border treaty with Lithuania. Yeltsin's plans to sign a border treaty with Lithuania provoked a heated response from the Russian Duma, which issued a written appeal to the president not to sign. The main point of conflict is the legal status of Klaipeda, a city on the Baltic Sea that originally belonged to Germany but was ceded to the USSR who incorporated it into the Lithuanian SSR on May 8, 1924. After WWII and the withdrawal of Germany from the eastern regions, Klaipeda remained a part of Lithuania. The Duma claimed that Klaipeda does not belong to Lithuania because Lithuania gained Klaipeda as a result of Soviet authority. Since Lithuania does not recognize the legality of the Soviet period, Russia can have no legal claim to Klaipeda.[91]

According to the Duma, Lithuania wants to sign a border treaty with Russia and avoid the issue of overland transit between Russia and Kaliningrad. Russian representatives regard these two issues as inseparable.[92] In addition it was perfectly clear to Duma deputies and the Russian media that the formal signing and demarcation of the border would remove the main obstacle to NATO membership, an outcome expressed as undesirable by Russia.[93]

The reaction on the Lithuanian side was negative and emotional. This is somewhat unusual since it has typically been the practice of the Lithuanian leadership to ignore emotional declarations from Duma deputies. But in this instance the Duma's heated pronouncements stung because they turned the legal argument against Lithuania and raised the issue of overland transit through Lithuania to Kaliningrad Oblast. But worst of all, the signing of a formal border treaty with Russia would have removed a crucial obstacle in Lithuania's path to NATO membership.[94] Though Yeltsin and Lithuanian President Brazauskas went ahead and signed the border treaty October 24, 1997, the treaty has yet to be ratified by the parliaments of both countries. The former pronouncements of the Russian Duma and appeals from the Kaliningrad Oblast to the Duma to not ratify the treaty "for a hundred years" cast doubt on the outcome of the border treaty.[95]

PROSPECTS FOR INDEPENDENCE

The prospects for the Baltic States' independence from Russia is on balance favorable, though Russia remains the principal security concern for the Baltic governments. Russia continues to exert considerable pressure on the Baltic States. Thus far, Russia has been the main obstacle in the realization of the most important goal of the Baltic countries: membership in the EU and NATO.

In the early to mid-1990s, Russia managed to delay withdrawing its troops and postpone signing formal border treaties to extract political concessions from the Baltic governments. Russia has successfully publicized to western states the discriminatory nature of Baltic citizenship laws as well as certain incidents involving clashes between Russian speakers and the national governments. Last, Russia explicitly stated that it considers NATO expansion to be a security threat. Russia gained this added leverage as a result of the NATO bombing of Serbia and now holds firm in its opposition to NATO expansion into the Baltic States.

In spite of all this pressure from their large neighbor, the Baltic States have managed to present a united front to Russia and Western States. The Baltic States regard the similarities among them to outweigh the differences. Relations among the Baltic countries have been more than cordial; Russian pressure applied to one becomes a potential threat to them all.

Russian-Estonian Relations

Estonian relations with Russia have been turbulent since independence. Estonia remained intransigent in its characterization of Russia as an aggressive imperial state. Russia for its part has attacked Estonia for its treatment of the Russian minority and has responded to Estonian territorial claims by making claims of its own, in particular claims to Narva and its environs. Russian success in publicizing Estonia's citizenship laws has resulted in numerous revisions of these laws, though their enforcement has done little to increase the number of Russian-speaking Estonian citizens.

As recently as June of 1998, Russia has accused Estonia of making token amendments to the citizenship statues that only create the illusion that Estonia is effectively dealing with the problem of statelessness among Russian speakers. The Russian government has been demanding that Estonia grant automatic citizenship to children born in Estonia and extend residency permits to senior citizens and retired military personnel.[96]

Estonia has concentrated its energies on expanding contacts with European organizations in its bid for EU and NATO membership. The Estonian Defense Minister publicly and enthusiastically announced Estonia's readiness and willingness to participate in the WEU in managing crises such as humanitarian aid operations in the Balkans. By participating in the operations of the WEU, Estonia hopes to build up its defense system and forge a working relationship with NATO. The Defense Minister expressed his view of the WEU as being a link between the EU and NATO.[97] In fact, the European Commission came to the decision to recommend Estonia as the only Baltic State for the fast track.[98] Deputy Speaker of the Austrian Parliament Heinrich Neisser publicly declared his country's conviction that Estonia should be among the first new countries admitted to the EU. He added that membership would give Estonia not only economic security but political security as well.[99] This decision has boosted foreign investment in Estonia, which further strengthens Estonia's position for membership.[100]

Russian-Latvian Relations

Latvian relations with Russia have been characterized as more cordial than those with Estonia. Nevertheless, Latvia's citizenship laws have been a major bone of contention between the two countries. It was Russia's opposition to Latvia's citizenship law that delayed Latvia's entry into the Council of Europe.[101] Recent incidents between Latvian government forces and Russian minority demonstrators have highlighted the internal political climate in Latvia. Russia publicized the event knowing it would tarnish Latvia's reputation with European countries. Likewise Russia has publicized evidence of Latvian fascism, claiming it would complicate Latvia's relations with Europe.

During the last 10 years, relations have been intermittently aggravated by events emotive for both sides. An incident involving Latvian policy and Russian pensioners postponed the chances for the successful resolution of the border issue and led to the boycott of Latvian goods by Russian businesses. On March 3, 1998, between 2,000 and 2,500 Russian military pensioners held an unauthorized rally that turned violent when Latvian police severely beat several pensioners. Demonstrators opposed hikes in the rates of municipal services such as electricity, water, and telephone services.[102] Russian pensioners are in the most precarious position since most of them are not citizens and are therefore unable to change residences, vote, or gain employment in the state sector. As non-citizens they are paid lower pensions. With fixed incomes, they are a group that would be most hurt by increases in the cost of living. Nevertheless the incident took on ethnic proportions because the demonstrators were Russian minorities who were denied citizenship.

Russian deputies and officials condemned the action in severe terms. Russian Foreign Minister Yevgeny Primakov called the incident a "flagrant violation of elementary human rights."[103] His statement was supported by Yeltsin who canceled a meeting with Latvian President Ulmanis and froze border talks.[104] The Latvian government countered Russian criticism by pointing out that the incident was not about ethnicity, but price hikes. It was claimed that many of the police who beat the pensioners were also Russian.[105] Prime Minister Guntars Krasts suggested that the whole incident might have been provoked by those in Russia who would like to tarnish Latvia's reputation abroad. Lastly, Riga Mayor Andris Berzins blamed the incident on the police themselves, stating that they were incapable of handling the situation in a civilized manner.[106]

Russia has also not hesitated to take advantage of incidents in Latvia involving Latvian Fascist organizations. On March 16, 1998, between 500 and 1,000 veterans of the Latvian SS Legion marched in Riga to commemorate the 55th anniversary of the establishment of the Latvian Corp of the Waffen SS, or Latvian SS Legion. It is a controversial group, as some regard it as a nationalist organization that fought against the Soviets while others view it as an instrument of Nazi terror responsible for carrying out Nazi crimes against the population.[107] For Latvia, the status or perception of the Corp is uncertain since

Latvia, along with Lithuania and Estonia, were caught between two brutal, oc-cupying forces. For Russia there is no ambiguity; Nazism is an unqualified evil, one that is so recognized by Western states including Germany. Germany took a very dim view of the march. The German Ambassador is on record as saying that the German government is critical of any Nazi veterans' groups.[108]

Latvia's reputation has not exactly been bolstered by several well-publicized trials of alleged Latvian Nazi war criminals. The latest case involves the prosecu-tion of Konrad Kalejs who was charged with crimes against humanity, genocide, and war crimes in October 2000. His arrest however was delayed by a Riga district court's refusal to issue a warrant.[109] Whatever the legality of the case, any per-ceived leniency towards Nazi war criminals is bound to have negative repercus-sions for Latvia's standing with the West. And Russia is well aware of this.

Russian-Lithuanian Relations

Relations between Lithuania and Russia have been relatively congenial since the irritants plaguing relations with Estonia and Latvia would seem to be absent. The Russian minority comprises only 8.2 percent of the population as of 1997.[110] Territorial claims are absent since Lithuania does not border Rus-sia proper. Nor is there any dispute with the western border with Kaliningrad Oblast, formerly the German territory of Königsberg.

The biggest area of contention is Lithuania's push for NATO membership. Russia has demonstrated its opposition in many ways. The issue of signing the border treaty is a case in point. Russia was fully aware that delaying the signing would hinder Lithuania's efforts to meet NATO membership guidelines. Fur-thermore, Lithuanian membership in NATO would allow NATO direct access to Vilnius and the encirclement of Kaliningrad Oblast.[111] Though Yeltsin signed, opposition from the Russian Duma has hindered its implementation. It is unclear as to whether Putin, who has been much more vehement in his op-position to NATO expansion, will honor arrangements concluded by the Yeltsin administration.

Lithuania, like Estonia and Latvia, remains committed to EU and NATO membership. At the security and foreign policy committee of the Baltic Assem-bly, Lithuanian parliamentarians submitted a proposal that all three Baltic dele-gations of parliamentarians urge their respective administrations not to reduce efforts to gain admittance to NATO. This action was in response to Russian pro-posals for an alternative security regime to NATO involving Russia and the Bal-tic States, where by Russia would guarantee Baltic security. The Baltic States were unanimous in rejecting Russia's offer.[112] Lithuania's recent elections have not changed its basic foreign policy line. The 1998 election of Valdas Adamkus as president did not alter Lithuania's foreign policy course toward integration into the EU and NATO.[113] In fact EU and NATO membership would have re-mained the principal foreign policy goals regardless of who won.

Baltic Unity

Cooperation among the Baltic States is evident in several spheres including economics, defense, and politics. In the face of Russian pressure, the Baltic States manage to present a united front. Each time one Baltic State is attacked the others immediately express solidarity and support. This fact is probably the best indicator that the Baltic States will eventually succeed in breaking away from Russia's sphere of influence.

The Baltic countries have signed several border protocols and agreements regulating trade and standardizing social polices and the mutual recognition of civil liability insurance and insurance polices of automobile owners.[114] In the area of defense, defense officials of the Baltic States finalized a treaty on the status of a joint peacekeeping battalion, BALTBAT. As the Baltic countries are small, their combined populations totaling a mere 7,813,000, their leaders obviously saw a military advantage in pooling their resources, especially personnel.[115] Agreements have been reached regarding the administration of the battalion and its members, wherever they might be stationed in the Baltic States. The three are also preparing documents on the use of the battalion in international peacekeeping operations. Treaties are also being prepared to form a joint naval squadron, BALTRON.[116]

The Baltic States have not been reticent about supporting one another in the face of Russian pressure. After Kozyrev made remarks about defending the Russian minorities with force, and later targeted Estonia in his assertions, then Latvian Foreign Minister Valdis Birkavs accused Russia of using the Russian ethnic card as a political weapon.[117] Lithuania's Foreign Ministry condemned the remarks and accused Russia of attempting to solve political problems with military means.[118] What is significant about Lithuania's reaction is that Kozyrev's remarks were clearly not directed at Lithuania which does not have a large Russian minority population and which does have an inclusive citizenship law.

After the incident in Latvia involving the beating of Russian pensioners, the Baltic Assembly condemned Russia's actions and statements as interference in Latvia's internal affairs. The resolution was adopted May 9 and recorded in a written document along with several other agreements among the Baltic States.[119] The Estonian Ministry of Foreign Affairs issued a statement condemning Russia threats against Latvia and rejected the notion that the rights of anyone had been violated. Furthermore, Russia's reaction was simply a strategy to prevent the Baltic countries from being admitted into the EU and NATO.[120]

On May 12, 1998, the three Baltic presidents publicly affirmed their solidarity and that despite difficulties with Russia, their common goals to be accepted into the EU and NATO would continue to unite them.[121] When the Baltic Assembly convened in Vilnius December 8–9, 2000, all three formally stated that early integration into NATO is necessary for European security. The significance lies not in the content of the statement but that the three acted as one.

They have also banded together in mutual support of EU membership. Estonia, the most likely candidate to be admitted first, will use its votes to help Latvia and Lithuania attain membership. Both Estonia and Latvia can be expected to assist Lithuania.

CONCLUSION

The Baltic States differ from the Slavic and Central Asian states in several ways that have a direct bearing on the relative success of the Baltic States in establishing viable, independent states. Though Russian interference is still very much felt by the Baltic States, their unity has helped them to withstand the pressure. But regardless of internal conditions that favor independence from Russia, the Baltic States would probably not have been so successful if it were not for international factors such as Western involvement and support for Baltic independence.

NOTES

1. "Latvian Interest in Kazakhstan Grows," *The Baltic Times*, May 21–27 (1998), p. 10.

2. *The Baltic States: A Reference Book* (Tallinn: Tallinn Book Printers, 1991) p. 6.

3. John Hiden and Patrick Salmon, *The Baltic Nations and Europe* (London: Longman, 1991) p. 11.

4. Walter C. Clemens, Jr., *Baltic Independence and Russian Empire* (New York: St. Martin's Press, 1991) p. 19.

5. Hiden and Salmon, *The Baltic Nations and Europe*, p. 16.

6. Ibid., p. 15.

7. Georg Von Raugh, *The Baltic State, The Years of Independence: Estonia, Latvia, Lithuania 1917–1940* (Berkeley: University of California Press, 1974) pp. 78–79.

8. Ibid., p. 77.

9. *FBIS-SOV*, 29 June (1992) p. 75.

10. Saulius Girnius, "The Economies of the Baltic States in 1993," *RFL/RE Research Reports*, vol. 3, no. 20 (1994) p. 1.

11. *FBIS-SOV*, 20 July (1992) p. 72.

12. Saulius Girnius, "The Economies of the Baltic States in 1993," p. 1.

13. Ibid., p. 2.

14. Ibid., p. 9.

15. *The Economist Intelligence Unit Country Report: Estonia, Latvia, Lithuania, 1st quarter* (London: The Economist Intelligence Unit, 1998) p. 6.

16. Saulius Girnius, "The Economies of the Baltic States in 1993," p. 10.

17. *The Economist Intelligence Unit Country Report: Estonia, Latvia, Lithuania, 1st quarter* (1998) p. 21.

18. Saulius Girnius, "The Economies of the Baltic States in 1993," pp. 6, 11–12.

19. *The Economist Intelligence Unit Country Report: Estonia, Latvia, Lithuania, 1st quarter* (1998) p. 35.

20. *FBIS-SOV*, 21 October (1997).

21. Ibid., pp. 12–6, 27–30, 43–46.
22. "On Yer Tank Transporters," *The Economist*, September 26 (1992) p. 56.
23. *FBIS-SOV*, 31 August (1992) p. 54.
24. Rasma Karklins, *Ethnopolitics and Transition to Democracy: The Collapse of the USSR and Latvia* (Washington, D.C.: The Woodrow Wilson Center Press, 1994) pp. 76–77.
25. *FBIS-SOV*, 31 August (1992) p. 54.
26. *FBIS-SOV*, 9 October (1992) p. 42.
27. *FBIS-SOV*, 8 November (1993) p. 83.
28. Walter C. Clemens Jr., "Baltic Identities in the 1990s: Renewed Fitness," in *National Identity and Ethnicity in Russia and the New States of Eurasia*, edited by Roman Szporluk (New York: M.E. Sharpe, 1994) pp. 196–197.
29. *FBIS-SOV*, 20 July (1992) p. 72.
30. *FBIS-SOV*, 21 July (1992) p. 53.
31. *FBIS-SOV*, 29 July (1992) p. 75.
32. *FBIS-SOV*, 31 August (1992) p. 54.
33. *FBIS-SOV*, 12 November (1992) p. 117.
34. *FBIS-SOV*, 28 October (1992) p. 115.
35. *FBIS-SOV*, 12 January (1993) p. 66.
36. *FBIS-SOV*, 7 October (1993) p. 70.
37. *FBIS-SOV*, 2 February (1993) p. 67.
38. *FBIS-SOV*, 2 February (1993) p. 67.
39. "On yer tank transporters," *The Economist*, p. 56.
40. *FBIS-SOV*, 26 May (1994) p. 13.
41. *FBIS-SOV*, 24 April (1995) p. 106.
42. *FBIS-SOV*, 24 April (1995) p. 103.
43. *FBIS-SOV*, 21 April (1995) p. 75.
44. *FBIS-SOV*, 20 April (1995) p. 73.
45. Paul Kolstoe, *Russians in the Former Soviet Republics* (Bloomington: Indiana University Press, 1995) p. 10.
46. Saulius Girnius, "Restraint and Resentment from the Baltic States," *Transition*, November 15 (1996) p. 17.
47. *FBIS-SOV*, 25 January (1994) p. 71.
48. *FBIS-SOV*, 12 January (1993) p. 66.
49. Villu Kand, "Estonia: A Year of Challenges," *RFE/RL Research Report*, vol. 3, no. 1 (1994) p. 92.
50. *The Economist Intelligence Unit Limited 2000: EIU Country Profile Estonia*, (London: The Economist Intelligence Unit, 2000) p. 5.
51. Dzintra Bungs, "Latvia: Transition to Independence Completed," *RFE/RL Research Report*, vol. 3, no. 1 (1994) p. 98.
52. *The Economist Intelligence Unit Limited 2000: EIU Country Profile Latvia 2000–01* (London: The Economist Intelligence Unit, 2000) p. 13.
53. Dzintra Bungs, "Russia Agrees to Withdraw Troops from Latvia," *RFE/RL Research Report*, vol. 3, no. 22 (1994) p. 5.
54. *The Economist Intelligence Unit Limited 2000: EIU Country Profile Lithuania* (London: The Economist Intelligence Unit, 2000) p. 11.
55. Saulius Girnius, "Lithuania: Former Communists Fail to Solve Problems," *RFE/RL Research Report*, vol. 3, no. 1 (1994) p. 101.

56. Peter Maass, "Baltic Russians Accept Secession," *The Washington Post*, February 24 (1991) p. A18.

57. Lowell Barrington, "The Domestic and International Consequences of Citizenship in the Soviet Successor States," *Europe-Asia Studies*, vol. 47, no. 5 (1995) p. 745.

58. Ibid.

59. Grant Gukasov, "From Soviet to State Assembly via 'Russian Question,' " *Moscow News Weekly*, no. 39 (1992) p. 5.

60. Ibid., p. 746.

61. Henn-Juri Uibopuu, "Dealing with the Minorities—a Baltic Perspective," *The World Today*, June (1992) pp. 109–110.

62. Celestine Bohlen, "Estonia Rattles Its Russian Residents With Its Insistence on 'Estonization,' " *The New York Times*, August 10 (1992) p. A6.

63. Lowell Barrington, "The Domestic and International Consequences of Citizenship in the Soviet Successor States," p. 733.

64. Saulius Girnius, "Restraint and Resentment from the Baltic States," p. 18.

65. Ibid.

66. Ibid.

67. Lowell Barrington, "The Domestic and International Consequences of Citizenship in the Soviet Successor States," p. 739.

68. Saulius Girnius, "Restraint and Resentment from the Baltic States," p. 18.

69. Dzintra Bungs, "Latvia: Transition to Independence Completed," p. 98.

70. Celestine Bohlen, "Estonia Rattles Its Russian Residents," p. A6.

71. "Russia continues attacks," *The Baltic Times*, May 28–June 3 (1998) p. 2.

72. "Citizenship amendments adopted," *The Baltic Times*, May 28–June 3 (1998) p. 1.

73. Press release by the USIS Riga, "Text: EU on Latvia Granting Citizenship to Stateless Children," from the homepage of the *U.S. Mission to Latvia: http://www.usis.bkc.lv*, 25 June (1998).

74. "Estonians Want Non-Estonians to Leave," *The Baltic Times*, vol. 5, no. 4, September 14–20 (2000), p. 4.

75. "Russian, nyet," *The Economist*, June 25 (1994) p. 52.

76. Dzintra Bungs, "Seeking Solutions to Baltic-Russian Border Issues," *RFE/RL Research Report*, vol. 3, no. 13 (1994) p. 25.

77. Ibid., p. 29.

78. Ibid.

79. Saulius Girnius, "Restraint and Resentment from the Baltic States," p. 18.

80. Ibid.

81. Dzintra Bungs, "Seeking Solutions to Baltic-Russian Border Issues," p. 29.

82. Ibid.

83. *FBIS-SOV*, 6 May (1994) p. 12.

84. *FBIS-SOV*, 16 March (1995) p. 58.

85. Dzintra Bungs, "Seeking Solutions to Baltic-Russian Border Issues," p. 30.

86. Ibid.

87. Saulius Girnius, "Restraint and Resentment from the Baltic States," pp. 18–19.

88. Dzintra Bungs, "Seeking Solutions to Baltic-Russian Border Issues," p. 30.

89. *The Economist Intelligence Unit Country Report: Estonia, Latvia, Lithuania, 1st quarter* (London: The Economist Intelligence Unit, 1998) p. 22.

90. Dzintra Bungs, "Seeking Solutions to Baltic-Russian Border Issues," pp. 26, 31.

91. "Kakuiu granitsy khotiat pereiti deputaty?" *Rossiiskaia gazeta*, October 4 (1997) p. 3.

92. Ibid.

93. Viktor Sokolov, "Dogovor o granitse neobkhodimakh," *Nezavisimaya gazeta*, October 10 (1997) p. 4.

94. Vladimir Zarovskii, "Reaktsiia iz Litvy ne zastavila sebia zhdat," *Rossiiskaia gazeta*, October 4 (1997) p. 3.

95. *The Economist Intelligence Unit Country Report: Estonia, Latvia, Lithuania, 1st quarter*, (London: The Economist Intelligence Unit, 1998) p. 39.

96. "Russia Continues Attacks," *The Baltic Times*, May 28–June 3 (1998) p. 2.

97. "Ready to Solve European Crises," *The Baltic Times*, May 14–20 (1998) p. 2.

98. *FBIS-SOV*, 9 October (1997).

99. "Support for Estonia's EU Bid," *The Baltic Times*, May 14–20 (1998) p. 4.

100. *FBIS-SOV*, 9 October (1997).

101. Dzintra Bungs, "Latvia: Transition to Independence Completed," p. 98.

102. Dmitrii Gornostaev, "V Latvii izbili russkikh pensionerov," *Nezavisimaya gazeta*, March 7 (1998) p. 1.

103. *The Current Digest of the Post-Soviet Press*, vol. 50, no. 10 (1998) p. 5.

104. Dmitrii Gornostaev, "Otnosheniia Moskvy i Rigi rezko obostrilis,'" *Nezavisimaya gazeta*, March 7 (1998) p. 6.

105. *The Current Digest of the Post-Soviet Press*, vol. 50, no. 10 (1998) p. 5.

106. Dmitrii Gornostaev, "Otnosheniia Moskvy i Rigi rezko obostrilis,' " p. 6.

107. Viktor Sokolov, "Den' legiona SS v Rige," *Nezavisimaya gazeta*, March 17 (1998) p. 1.

108. Maksim Iusin, "Nostal'giia po natsizmu oslozhnit put' Rigi v Evropy," *Izvestiia*, March 18 (1998) p. 3.

109. Coleman, Nick, "Kalejs Charged, Arrest Delayed," *The Baltic Times*, vol. 5, no. 227, October 5–11 (2000) pp. 1, 7.

110. *The Economist Intelligence Unit Limited 2000: EIU Country Profile Lithuania*, p. 12.

111. Viktor Sokolov, "Dogovor o granitse neobkhodimakh," p. 4.

112. *FBIS-SOV*, 8 October (1997).

113. Andrei Smirnov, "Litovskiie izbirateli ustali ot krainostei," *Segodnia*, December 23 (1997) p. 4.

114. "Baltic Assembly Condemns Russian Actions," *The Baltic Times*, May 14–20 (1998) p. 1.

115. *Statistical Handbook 1994: States of the Former USSR* (Washington, D.C.: The World Bank, 1994) pp. 167, 351, 399.

116. *FBIS-SOV*, October 17 (1997).

117. *FBIS-SOV*, 20 April (1995) p. 73.

118. *FBIS-SOV*, 20 April (1995) p. 74.

119. "Baltic Assembly Condemns Russian Actions," p. 1.

120. Il'ia Nikiforov, "Estoniia pomozhet Latvii," *Nezavisimaya gazeta*, March 19 (1998) p. 6.

121. Tanya R. Neuman, "Baltic Unity Remains Undivided: Baltic Presidents Reconfirm their Commitments," *The Baltic Times*, May 14–20 (1998) p. 1.

Chapter 8

Conclusion

Though the former Republics achieved de facto independence, the post-independence period was characterized mainly by the continuation of the administrative links established during the Soviet period. Conditions necessary to break thee links exist only in the case of the Baltic States, and their relative success, in large part, was the result of the existence of an alternative security regime in Europe and North America and their efforts to become a part of it.

Interactions between the various components of an empire have direct implications for the emergence of relations between newly established states. The center of an empire holds power over its periphery. Certain conditions in the center and periphery must be present in order to facilitate the establishment and maintenance of an empire. When an empire dissolves from internal causes, borders may change, but the balance of power between the center and periphery does not. Once the various territories of the former periphery gain independence as states, it can be expected that the center will continue to interfere in these areas. Though the center may not be able and willing to reform the old empire into one coherent, integrated political system, that does not mean that the center will not continue to dominate the periphery in other, more indirect ways. The ability for the center to do this in many ways depends on the conditions in the periphery. Still the impetus for projecting power emanates from the center.

The territories significantly differed from one another. These differences support the idea that the former center's domineering behavior is the direct result of the nature of the political system of which they were all a part. By comparing the former territories and stressing the differences among them, the one common denominator that unites them is underscored. This singular commonality is the center's treatment of them as inferior powers.

THE SOVIET UNION

Conditions in Russia in the latter half of the 1980s resulted in independence for the former Republics. The lack of imperial drive and its current political and economic disarray diminished both Russia's will and ability to restore the empire via traditional administrative and military means. What was left was confusion among Russian intellectuals and politicians about Russia's national identity and hence the basis for the Russian Federation. To take one small example, some reject the entire Soviet era as an aberration in Russia's national development while others feel the Soviet era was a more or less natural outgrowth of the tsarist Russian Empire.

But while this lack of national unity in the center has not led to the formal restoration of the empire, it has not changed the balance of power between Russia and the former Republics. Russia certainly regards the former Republics as within its sphere of influence. Russia remains a great power and has demonstrated intolerance to the involvement of outside powers in the areas of the former Soviet Union.

The Slavic, Central Asian and Baltic regions have distinctive characteristics that will influence their national development in the post-Soviet period. The Slavic states exhibit a nationalism that is ambivalent in its relationship to Russia. This ambivalence does not stem from the lack of a distinct ethnic background and nationality. National identity itself is not in question: Ukrainians and Belarusians have their own languages and shared historic experience apart from Russia. However, there is no consensus about Russia in either of them. In Belarus, Lukashenka clearly favors close ties with Russia while the political opposition supports mending relations with Europe. Ukraine is similarly divided on the issue, with sharp ideological divisions between western and eastern Ukraine.

The nations of Central Asia by contrast can certainly not be confused with Russia. Being the most different from Russia in race, linguistic affiliations, and religion, the Central Asian states find themselves in a difficult position similar to that of West Africa following independence from France. Economic, political and social indicators all place the Central Asian states in the same category as the developing world. Given the artificial nature of the borders of these states and low levels of national consciousness, the Central Asian states are faced with the task of forging national cohesiveness within the confines of their current borders. Enduring clan and kinship loyalties that permeate political and economic life complicate this task. Meanwhile, international indifference and geographical isolation forced the Central Asian governments to rely on the former center for economic and security needs.

The Baltic States are in the most fortunate position vis-à-vis Russia for several reasons. First, their smallness and distinct ethnic identity have fostered a tight-knit sense of national solidarity among the population and governments. This solidarity has resulted in a determination to break away from Russia's dominance and a willingness to accept the difficulties of the transition. Second, the geographic proximity of the Baltic States to Europe has provided these small states with an alternative to cooperation with Russia. The path to Europe presents an opportunity to become a part of its economic and security regimes. European powers and the United States have demonstrated a willingness to accommodate the Baltic States, providing cordial relations with Russian can be maintained in the process.

Empires are anachronisms in the twenty-first century. They are non-democratic, centralized political systems formed in earlier historic periods. As ancient political systems, empires are incompatible with twenty-first-century mass ideologies such as nationalism. The maintenance of empires *depends* on the non-participation of the masses. Empires that survived into the twenty-first century faced new challenges to continued survival. International relations in the new millennium are characterized by the political participation of the masses and the rise of nationalism. Nationalism as an ideology, as a political phenomenon, is based on the idea of popular sovereignty. It becomes the justification of the state. And where there is no "natural" basis of national unity, such as a common religion, language, etc., *states* create nations. Either way nationalism becomes the *raison d'être* of governments. And governments always claim to rule on behalf of the people, even when they are not democratic.

Selected Bibliography

BOOKS

The Baltic States: A Reference Book (Tallinn: Estonian Encyclopaedia Publishers; Riga: Lativian Encyclopaedia Publishers, 1991).

Bater, James H. *Russia and the Post-Soviet Scene* (London: Arnold, a member of the Hodder Headline Group, 1996).

Benningsen, Alexandre A. and Wimbush, S. Enders. *Muslim National Communism in the Soviet Union: A Revolutionary Strategy for the Colonial World* (Chicago: The University of Chicago Press, 1979).

Berlin, Isaiah. *Russian Thinkers* (New York: Viking Press, 1978).

Blum, Douglas W. *Russia's Future: Consolidation or Disintegration* (Boulder: Westview Press, 1994).

Bremmer, Ian and Taras, Ray (eds.). *New States, New Politics: Building the Post-Soviet Nations* (Cambridge: Cambridge University Press, 1997).

Breuilly, John. *Nationalism and the State*, 2nd ed. (Manchester: Manchester University Press, 1994).

Buttino, Marco. *In a Collapsing Empire: Underdevelopment, Ethnic Conflicts and Nationalisms in the Soviet Union* (Milan: Fondazione Giangiacomo Feltrinelli, 1993).

Cardoso, Fernando and Faletto, Enzo. *Dependency and Development in Latin America* (Berkeley: University of California Press, 1979).

Carter, Stephen. *Russian Nationalism: Yesterday, Today, Tomorrow* (New York: St. Martin's Press, 1990).

Clemens, Walter C. Jr. *Baltic Independence and Russian Empire* (New York: St. Martin's Press, 1991).

Coates, W. P. and Coates, Zelda K. *Soviets in Central Asia* (Westport, Connecticut: Greenwood, 1969).

Comrie, Bernard and Corbett, Greville G. (eds.). *The Slavonic Languages* (New York: Routledge, 1993).

Conquest, Robert. *The Last Empire: Nationality and the Soviet Future* (Stanford: Hoover Institution Press, 1986).

Cyzevs'kyj, Dmytro. *A History of Ukrainian Literature* (Littleton, Colorado: Ukrainian Academic Press, 1975).

Dawisha, Karen and Parrott, Bruce (eds.). *Russia and the New States of Eurasia: The Politics of Upheaval* (Cambridge: Cambridge University Press, 1994).

Dawisha, Karen and Parrott, Bruce (eds.). *The End of Empire? The Transformation of the USSR in Comparative Perspective* (New York: M. E. Sharpe, 1997).

Dawisha, Karen and Parrott, Bruce (eds.). *Democratic Changes and Authoritarian Reactions in Russia, Ukraine, Belarus, and Moldova* (Cambridge: Cambridge University Press, 1997).

Denber, Rachel. *The Soviet Nationality Reader: The Disintegration in Context* (Boulder: Westview Press, 1992).

D'Encausse, Helene Carrere. *Decline of an Empire: The Soviet Republics in Revolt* (New York: Newsweek Books, 1979).

D'Encausse, Helene Carrere. *The End of the Soviet Empire: The Triumph of the Nations* (New York: BasicBooks, 1993).

D'Encausse, Helene Carrere. *Islam and the Russian Empire: Reform and Revolution in Central Asia* (London: I.B.TAURIS 7 Co Ltd Publishers, 1988).

Deutsch, Karl. *Nationalism and Social Communication*, 2nd ed. (Cambridge: The Massachusetts Institute of Technology, 1953).

Doyle, Michael W. *Empires* (Ithaca: Cornell University Press, 1986).

Eisenstadt, S. N. *The Decline of Empires* (New Jersey: Prentice-Hall, 1967).

Eisenstadt, S. N. *The Political Systems of Empires* (New York: Free Press of Glencoe, 1963).

Enloe, Cynthia. *Ethnic Conflict and Political Development* (United States: Little, Brown and Company, 1973).

Furtado, Charles F. Jr. and Chandler, Andrea. *Perestroika in the Soviet Republics: Documents on the National Question* (Boulder: Westview Press, 1992).

Geertz, Clifford. *Old Societies and New States: The Quest for Modernity in Asia and Africa* (New York: Free Press, 1963).

Gellner, Ernest. *Nations and Nationalism* (London: Basil Blackwell, 1983).

Geyer, Georgie Ann. *Waiting for Winter to End: An Extraordinary Journey Through Central Asia* (Washington-London: Brassey's, 1994).

Gleason, Abbott. *Young Russia* (New York: Viking Press, 1978).

Greenstein, Fred and Polsby, Nelson. *Handbook of Political Science: vol. 3, Macropolitical Theory* (Reading, MA: Addison-Wesley Press, 1975).

Hellie, Richard. *Enserfment and Military Change in Muscovy* (Chicago: University of Chicago Press, 1971).

Hiden, John and Salmon, Patrick. *The Baltic Nations and Europe* (London: Longman, 1991).

Hobson, J. A. *Imperialism* (Ann Arbor: reprinted by the University of Michigan, 1965).

Hunter, Shireen T. *Central Asia Since Independence* (Westport, Connecticut: Praeger, 1996).

Hutchinson, John and Smith, Anthony D. *Nationalism* (Oxford: Oxford University Press, 1994).

Karasik, Theodore W. *Russia and Eurasia Facts & Figures Annual: Volume 19* (Gulf Breeze, FL: Academic International Press, 1994).

Karklins, Rasma. *Ethnic Relations in the USSR: The Perspective from Below* (Boston: Allen & Unwin, 1986).

Karklins, Rasma. *Ethnopolitics and Transition to Democracy: The Collapse of the USSR and Latvia* (Washington, D.C.: The Woodrow Wilson Center Press, 1994).

Katzner, Kenneth. *The Languages of the World* (New York: Funk & Wagnall's, 1975).

Kohn, Hans. *The Idea of Nationalism* (New York: Collier Books, 1948).

Kolstoe, Paul. *Russians in the Former Soviet Republics* (Bloomington: Indiana University Press, 1995).

Kolycheva, E. I. *Agrarnyiu stroi Rossii XVI veka* (Moscow: Nauka, 1987).

Krasnov, Vladislav. *Russia Beyond Communism: A Chronicle of National Rebirth* (Boulder: Westview Press, 1991).

Lempert, David H. *Daily Life in a Crumbling Empire: The Absorption of Russia into the World Economy* (Boulder: East European Monographs, 1996).

Lenin, V. I. *Imperialism: The Highest Stage of Capitalism* (New York: reprinted by International Publishers, 1939).

Lewis, Robert A. *Geographic Perspectives on Soviet Central Asia* (London: Routledge, 1992).

Lieven, Anatol. *Chechnya: Tombstone of Russian Power* (New Haven: Yale University Press, 1998).

Melvin, Neil. *Forging the New Russian Nation* (London: The Royal Institute of International Affairs, 1994).

Melvin, Neil. *Regional Foreign Policies in the Russian Federation* (London: The Royal Institute of International Affairs, 1995).

Mirsky, Georgiy I. *On the Ruins of an Empire: Ethnicity and Nationalism in the Former Soviet Union* (Westport, Connecticut: Greenwood Press, 1997).

Motyl, Alexander J. *Thinking Theoretically About Soviet Nationalities: History and Comparison in the Study of the USSR* (New York: Columbia University Press, 1992).

Natsional'nyi sostav neseleniia SSSR (Moscow: Nauka, 1991).

Olcott, Martha Brill. *Central Asia's New States: Independence, Foreign Policy, and Regional Security* (Washington, D.C.: United States Institute of Peace Press, 1996).

Palmer, Monte. *Dilemmas of Political Development: An Introduction to the Politics of Developing Areas 4th edition* (Itasca: F. E. Peacock Publishers, 1989).

Park, Alexander. *Bolshevism in Turkestan, 1917–1927* (New York: Columbia University Press, 1957).

Pierce, Richard A. *Russian Central Asia 1867–1917: A Study in Colonial Rule* (Berkeley: University of California Press, 1960).

Plyushch, Leonid. *History's Carnival* (New York: Harcourt Brace Jovanovich, 1977).

Rudolph, Richard L. and Good, David F. (eds.) *Nationalism and Empire: The Hapsburg Monarchy and the Soviet Union* (Minnesota: St. Martin's Press, 1992).

Rywkin, Michael. *Moscow's Muslim Challenge: Soviet Central Asia* (New York: M. E. Sharpe, 1982).

Schumpeter, Joseph. *Imperialism and Social Classes* (New York: Meridian Books, 1951).

Seton-Watson, Hugh. *Nations and States* (Boulder: Westview Press, 1977).

Shlapentokh, Vladimir, Sendich, Munir and Payin, Emil (eds.). *The New Russian Diaspora* (Armonk: M. E. Sharpe, 1994).

Simon, Gerhard. *Nationalism and Policy Toward the Nationalities in the Soviet Union: From Totalitarian Dictatorship to Post-Stalinist Society* (Boulder: Westview Press, 1991).

Smith, Anthony. *The Ethnic Origins of Nations* (London: Basil Blackwell, 1986).

Statistical Handbook 1994: States of the Former USSR (Washington, D.C.: The World Bank, 1994).

Suny, Ronald Grigor. *The Revenge of the Past* (Stanford, California: Stanford University Press, 1993).

Symons, Leslie. *The Soviet Union: A Systematic Geography* (New York: Routledge, 1983).

Szporluk, Roman. *National Identity and Ethnicity in Russia and the New States of Eurasia* (New York: M. E. Sharpe, 1994).

Thornton, A. P. *Imperialism in the Twentieth Century* (Minneapolis: University of Minnesota Press, 1977).

Ulam, Adam B. *Stalin: The Man and His Era* (Boston: Beacon Press, 1989).

Vakar, Nicholas P. *Belorussia: The Making of a Nation* (Cambridge: Harvard University Press, 1956).

Vernadsky, George. *Russian Historiography: A History* (Massachusetts: Nordland Publishing Company, 1978).

Von Raugh, Georg. *The Baltic States, The Years of Independence: Estonia, Latvia, Lithuania 1917–1940* (Berkeley: University of California Press, 1974).

Wallerstein, Immanuel. *The Capitalist World-Economy* (Cambridge: Cambridge University Press, 1979).

Yoffee, Norman and Cowgill, George L. *The Collapse of Ancient States and Civilizations* (Tucson: The University of Arizona Press, 1988).

Zviagelskaia, Irina. *The Russian Policy Debate on Central Asia* (London: The Royal Institute of International Affairs, 1995).

ARTICLES

Akbarzadeh, Shahram. "The Political Shape of Central Asia," *Central Asian Survey* vol. 16, no. 4 (1997).

Barrington, Lowell. "The Domestic and International Consequences of Citizenship in the Soviet Successor States," *Europe-Asia Studies* vol. 47, no. 5 (1995).

Birgerson, Susanne M. and Kanet, Roger E. "East-Central Europe and the Russian Federation," *Problems of Post-Communism.* vol. 42, no. 4, July-August (1995).

Boss, Helen and Havlik, Peter. "Slavic (dis)union: Consequences for Russia, Belarus, and Ukraine," *Economics of Transition* vol. 2, no. 2, June (1994).

Bremmer, Ian. "The Politics of Ethnicity: Russians in the New Ukraine," *Europe-Asia Studies* vol. 46, no. 2 (1994).

D'Anieri, Paul. "Dilemmas of Interdependence: Autonomy, Prosperity, and Sovereignty in Ukraine's Russia Policy," *Problems of Post-Communism.* January/February (1997).

Galtung, Johan. "A Structural Theory of Imperialism," *Journal of Peace Research* no. 2 (1971).

Goltz, Thomas. "Letter from Eurasia: The Hidden Russian Hand," *Foreign Policy* no. 92, Fall (1993).

Harris Chauncy D. "Ethnic Tensions in the Successor Republics in 1993 and Early 1994," *Post-Soviet Geography* vol. 35, no. 4 (1994).

Huntington, Samual P. "Political Development and Political Decay," *World Politics* vol. 17, no. 3 (1965).

Hyman, Anthony. "Turkestan and pan-Turkism Revisited," *Central Asian Survey* vol. 16, no. 3 (1997).

Kosikova, Lidiya and Mikhalskaya, Anna. "Problems of State Regulation of Trade Between Russia and the Near Abroad Countries," *Foreign Trade* 11–12 (1992).

Lieven, Anatol. "Russia's Military Nadir," *The National Interest.* Summer (1996).

Metcalf, Lee Kendall. "The (Re)Emergence of Regional Economic Integration in the Former Soviet Union," *Political Research Quarterly* (1997).

Olcott, Martha Brill. "Post-Soviet Kazakhstan: The Demographics of Ethnic Politics," *Problems of Post-Communism.* March/April (1995).

Olcott, Martha Brill. "Youth and Nationality in the USSR," *Journal of Soviet Nationalities* vol. 1, no. 1 (1990).

Press release by the USIS Riga. "Text: EU on Latvia Granting Citizenship to Stateless Children," from the homepage of the *U.S. Mission to Latvia: http://www.usis.bkc.lv.* 25 June (1998).

Roeder, Philip. "Soviet Federalism and Ethnic Mobilization," *World Politics* vol. 43, January (1991).

Rudnytsky, Ivan L. "Observations on the Problem of 'Historical' and 'Non-Historical' Nations," *Harvard Ukrainian Studies* vol. 5, no. 3 (1981).

Sartori, Giovanni. "Totalitarianism, Model Mania and Learning From Error," *Journal of Theoretical Politics.* vol. 5, no. 1 (1993).

Stebelsky, Ihor. "The Toponymy of Ukraine," *Post-Soviet Geography and Economics* vol. 38, no. 5 (1997).

Wright, Robin. "Report from Turkestan," *The New Yorker*, 6 April (1992).

NEWSPAPERS AND JOURNALS

The Baltic Times
Central Asian Monitor
Central Asian Survey
The Current Digest of the Post-Soviet Press
Economics of Transition
The Economist
Europe-Asia Studies
Foreign Broadcast Information Service, Central Eurasia
Foreign Policy
Foreign Trade
Harvard Ukrainian Studies
Izvestiia
Journal of Peace Research
Journal of Soviet Nationalism
Journal of Theoretical Politics

Moscow News Weekly
Moscow Times
Moskovskii Novosti
The National Interest
The New York Times
The New Yorker
Nezavisimaya gazeta
Novaya gazeta
Political Research Quarterly
Post-Soviet Geography
Pravda
Pravda-5
Problems of Post-Communism
Rossiiskaya gazeta
Segodnya
The Times
Transitions
The Washington Post
World Politics

REPORTS

Economist Intelligence Unit Country Report: Belarus/Moldova, 1st quarter 1998
Economist Intelligence Unit Country Report: Belarus/Moldova, 1st quarter 2000
Economist Intelligence Unit Country Report: Belarus/Moldova, 4th quarter 1996
Economist Intelligence Unit Country Report: Estonia, Latvia, Lithuania, 1st quarter 1998
Economist Intelligence Unit Country Report: Estonia, Latvia, Lithuania, 1st quarter 2000
Economist Intelligence Unit Country Report: Kazakhstan, 1st quarter 1998
Economist Intelligence Unit Country Report: Kazakhstan, 2000
Economist Intelligence Unit Country Report: Kazakhstan, annual report 1998
Economist Intelligence Unit Country Report: Kyrgyz Republic, Tajikistan, Turkmenistan, Uzbekistan, 1st quarter 1996
Economist Intelligence Unit Country Report: Kyrgyz Republic, Tajikistan, Turkmenistan, Uzbekistan, 4th quarter 1996
Economist Intelligence Unit Country Report: Kyrgyz Republic, Tajikistan, Turkmenistan, Uzbekistan, 1st quarter 1998
Economist Intelligence Unit Country Report: Ukraine, 1996–97 annual report
Economist Intelligence Unit Country Report: Ukraine, 1st quarter 1998
Economist Intelligence Unit Country Report: Ukraine, 1st quarter 2000
Economist Intelligence Unit Limited: EIU Country Profile 1999–2000, Ukraine
Economist Intelligence Unit Limited: EIU Country Profile 2000, Belarus
Foreign Broadcast Information Service, Central Eurasia
Natsional'nyi sostav neseleniia SSSR
Radio Free Europe/Radio Liberty, RFE/RL Newsline
RFE/RL Research Report
Russia & Eurasia Facts & Figures Annual
Stratfor Global Intelligence Update, http://www.stratfor.com/service/GIU/102299

Index

About the Author

SUSANNE MICHELE BIRGERSON is an independent researcher who began working and writing on Eastern Europe and the former Soviet Union in the decade after the Soviet Union collapsed. Dr. Birgerson's research has been published in various academic journals such as *Problems of Post-Communism, Asian Affairs: An American Review, Communist and Post-Communist Studies,* and *Revue d'Etudes Comparatives Est-Ouest.*